Christopher Rowland is Professor of the Exegesis of Holy Scripture, Queen's College, Oxford. Crispin Fletcher-Louis is Honorary Research Fellow at Wycliffe Hall, Oxford.

JOURNAL FOR THE STUDY OF THE NEW TESTAMENT
SUPPLEMENT SERIES
153

Executive Editor
Stanley E. Porter

Sheffield Academic Press

Understanding, Studying and Reading

New Testament Essays in Honour of John Ashton

edited by
**Christopher Rowland
& Crispin H.T. Fletcher-Louis**

Journal for the Study of the New Testament
Supplement Series 153

Copyright © 1998 Sheffield Academic Press

Published by Sheffield Academic Press Ltd
Mansion House
19 Kingfield Road
Sheffield S11 9AS
England

Printed on acid-free paper in Great Britain
by Bookcraft Ltd
Midsomer Norton, Bath

British Library Cataloguing in Publication Data

A catalogue record for this book is available
from the British Library

ISBN 1-85075-828-X

CONTENTS

Dear John,

In other contexts, a Dear John letter signifies (or used to) a parting of ways. Not here. Your remaining in Oxford in retirement promises continuing friendships and opportunities for even closer collaboration, once relieved of other time-filling activities. This letter represents the friendship of non-contributors as well as the appreciation of the writers whose pieces it introduces, and is the letter-writer's reward for failing to meet a deadline and so reducing the weight of the volume. Since writing it is a pleasure this must be a reward, not a punishment administered by our chairman Chris Rowland.

You were already an Oxford-based scholar with other Oxford antecedents on that memorable 1984 day on which you were voted into a University lectureship. It is therefore possible to look back with delight over fourteen rather than merely your twelve years in post. Some can look right back into your Oxford past—to when you were being tutored in philosophy for Greats by Iris Murdoch—but most of the NT seminar are more recent acquisitions, so I will leave ancient history to the ancients and attend to *Zeitgeschichte* and start with autobiography. For me one of the great pleasures and privileges of 1984, prior to your appointment, was reading the half-completed manuscript of *Understanding the Fourth Gospel* and reporting on its excellence, and one of the great pleasures of 1991 was receiving the completed and handsomely published work and attending a party of celebration. One of the guests was your distinguished philosophy tutor herself. Another of them (anonymous) was so impressed by the value of the work, or intimidated at the cost, as to remove the copy that was on display. Well friendship takes many forms, and occasionally liberties too—like Wilma's dinner guest who in the excitement of argument once provided you with what must be the least appropriate political characterization you have ever received.

But more seriously: your time among us (to date—and we trust it may be long extended) has been marked by the trust and confidence and affection you inspire, both as a teacher and as a colleague. One of the hall-marks of an Oxford tutor, and much of the value of that financially threatened system, consists in the level of commitment towards the individual being taught found among the teachers. Some of the most important educational ideals are best exemplified in this highly privileged system. This combination of friendship, personal interest, and professional distance is not always easy for non-tutorial fellows outside the undergraduate colleges to maintain, especially as the age gap widens. Perhaps your late arrival helped you, but you have shown the rest of us how admirably it can mature even as we move towards retirement. Here as in other areas, your work has been a true reflection of the person. Among graduate students, several of whom are expressing their appreciation here, your willingness to spend long periods reading drafts and theses of those you were not yourself supervising has been similarly inspired by your interest in the writers and their progress, as well as a high sense of the responsibilities of your post which goes far beyond the duties as laid down by statute.

Post-holders are of course committed to some administration. Your time as librarian involved a difficult juggling act, but you emerged unscathed and helped prepare the way for an easier future for your successors. On the Board your contribution as a disinterested and fair-minded judge on whatever came up will be remembered appreciatively by some, and your stints as Chairman of Examiners provided material for the raconteur in you. Wolfson has also learned to value and use your calmness and good judgment in even quite tedious administrative chores. These too can be a way of mixing with colleagues and nurturing friendships.

But in the context of these essays it is your scholarly achievement that shines most brightly, so I must forbear to recall details of other significant achievements such as your recent high-speed ascent of Snowdon, 'I only came for conversations with friends and it turned out to be a hiking holiday'.

The Big Book will continue to occupy us for a long time. Its style as well as its content have been sufficiently praised—an ironic comment in the acknowledgments suggests that this praise will have been no surprise. Modesty is all very well, but truthfulness is the primary obligation. I have personal reasons to take special pleasure also in your edited collection, *The Interpretation of John* (London, 1986, second and enlarged edition forthcoming) and the collection of superb articles, *Studying John* (Oxford, 1994). They kept Johannine studies in the forefront of our local concerns at a time when Ed Sanders's dazzling contributions on Paul and Jesus were exciting us. Like his epoch-making studies yours too have made recent advances in the study of early Judaism richly fruitful for New Testament studies. Like him you have been content to let systematic theologians make what they will of your historical and exegetical work. If he, like Dodd in mid-career (1935), enlarged our understanding of the kingdom of God in the preaching of Jesus, you, like Dodd in his maturity (1953) have made a decisive contribution to the interpretation of the Fourth Gospel, and like Dodd in later years (especially 1963) have continued to advance our understanding of this most significant religious text. Yet it is not Dodd but Bultmann who remains our primary point of reference in twentieth-century Johannine studies. Bultmann as theologian you would not care to emulate, despite having much in common with him from some perspectives, but you do rise to the challenge of his incisive questioning and of his elegant total solution. You identify its errors, and apply the brilliant advances of Lou Martyn and Wayne Meeks and the solid commentary work of Ray Brown and Barnabas Lindars among others, to direct the light that has been generated by studies on the Johannine community into the relatively obscure and far more important areas of the evangelist's religious language and theological understanding.

The value of the work you have done will be increasingly recognized. Those who have benefited from your teaching and stimulating conversations have high hopes too for the work in progress, on Paul and on hermeneutics. Which is as much as to say that retirement is only one more step along the road we go, those of us fortunate enough to reach it, clutching our bus and rail passes but not taking advantage of them to ride out into the sunset. The rest of us still need your input, so we hope the philosopher's lodgings in Park Town will be a seed-bed for ideas and reflection on the New Testament also. As you dash off today to examine in Dublin, within minutes of giving the seminar your valedictory on Luz and Gadamer, we offer you in return this small token of affection as in-flight reading, without overloading your baggage allowance. Go well—and return safely.

As ever
pro nobis omnibus

Bob Morgan

ABBREVIATIONS

AB	Anchor Bible
ABD	David Noel Freedman (ed.), *The Anchor Bible Dictionary* (New York: Doubleday, 1992)
BAGD	W. Bauer, W.F. Arndt, F.W. Gingrich and F.W. Danker, *Greek–English Lexicon of the New Testament*
BETL	Bibliotheca ephemeridum theologicarum lovaniensium
Bib	*Biblica*
BK	*Bibel und Kirche*
BNTC	Black's New Testament Commentaries
CBQ	*Catholic Biblical Quarterly*
EBib	Etudes bibliques
ETL	*Ephemerides theologicae lovanienses*
ExpTim	*Expository Times*
FRLANT	Forschungen zur Religion und Literatur des Alten und Neuen Testaments
GTJ	*Grace Theological Journal*
HTKNT	Herders theologischer Kommentar zum Neuen Testament
ICC	International Critical Commentary
IDB	G.A. Buttrick (ed.), *Interpreter's Dictionary of the Bible*
JBL	*Journal of Biblical Literature*
JRS	*Journal of Roman Studies*
JSNT	*Journal for the Study of the New Testament*
JSNTSup	*Journal for the Study of the New Testament*, Supplement Series
JTS	*Journal of Theological Studies*
Judaica	*Judaica: Beiträge zum Verständnis...*
MNTC	Moffatt NT Commentary
NCB	New Century Bible
NICNT	New International Commentary on the New Testament
NIGTC	The New International Greek Testament Commentary
NovT	*Novum Testamentum*
NovTSup	*Novum Testamentum* Supplements
NTG	New Testament Guides
NTS	*New Testament Studies*
OrChr	*Oriens christianus*
OTL	Old Testament Library
PNTC	Pelican New Testament Commentaries
RB	*Revue biblique*
SH	Scripta Hierosolymitana

SJLA	Studies in Judaism in Late Antiquity
SJT	*Scottish Journal of Theology*
SUNT	Studien zur Umwelt des Neuen Testaments
TDNT	G. Kittel and G. Friedrich (eds.), *Theological Dictionary of the New Testament*
TDNT I	G. Bromley (ed.), *Theological Dictionary of the New Testament Abridged in one volume*
TQ	*Theologische Quartalschrift*
TynBul	*Tyndale Bulletin*
WBC	Word Biblical Commentary
WUNT	Wissenschaftliche Untersuchungen zum Neuen Testament
ZTK	*Zeitschrift für Theologie und Kirche*

Ian Boxall, St Stephen's House

Sebastian Brock, Wolfson College, Oxford

David Catchpole, Exeter University

Mark Edwards, Christ Church College, Oxford

Steve Finamore, Regents Park College, Oxford

Crispin H.T. Fletcher-Louis, Keble College, Oxford

Eric Franklin, St Stephen's House

Alan Le Grys, Ripon College, Cuddesdon

Christine E. Joynes, St Hugh's College, Oxford

Larry J. Kreitzer, Regent's Park College, Oxford

John Muddiman, Mansfield College, Oxford

Joseph A. Munitiz, Campion Hall, Oxford

Peter Oakes, Northern College, Manchester

Christopher Rowland, The Queen's College, Oxford

Henry Wansbrough, St Benet's Hall, Oxford

David Wenham, Wycliffe Hall, Oxford

Trevor Williams, Trinity College, Oxford

A QUESTION OF IDENTITY: 'WHO DO PEOPLE SAY THAT I AM?'
ELIJAH, JOHN THE BAPTIST AND JESUS IN MARK'S GOSPEL

Christine E. Joynes

The purpose of this essay is to examine how appropriate it is to
describe John the Baptist as Elijah redivivus. For reasons of brevity
and to provide a clear focus for discussion, I shall concentrate on
Mark's Gospel, although the conclusions reached have wider implications. Three main issues will be addressed. First, an analysis of Mark
is required to see if John the Baptist is associated with Elijah. Secondly, I will ask if this association is best defined using the term
'Elijah redivivus'. Thirdly, I will see if the associations are exclusively applied to John the Baptist, making this a distinctive feature of
his identity. In Part I, I shall outline various questions and general
problems, then in Part II, I shall concentrate on four key passages in
Mark: 1.1-15; 6.14-29; 8.27–9.13 and 15.33-39.

Reviewing the Status Quaestionis

Preliminary Observations
New Testament scholarship usually accepts that John the Baptist is to
be identified as Elijah and moreover, that there was a predominant
expectation of Elijah as the forerunner of the Messiah in Second
Temple Judaism.[1] The identification of John with Elijah can be interpreted in two ways: at a redactional level, that is, in terms of how the
Synoptics portray John the Baptist, and at the historical level, relating
to John's 'Elijah consciousness'. I shall press the question further at
the redactional level, asking how Mark interprets the eschatological
role of Elijah and how this is related to Christology.

The importance of analyzing the role of Elijah is apparent when we

1. Recently challenged by M. Faierstein, 'Why Do the Scribes Say that Elijah
Must Come First?', *JBL* 100 (1981), pp. 75-86.

recognize the wide range of literature in which he is mentioned. Elijah features in pre-Christian Jewish writings, in the New Testament, in the Early Church Fathers and in Rabbinic material. However, whilst this indicates the significance of the subject I am considering, we should not be too hasty to conflate the material. Methodological questions must be asked about date and prevalence and how far the evidence can be compared, thus resisting the allure of 'parallelomania'.

Old Testament Background
The translation of the ninth-century prophet Elijah to heaven in a fiery chariot is described in 2 Kgs 2.11-12. No mention is made there of his future return; indeed his succession by Elisha might fairly be thought to exclude the idea. However, it becomes the key point in Malachi's prophecy, Mal. 4.5-6: 'Behold, I will send you Elijah the prophet before the great and terrible day of the Lord comes. And he will turn the hearts of fathers to their children and the hearts of children to their fathers, lest I come and smite the land with a curse.'[2] This prophecy is enlarged upon in Ecclus. 48.9-10, where we are told that Elijah will come to allay the divine wrath before its final fury and to restore the tribes of Jacob. Ecclesiasticus also emphasizes Elijah's fame as a miracle worker, a feature which was later taken up in Rabbinic literature.[3]

Elijah Redivivus?
It is symptomatic of the confusion concerning this subject that when talking of Elijah as an eschatological figure scholars use the term 'Elijah *redivivus*'.[4] This is inappropriate when applied to Elijah, since the whole point is that Elijah did not die, he was taken up to heaven. This is a fairly distinctive trait, since Enoch is the only other Old Testament figure who escaped death and ascended to heaven.[5] 'Elijah reditus' or the 'returning Elijah' would be a more suitable expression.

---

2.   All Malachi references are to the English translation.

3.   H.L. Strack and P. Billerbeck, *Kommentar zum Neuen Testament aus Talmud und Midrash* (Munich: C.H. Beck'sche Verlagsbuchhandlung), IV.2, p. 769.

4.   There are references to Solomon redivivus, Paul redivivus and Nero redivivus, the latter being the only instance where the term could be applicable.

5.   Gen. 5.24.

Not only is 'redivivus' an unsuitable term to use, it is customarily used without questioning its implications. If we overlook the terminological confusion and accept that most scholars use 'redivivus' to refer to Elijah returned from heaven, not from the dead, this seldom strikes commentators as an unusual occurrence! So for example we find, 'John the Baptist is not just a new Elijah, but Elijah himself.'[6] Similarly, T.L. Wilkinson believes that this was a real possibility and interprets the Fourth Gospel's denial that John the Baptist is Elijah as an attempt to avoid the literalistic identification of John the Baptist as the historical Elijah the Tishbite reditus. This is not to deny, argues Wilkinson, that John fulfils the *function* of Elijah as the forerunner of the Messiah.[7]

The notion of 'redivivus' is sometimes even applied to prophets in general.[8] This blurs the distinction between Elijah who was translated to heaven and other prophets who died. The above discussion illustrates that the debate has important implications for our understanding of resurrection and eternal life in Second Temple Judaism.

Typology

When examining the relevant texts we need to ask whether a prophetic typology or an eschatological use of Elijah terminology is being applied and what the function of the Elijah references is in the overall context of the narrative.

Knowles argues, 'As Elijah's antitype, John the Baptist does not just reflect his biblical antecedent, he fulfils and surpasses it.'[9] This brings me to a brief consideration of the nature of typology. If typology is defined as 'the perception of significant correspondences between the

6. G. Molin, 'Elijahu: Der Prophet und sein Weiterleben in den Hoffnungen des Judentums und der Christenheit', *Judaica* 8 (1952), p. 89.

7. T.L. Wilkinson, 'The Role of Elijah in the New Testament', *Vox Reformata* 10 (1968), p. 5.

8. K. Berger, *Die Auferstehung des Propheten und die Erhöhung des Menschensohnes* (Göttingen: Vandenhoeck & Ruprecht, 1976), p. 21. 'The identification of Jesus with one of the prophets in Mk 6.15 probably indicates that he is thought to be one of the prophets in bodily form, brought from heavenly existence. This is not necessarily an eschatological event, but a special hallmark of holy time (*Heilszeit*).' (My translation.)

9. M. Knowles, *Jeremiah in Matthew's Gospel: The Rejected Prophet Motif in Matthaean Redaction* (JSNTSup, 68; Sheffield: JSOT Press, 1993), p. 230.

characters and circumstances of two *different* historical individuals…so that each is understood either as an anticipation or as a
fulfilment of the other', then following the usual assumption that
Elijah reditus is a reference to the *same* individual, we cannot look at
the New Testament narratives simply in terms of typology.[10] Hence, a
more nuanced categorization of the Elijah material is required.

We should also ask how obvious the Old Testament allusions were
for the Evangelists' audiences.[11] Many proposed interpretations are
over-subtle in their analysis and fail to take into account the fact that
the original audiences would have heard rather than read the Gospels.
Oral delivery is less conducive to meditation on Old Testament allusions than visual reading.

The brief overview above illustrates the need for clarity when
interpreting the Elijah material. First, we can identify a typological
use of the Elijah traditions, where language is used in a metaphorical
or literary sense. In this context we should abandon reference to
'Elijah reditus', since there are no metaphysical connotations implied.
Secondly, the relationship of Elijah to a successor could be perceived
on the model of that with Elisha, that is, the receiving of a 'double
portion' of his spirit. The implication of this view is that Elijah lives
on through the transfer of his spirit, rather than through the
expectation of a future return from heaven.[12] This does not imply the
problem of the conflict of two persons; it can be interpreted as a non-
personal enhancement of an individual's prophetic powers. Thirdly,
the notion of Elijah's return could suggest a heavenly being taking
over another human individual who is rendered passive.[13] The four
key Markan passages examined below illustrate this diversity in the
application of the Elijah tradition.

10. Knowles, *Jeremiah*, p. 223. My italics. See further D.C. Allison, *The New Moses: A Matthean Typology* (Edinburgh: T. & T. Clark, 1993), pp. 15-16.
11. The Gospels address different audiences, although they were not restricted to one context.
12. W.C. Kaiser ('The Promise of the Arrival of Elijah in Malachi and the Gospels', *GTJ* 3 [1982], pp. 221-33), describes this idea as 'generic prophecy', suggesting that we still await other Elijahs. Also R. Hammer, 'Elijah and Jesus: A Quest for Identity', *Judaism* 19 (1970), p. 210, 'Elisha seeks to *incarnate* Elijah and continue his work'.
13. This is the logical conclusion of Molin's assertion that John the Baptist was not a new Elijah but Elijah himself.

Mark's Gospel: A Quest for Identity

Mark 1.1-15. The Prologue

John the Baptist appears in the wilderness in rather odd attire, preaching a baptism of repentance for the forgiveness of sins. Here in the opening chapter of Mark is an allusion to Elijah, assuming that we accept that the messenger of Mal. 3.1, quoted here, is the same as Elijah who is named in Mal. 4.5. A further allusion to Elijah is apparent in the description of John's dress (2 Kgs 1.8; Mk 1.6).[14] John appears aiming for national repentance, which is another feature associated with Elijah reditus.[15]

Whilst these allusions to Elijah are not particularly contentious, the proposed parallels between Jesus and Elijah in 1.12-13 are more so. Reference is made to being cast out by the Spirit in 1 Kgs 18.12 and 2 Kgs 2.16. 1 Kings 19 describes both a 40-day period (v. 8) and nourishment by an angel.[16]

1.14-15 forms a hinge between the opening thirteen verses and what follows. Jesus, like John, preaches repentance. The verb παραδίδωμι used in 1.14 to describe John's arrest is also used to refer to Jesus' passion in 9.31; 10.33; 14.21 and 14.41. The parallelism is here only hinted at, but it indicates that the Elijah motif is not exhaustively fulfilled in John the Baptist; it is carried over to interpret the character and fate of Jesus too.

The allusions to Elijah in Mk 1.1-15 are reasonably clear. The Malachi quotation suggests we are dealing with an Elijah reditus tradition.

---

14. J.A.T. Robinson ('Elijah, John and Jesus: An Essay in Detection', in *idem*, *Twelve New Testament Studies* [London: SCM Press, 1962], p. 29) denies this latter parallel, referring to Zechariah, where such clothing is associated with false prophets. Since this does not fit the portrayal of John the Baptist in Mark it is more convincing to accept a reference here to Elijah.

15. K. Brower ('Elijah in the Markan Passion Narrative', *JSNT* 18 [1983], p. 87) claims that *all* Judaea was baptized because Elijah is the restorer of *all* things. Further appeal to Elijah and Elisha has been suggested with reference to the River Jordan, although this feature is obviously not confined to their ministry. See H. Anderson, *The Gospel of Mark* (Grand Rapids: Eerdmans, 1976), p. 72.

16. Mahnke's objections to these parallels (cited in R.H. Gundry, *Mark: A Commentary on his Apology for the Cross* [Grand Rapids: Eerdmans, 1993], p. 62) are unconvincing, whilst illustrating the subjectivity of typology.

But since Elijah typology is used of Jesus in the wilderness, we have two different uses of the Elijah traditions side by side.[17] Furthermore, we could focus on the parallels drawn between John and Jesus, together with the emphasis on chronological succession in Mk 1.14 ('After John was arrested, Jesus came into Galilee preaching the gospel of God'), and see their relationship in terms of Jesus as John's successor as Elisha succeeded Elijah. Therefore 1.1-15 illustrates the three different ways I noted earlier in which the Elijah traditions can be interpreted.

Mark 6.14-29. The Death of John the Baptist
The picture becomes more confused in Mk 6.14-29. This narrative of the death of John the Baptist is usually dismissed as a time-filling device between the sending out of the Twelve on their mission and their return.[18] However, Mark's intercalation technique has a theological, not just a narrative function.[19] Mark was not forced to write this episode because he had nothing else to say. 6.14-16 consists of more than preliminary story-setting details, since the three prevailing opinions about Jesus are repeated in 8.28 and are quoted in all the Synoptic Gospels, indicating that we must explain their function in the narrative.[20]

> King Herod heard of it; for Jesus' name had become known. Some said, 'John the baptizer has been raised from the dead; that is why these powers are at work in him.' But others said, 'It is Elijah.' And others said, 'It is a prophet, like one of the prophets of old.' But when Herod heard of it he said, 'John, whom I beheaded, has been raised' (6.14-17).

The first remarkable point to note is that some people say that John the Baptist has been raised from the dead. Familiarity with the story reduces the shock factor of v. 14, which is designed to bewilder us. We have not been told that John is dead, yet we hear reports that he has risen. Although several scholars suggest that this is just Herod's

17. A. Farrer, *A Study in St Mark* (Westminster: Dacre Press, 1951), p. 62.
18. M. Hooker, *The Gospel According to St Mark* (London: A. & C. Black, 1991), p. 158.
19. J.R. Edwards, 'Markan Sandwiches: The Significance of Interpolations in Markan Narratives', *NovT* 31 (1989), pp. 193-216.
20. Contra A.E.J. Rawlinson (ed.), *St Mark* (Westminster Commentary, 41; London: Methuen, 1925), p. 82, who dismisses 6.14-16 as unedifying report and market-place rumour.

guilty conscience plaguing him, Mark introduces the opinion on the lips of other people that Jesus can be identified with John the Baptist raised from the dead.[21] Herod then reiterates this. This identification of John and Jesus could only be reached by those who did not know that they were alive at the same time, whilst it points to the similarity between them. Since the audience knows that John baptized Jesus, we cannot accept Herod's conclusion.

The second noteworthy feature of this passage is that Elijah and John the Baptist are presented as two *alternative* possible identifications of Jesus, not as synonymous. This is good evidence against the assertion that 'The association of Elijah and the Messiah was taken so much for granted by the whole people that when Jesus appeared, his pupils and disciples regarded John the Baptist as the returned Elijah.'[22] The reference to John the Baptist is associated with ideas about resurrection, whereas Elijah is connected with the notion of return from heaven.[23]

Mark 6.14-29 is introduced with reference to Jesus' reputation as a miracle worker. This theme forms a connection with the rest of the Markan sandwich, the mission of the Twelve. Mark underlines the lengths to which people went in order to explain Jesus' miracles without becoming disciples. As Gundry comments, 'What mighty powers must be at work in Jesus, to push the king into identifying [Jesus] with a man whose head the king himself had seen delivered on a platter to his own dining room.'[24]

An alternative reason for Herod's identification of Jesus with John the Baptist could be their criticism of his marriage to Herodias. Mk 10.10-12 may be evidence that Jesus also criticized the marriage, as John had done. This avoids the problem of explaining why Herod should identify John and Jesus on the basis of Jesus' reputation as a

21. Are we dealing here with resurrection understood as resuscitation, like the raising of Jairus's daughter narrated in the previous chapter? If so, how do we explain Luke's addition, 'one of the prophets has risen' (Lk. 9.9), since this surely refers to the more distant past? R. Pesch compares the allusion to John's resurrection with that of Jesus, using this passage to illustrate the possibility of speaking about the resurrection of an individual without mentioning an empty tomb ('Zur Entstehung des Glaubens an die Auferstehung', *TQ* 153 [1973], p. 206).

22. A. Wiener, *The Prophet Elijah in the Development of Judaism: A Depth-Psychological Study* (London: Routledge & Kegan Paul, 1978), p. 178.

23. Gundry, *Mark*, p. 304.

24. Gundry, *Mark*, p. 306.

miracle worker, since we have no evidence that John performed miracles and this is explicitly denied in the Fourth Gospel.[25] However, it does not account for the popular belief given in Mark, that Jesus is John the Baptist raised from the dead, which is repeated in 8.28 where Herod is not mentioned.

The wider context points to the Elijah tradition applied to Jesus, perhaps providing justification for the popular identification of Jesus and Elijah cited at 6.15. The rejection at Nazareth echoes the rejection of Elijah, particularly in view of the immediately preceding account of the raising of Jairus's daughter (5.35-43), which resembles 1 Kings 17 where Elijah raises the widow of Zarephath's son from the dead.[26] 1 Kings 17 also refers to a miraculous multiplying of food which is the next miracle to occur in Mark's Gospel after the death of John the Baptist. Herod's banquet is implicitly contrasted with the messianic banquet, symbolized by the feeding of the five thousand. Mk 6.30-44 also echoes 2 Kgs 4.42-44 where Elisha feeds 100 men with 20 loaves.[27] In contrast, Jesus feeds 5,000 men with 5 loaves and has 12 baskets of scraps left over, demonstrating that he far surpasses Elisha, who in turn has received a double portion of Elijah's spirit. Thus, there are various connections between the stories reported from 5.21–6.43, contrary to the claim that the death of John the Baptist fits superficially into its present context.[28]

Mark's intercalation of 6.14-29 indicates the connection between mission and martyrdom, with parallels drawn between the fates of John the Baptist, Jesus and the disciples. There are clear links between Mk 6.14-29 and Jesus' passion.[29] Both John and Jesus are seized and a delay in execution follows due to fear on the part of officialdom. John's head on a platter at Herod's banquet prefigures Jesus'

25. E. Bammel, 'John Did No Miracle', in C.F.D. Moule (ed.), *Miracles: Cambridge Studies in their Philosophy and History* (London: Mowbray, 1965), pp. 181-202. Contra O. Cullmann, *The Christology of the New Testament* (London: SCM Press, 1959), p. 32.

26. The use of κοράσιον in 5.41 and 6.22 provides another link between the episode of Jairus's daughter and the death of John the Baptist.

27. This is a closer parallel than 1 Kgs 17.

28. For reference to the Elijah tradition see R.E. Brown, 'Jesus and Elisha', *Perspective* 12 (1971), p. 89, and B. Lindars, 'Elijah, Elisha and the Gospel Miracles', in Moule (ed.), *Miracles*, p. 66.

29. C. Myers, *Binding the Strong Man: A Political Reading of Mark's Story of Jesus* (New York: Orbis Books, 1988), p. 217. Contra Gundry, *Mark*, p. 312.

self-giving, portrayed as the giving of his body.[30] Both 6.21 and 14.11 mention that an opportune moment occurred, and after their deaths both individuals are buried. The last parallel is really a contrast, since John's disciples come and reverently place him in a tomb whereas Jesus' male disciples all flee and the women followers who remain do not bury him. A contrast between the deaths of John and Jesus is also apparent in the political parody in 6.14-29 where, 'among all these powerful men, a dancing girl determines the fate of John the Baptist'.[31]

Mark 6.14-29 excludes the identification of John the Baptist with Elijah reditus, presenting them as *alternative* identifications of Jesus. This passage focuses on John the Baptist raised from the dead, rather than on the Elijah reditus motif. On the other hand, the passage is a flash-back to the prologue where the association of John and Elijah is clear, filling in the brief allusion to the arrest of the Baptist (1.14) and explaining the sequel. The Elijah tradition is applied typologically in 6.14-29 with strong parallels between Herodias and Jezebel.[32]

It is surprising that in the context of the narration of John the Baptist's death, we find Elijah typology applied to Jesus. This may point to a bequeathing of spirit, with John passing on to Jesus the legacy of his unfinished work.[33]

This passage refers backwards to the prologue and forwards to the Transfiguration and the subsequent discussion about Elijah and John the Baptist in 9.11-13. Only in 9.9-13 is the connection between John the Baptist as Elijah and the significance of his death drawn out. 6.14-29 is not a superficial, incidental episode. On the contrary, it is important in the shape of Mark's storyline.

Mark 8.27–9.13. The Transfiguration
The initial question 'Who do *people* say that I am?' before attention is focused on Peter's confession connects this passage to 6.14-29 and also

30. J.C. Anderson, 'Feminist Criticism: The Dancing Daughter', in S.D. Moore and J.C. Anderson (eds.), *Mark & Method: New Approaches in Biblical Studies* (Minneapolis: Fortress Press, 1992), p. 133.

31. Myers, *Binding*, p. 216.

32. Contra R. Aus, *Water into Wine and the Beheading of John the Baptist* (Atlanta: Scholars Press, 1988), p. 73.

33. Myers, *Binding*, p. 217. 'Herod is wrong about Jesus. But not entirely... Jesus indeed took up John's mantle and message upon his arrest.'

echoes the prologue, resituating the story around a new theme.[34] We begin to anticipate, therefore, some resolution of the puzzle posed by the earlier texts. However, confusion abounds concerning the relationship between the Transfiguration and 9.11-13. The implicit identification of John the Baptist and Elijah is usually highlighted in 9.11-13 without relating it to the immediately preceding appearance of Elijah at the Transfiguration.

The appearance of Elijah and Moses in the Transfiguration account is often explained with reference to their distinctive role as the only Old Testament figures who ascended Sinai and received divine revelation there.[35] Or Elijah is regarded as a champion of Yahweh against false gods, purifying the covenant which Moses, the great legislator, had established between God and Israel. The latter suggestion implies that the Transfiguration is an anticipation of the new covenant.

The presence of Elijah and Moses at the Transfiguration could also be explained with reference to Malachi 3–4. In Mal. 4.4-5 Moses is mentioned as the Lawgiver and Elijah as the eschatological prophet of the end-time. In Mal. 3.2, the Lord who will come suddenly to his Temple (v. 1) is described in terms of refiner's fire and fuller's soap. Mk 9.3 mentions that Jesus' garments were glistening white, such as no fuller *on earth* could bleach them. Moreover, Mk 8.27–9.13 marks a turning point in the narrative, with Jesus moving towards Jerusalem where he acts decisively in the Temple. Therefore, the Transfiguration is a representation of the fulfilment of the prophecy of Malachi in the ministry of Jesus.[36]

If we accept 9.2-8 as an indication of prophetic fulfilment of Malachi 3–4, then I suggest that we can interpret vv. 9-13 as continuing along a similar track. 9.12 could be punctuated as an interrogative, 'Does Elijah come first to restore all things?', expecting a partly negative response.[37] Jesus challenges the assumption that Elijah comes

---

34. Myers, *Binding*, pp. 236-37.

35. Gundry (*Mark*, p. 478) cannot be right when he says, 'Since Mark does not describe Elijah and Moses as transfigured human beings who were translated to heaven, cross-reference to the Old Testament and later Jewish literature concerning their translations and transfigurations are relevant neither to pre-Marcan tradition concerning the Transfiguration, nor Mark's version of it.'

36. However, this is not in terms of midrash, as suggested by M. Black, 'The Theological Appropriation of the Old Testament by the New Testament', *SJT* 39 (1986), pp. 1-17.

37. J. Marcus, *The Way of the Lord* (Edinburgh: T. & T. Clark, 1993), p. 99.

first to restore all things, since this would leave no place for the suffering of the son of Man. However, Elijah has already come and suffered, thus inverting popular expectations in the same way that Jesus radically altered the definition of messiahship through his sufferings.[38]

This raises the question of the *function* of Elijah reditus. Here I should briefly mention Mk 11.27-33, where there is a clear connection between restoring things, cleansing the Temple and purifying the cult and the figure of John the Baptist. The implication of this passage is that Jesus cleansed the Temple using the authority of John the Baptist as his justification. Thus, Mk 9.11-13 could be interpreted as an assertion that although all things were done to John the Baptist as Elijah reditus, he did not complete his programme because his life was cut short.[39] Consequently, his task of restoration was incomplete and Jesus took on the legacy of this unfinished work.[40]

Although the disciples' question grew out of the reference to resurrection, Jesus switches the focus to the passion which illustrates that this is the main focus of the debate.[41] 'Jesus has power to predict his own death even against the apparent implication of the scribes' scripturally based expectation concerning Elijah.'[42]

Verse 13 'as it is written of him' has puzzled commentators, since there is no known scriptural precedent for the martyrdom of Elijah. 1 Kings 19 is hardly typologically predictive of the maltreatment of Elijah.[43] Nor is there substantial evidence for the tradition of the martyrdom of Elijah.[44]

---

38. Contrast this with scholars who uphold the tradition of a suffering Elijah. J. Jeremias, ''Ηλ(ε)ιας', *TDNT*, II, pp. 939-40; Pesch, 'Zur Entstehung des Glaubens', p. 222; Berger, *Die Auferstehung*, p. 376; U. Wilckens, *Resurrection: Biblical Testimony to the Resurrection: An Historical Examination and Explanation* (trans. A.M. Stewart; Atlanta: John Knox Press, 1977), pp. 108-109.

39. ἀποκαθιστανει (v. 12) is a present indicative that rules out past accomplishment of restoration, and requires that it should be interpreted as futuristic. Cf. Mt. 17.11 where the future is used.

40. This is ironic; Elijah returns to complete something which was left undone before he was taken up to heaven, and second time round he is again thwarted!

41. Myers's chiastic analysis (*Binding*, p. 253) supports this point.

42. Gundry, *Mark*, p. 464.

43. Contra Hooker, *St Mark*, p. 221; Farrer, *St Mark*, p. 92.

44. R.J. Bauckham, 'The Martyrdom of Enoch and Elijah: Jewish or Christian?', *JBL* 95 (1976), pp. 447-48. It is suggested that a tradition similar to Rev. 11.3-12 was circulating at the time when Mark wrote which portrayed Elijah returning at the

Jesus' affirmation that John the Baptist is Elijah could be an indirect messianic claim, if we accept the connection between Elijah and the forerunner of the Messiah.[45] Therefore, Peter's confession, the Transfiguration and the debate about Elijah are all relevant to the discussion of identity, with the question of death and resurrection and the role of Elijah all integral parts of the debate.

The connection between Elijah in the Transfiguration account and John the Baptist, who is referred to in the discussion on the way down the mountain after the Transfiguration, is highly significant. For the first time a clear distinction is drawn between Jesus as the son of Man and John the Baptist as Elijah.[46] The reditus concept is applied to John the Baptist and the notion of the bequeathing of spirit is evident in the transference of the Malachi prophecy to Jesus.

Mark 15.33-39. Eloi, Eloi, lama sabachthani?
We now move to the third apocalyptic moment in the Gospel of Mark, the crucifixion, focusing specifically on 15.33-39. This is widely quoted as the earliest evidence for the view that Elijah was regarded as helper of righteous sufferers.[47] It is not clear what the implication is behind the request of the bystanders. Possibly they try to keep Jesus alive a bit longer in case Elijah comes to rescue him from death. Alternatively, Elijah's function may be to ease Jesus through death and transport him to bliss in heaven. In either case, this is a new element introduced into the Elijah tradition in comparison with the references in the rest of the gospel.

end of time, performing miracles, suffering martyrdom and rising from the dead. The dating of this tradition is debatable and cannot be assumed to be pre-Christian.

45. D.C. Allison, 'Elijah Must Come First', *JBL* 103 (1984), p. 258; C.K. Barrett, *The Gospel according to St John* (London: SPCK, 1978), p. 173; Jeremias, 'Ηλ(ε)ιας', p. 938. Contra J.A. Fitzmyer, 'More about Elijah Coming First', *JBL* 104 (1985), p. 296, and Robinson, 'Elijah, John and Jesus', p. 36.

46. Hammer ('Elijah and Jesus', p. 216) suggests that at this point Jesus faced an identity crisis, since up until then he had thought that he was Elijah!

47. Strack and Billerbeck, *Kommentar*, IV.2, p. 770; Jeremias, 'Ηλ(ε)ιας', p. 930; J. Nützel, 'Elija und Elischa im Neuen Testament', *BK* 41 (1986), p. 163. This is taken up in Rabbinic Judaism with many stories of Elijah intervening in different guises to help the poor and afflicted. See M.-J. Stiassny, 'Le prophète Elie dans le judaïsme', in *Elie le Prophète* (2 vols.; Etudes Carmélitaines; Paris: Desclée de Brouwer, 1956), pp. 199-255.

Myers's table below illustrates the similarities between the three apocalyptic moments of baptism, Transfiguration and crucifixion.[48]

Baptism	*Transfiguration*	*Crucifixion*
a) heavens rent	garments turn white	sanctuary veil rent
dove descends	cloud descends	darkness spreads
b) voice from heaven	voice from cloud	Jesus' great voice
c) 'You are my	'This is my son,	'Truly this man was
beloved son'	beloved'	son of God'
d) John the Baptist	Jesus appears with	'Is he calling Elijah?'
as Elijah	Elijah	

The peculiarity of Mk 15.33-39 is striking, since we would expect Jesus' cry, 'My God, my God, why have you forsaken me?' to be the climax. Instead our attention is diverted to a popular superstition about Elijah.[49] Whether or not it was possible to mishear 'Elijah' for 'Eloi' ('My God') undoubtedly this is what Mark asserts. The episode reveals typical Markan irony, since at 9.13 we have been told that Elijah has come and been killed. Now as Jesus is undergoing the same fate, the bystanders misunderstand and think that Jesus is calling on Elijah.

The irony is heightened when we consider the wider context, placing the suggestion of the bystanders in 15.36 alongside 15.31 and also 8.35. It is precisely by not saving himself that Jesus is able to save others. 'In Mark's view, the day of the Lord has arrived in the cross of Jesus.'[50] The dawning of the day of the Lord reminds us once more of Mal. 4.5 and the promise that *Elijah* would come before the great and terrible day of the Lord, again pointing back to 9.9-13.

The confession of the centurion in this passage further highlights the importance of the question of identity.[51] The acknowledgment of Jesus as the son of God also echoes the opening verse of Mark, 'the beginning of the gospel of Jesus Christ, the Son of God.'

The tearing of the Temple veil is related back to the Temple cleansing in ch. 11, which is directly connected with John the Baptist. The tearing of the Temple veil may signify access for non-Jews to the

48. Myers, *Binding*, p. 391. The differences should also be noted, since at the cross those who deride Jesus mention Elijah and the heavenly portents are replaced by an earthly one, the tearing of the Temple curtain.

49. See Myers's chiastic analysis of this passage, *Binding*, p. 389.

50. Brower, 'Elijah', p. 95.

51. Cf. the confession of messiahship at 8.27-28.

Jewish God, parallel to the emphasis in ch. 11 on the Temple as a house of prayer for *all* nations.[52] It could also be interpreted as a sign of destruction. These are not mutually exclusive alternatives.

The Elijah reference in the crucifixion scene is seldom acknowledged to be important. At best, commentaries devote a few sentences to the likelihood of hearing Elijah instead of Eloi, and occasionally mention Markan irony and the theme of misunderstanding. The significance of the popular belief about the function of Elijah is again separated from the question of the relationship between John the Baptist and Elijah.

Since the previous reference to Elijah in Mark was directly linked to John the Baptist, the cry from the cross and the bystanders' mishearing should be seen in the context of the debate about the relationship between John the Baptist and Elijah. By explicitly naming Elijah, this reminds us of the other Elijah references mentioned so far. A further reminder is given by the reference to the tearing of the Temple curtain. Interestingly, Jesus is no longer confused with Elijah, in contrast to 6.15 and 8.28. The relationship between John the Baptist and Jesus is indirectly alluded to, with the echo of ch. 11 raising the question of the respective functions of John and Jesus in regard to the purification of the cult. Mark uses the popular belief about Elijah ironically, to illustrate the misunderstanding of the onlookers. This is not his central understanding of the role of Elijah.

Conclusion

The above analysis demonstrates the variety of possible ways of applying the Elijah tradition. First, by means of typology, without any metaphysical connotation. Secondly, in terms of the transfer of spirit, as a non-personal enhancement of prophetic powers. Thirdly, with reference to Elijah reditus, interpreted as Elijah returning from heaven in the guise of another person, i.e. John the Baptist. Finally, Elijah is mentioned in Mark's Gospel as a heavenly being who comes to take a person to heaven or save someone from death. All of the above motifs are present in Mark's Gospel and we cause more problems than we solve when we try to understand the material simply in terms of *one* category.

This diversity illustrates that the whole issue is more complex than

---

52. Supported by the confession at the cross made by a *Gentile* centurion.

it is usually perceived to be. Furthermore, it cannot be solved by saying that if John the Baptist is not straightforwardly to be identified as Elijah reditus, then *Jesus* originally saw himself as fulfilling that role! This is equally unsatisfactory and does not take account of the diverse ways of interpreting the Elijah traditions. We have clearly identified an Elijah tradition in Mark's Gospel which is applied to both John and Jesus.[53]

The specific question of the Elijah tradition in Mark relates to the larger issue of the interpretation of the Gospel as a whole. Christology, eschatology and soteriology (martyrdom and suffering) have often been polarized as separate issues, each of which provides the 'key to the Gospel'. The Elijah motif illustrates that these three areas need to be integrated, not separated.

53. Contra W. Roth, *Hebrew Gospel: Cracking the Code of Mark* (Oak Park, IL: Meyer-Stone Books, 1988), I do not regard this as a compositional constraint on the Evangelist.

A PASSION NARRATIVE FOR Q?

Eric Franklin

One of the most striking things about discussions of the alleged document Q in the last few years has been the way in which very many of its advocates have moved from acknowledging it as a hypothesis to treating it as a fact. There are of course prominent exceptions to the general stance. Nevertheless these are rather lonely voices in what otherwise appears either as a somewhat dour rigidity or as raucous certainty. F. Neirynck, himself an example of those who approach the reconstruction of its text with a confidence born out of a conviction of the realism of the exercise, nevertheless expresses his own reservations about some of the approaches of his fellow Q advocates, when he says that 'the shift from Q source to Gospel is most remarkable'.[1] The purpose of this essay is simply to question the 'Q consensus' at one point to suggest that this hypothetical document might well have contained some form of passion narrative and that it could in fact be found in Luke's Gospel.

It is of course generally conceded, though not always given adequate acknowledgment, that Q was almost certainly more extensive than that part of it which can be reconstructed out of material common to Matthew and Luke.[2] The hazardous nature of such an enterprise is obvious from any parallel exercise in trying to reconstruct Mark out of Matthew, Luke and Q. We would probably deny all of Mk 6.45–8.26 to him on the grounds that, since Luke did not contain it, it is best accounted for as a Matthaean insertion which he included because he liked doubling up and was always open to adding

---

1. 'Q: From Source to Gospel', *ETL* 72 (1995), pp. 421-30.
2. P. Vassiliadis, 'The Nature and Extent of the Q-Document', *NovT* 20 (1978), pp. 48-73. H. Schürmann, 'Zum Komposition der Redenquelle: Beobachtungen an der lukanischen Q-Vorlage', in C. Bussman and W. Radl (eds.), *Der Treue Gottes Trauen* (Freiburg: Herder, 1991).

anti-Jewish material. On the other hand, since we would be without our copies of John, we might well think that a gospel had to include an infancy narrative, that Mark's was probably lost but that it must have included at least those eleven points which Brown finds that Matthew and Luke have in common. Clearly, an attempt to give Q a narrative ending is not something that must inevitably be ruled out of court. Indeed, just how strong is the theoretical possibility of such an ending is acknowledged by N.T. Wright when he says, 'It would be well to keep on a tight rein any theories which depend on the significance of, for instance, Q's not having a passion narrative. Proceeding down that sort of road is like walking blindly into a maze without a map.'[3] There is in fact every reason to wonder whether Q did have a passion narrative. I hope to show that it is not entirely unreasonable to believe that Luke's Gospel provides us with an answer.

F.C. Burkitt of course argued precisely that in 1906.[4] He maintained that since for the passion narrative Luke was following a source other than Mark, 'the question arises whether this narrative of the passion may not have been derived from the same source as most of Luke's non-Markan material, i.e. from Q itself'.[5] There is little direct evidence in Matthew for Q at this point because he is following Mark closely. Nevertheless, Lk. 22.24-35 does support the hypothesis and, since Q contains some narrative, 'there is nothing surprising that it should have given an account of the last scenes'.[6]

Vincent Taylor notes that Burkitt's suggestion has not had much following. He himself is anxious to find some source behind Luke's passion narrative but rejects Burkitt's advocacy of Q at this point because it 'leaves unexplained the neglect of the presumed passion narrative by Matthew'.[7] Yet more weight than Taylor allows should be given to Burkitt's reasons for this. Matthew is following Mark closely: he makes him his guide. Luke's narrative is very different at

3. N.T. Wright, *The New Testament and the People of God* (London: SPCK, 1992), p. 441.

4. *The Gospel History and its Transmission* (Edinburgh: T. & T. Clark, 3rd edn, 1911).

5. *The Gospel History and its Transmission*, p. 134.

6. *The Gospel History and its Transmission*, p. 135.

7. *The Passion Narrative of St Luke* (Cambridge: Cambridge University Press, 1972), p. 4.

fundamental points and this allows little space for a great use of it. It is not easily assimilated to that of Mark.

Nevertheless, in spite of this inhibition, there is in fact more evidence of contact between Matthew and Luke than either Burkitt or Taylor allowed. Perhaps the place at which to begin to uncover this is the notorious minor agreement between Matthew and Luke at the mockery of Jesus which Michael Goulder's discussions have moved to the centre of the stage.[8] At that point both Matthew and Luke have 'Prophesy! Who is it that struck you?' in place of Mark's simple 'Prophesy!' (Mt. 26.28; Lk. 23.63; Mk 14.65). Here then is a candidate for Q. But we can go further. Luke's version is embedded in his narrative which virtually demands the challenge to be made in this form. He tells of a mockery, not by the Council, but by members of the guard who received him, and it takes place before the questioning and rejection of him by the council. That questioning by them in both Mark and Luke leads to Jesus' declaration of his status and in Mark it issues in their description of it as blasphemy. Jesus' claim to a special relationship with God is rejected. Their mockery in Mark is a part of their rejection and their call to prophesy is a further challenge to him to demonstrate his claimed powers in an unambiguous manner. It is on a higher level than that horseplay of the guards which Luke records and which gives little understanding of the reality of the charge brought against their prisoner. 'Who is it that struck you?' rightly captures the meaning of the narrative that Luke is unfolding.

It is somewhat different however in Matthew's story. He is following Mark and, in his narrative, 'Who is it who struck you?' undercuts the awesomeness of what Mark is conveying and which in his story brings out the tragedy of the Jewish leaders' rejection of Jesus, to take all dignity from them. In Matthew, they actually seek out false witnesses, perversely refuse to accede to what they really acknowledge and now engage in immodest, moronic horseplay. Perhaps even the lack of a blindfold is an intentional added insult against them: they are just buffeting him and simply setting out to confuse him totally. By taking over the words from Luke, Matthew has transformed the Markan scene and reduced both its dignity and its true drama.

At this point Q is an attractive hypothesis. Luke is following Q rather than Mark in order to make a consistent narrative. Matthew, on

---

8. M. Goulder, 'On Putting Q to the Test', *NTS* 24 (1978), pp. 218-34; *Luke: A New Paradigm* (2 vols.; JSNTSup, 20; Sheffield: JSOT Press, 1989).

the other hand, depends upon Mark but he takes over from Q what can serve to revise Mark in the light of his own particular emphases.

Moving back from this significant agreement, we come in the Third Gospel to the episode of the denial by Peter. Here there are two agreements of Matthew and Luke against Mark: both have the single cockcrow in place of the Markan two, and both end with 'And he went out and wept bitterly'.

If the first agreement is to be explained by the desire of both Evangelists to reduce the blame of Peter, the second increases that moment as the point of his conversion. Goulder has shown that though this is textually uncertain in Luke, some such response is demanded by the Lord's turning and looking upon him.[9] It is inconceivable that Luke could have left that movement without any mention of its results.

Again, these agreements are found at points in Luke where the narrative virtually demands them. Luke's story has Peter's denial take place before Jesus' own witness from which it is separated by the story of the mockery and so avoids the contrast which in Mark makes Peter's lack of acknowledgment so stark. One cockcrow only means that there is less to act as a constraint and so to make Peter's continuing in his apostasy so dramatic. All is in keeping with the earlier recognition that the disciple does not actually fall into the grasp of Satan: he does not go into the depths (Lk. 22.31-2). The narrative is of one piece.

In Matthew however this is not so. He follows Mark's stark sequence and contents but, in his customary desire to mellow the disciples' weaknesses, he does what he can to soften the story. Once more, dependence would seem to be on his side. Luke would seem to be reproducing Q out of conviction. Matthew uses it to tone down Mark. He takes the opportunity offered by it to introduce only one cockcrow and, rightly defining the significance of the Q ending, uses it to replace Mark's, even though for him it is strictly out of place since following Mark he has already moved Peter. He makes Peter's action conform to a pattern already made clear at Caesarea-Philippi and at the walking on the water, but now as a climax it represents something of a conversion. He alone of the Synoptics does not have the suggestion of a resurrection appearance to Peter since for him the point of change has already taken place.

Agreements against Mark are to be found in the episode where

9. 'On Putting Q to the Test', pp. 228-29.

Christ is taken captive. Matthew and Luke both have Jesus address Judas, Matthew after he has been kissed by him and Luke before he can do so. In Luke the initiative of Jesus is absolutely essential, for some action to identify Jesus is required. Jesus is in control. Matthew takes over this idea for, in the light of the authority expressed in v. 50, ἐφ᾽ ὃ πάρει is to be understood as a command rather than as a question. It is different from the form found in Luke because Matthew's following of Mark means that Judas has already kissed him.

In the episode of sword aggression where Mark offers no response of Jesus, both Matthew and Luke have Jesus' command to cease from violence. Luke has the episode of Jesus' healing of the slave's ear. Matthew, true to form, does not incorporate extra events into Mark's narrative, but justifies the command to desist on the ground of ethics. He adds v. 52 which parallels the Lukan presentation of Jesus' control whilst his additional reference to the fulfilment of Scripture in v. 54 might suggest a knowledge of Lk. 22.37.

This brings us to Jesus' agony in Gethsemane. Matthew's version is clearly based on that of Mark, whilst Luke's stands on its own in having the single prayer of Jesus and ending with Jesus' call to the disciples to 'Rise and pray that you may not enter into temptation'. He thus moves the temptation of the disciples away from the sleeping in the garden to watching with Jesus at his trials. Peter is the only disciple who is able to do this. Mark on the other hand emphasizes both the weakness of the disciples and the enduring struggle of Jesus. Luke has such a struggle but it is represented as a single combat that is witnessed by the angel and which is concluded successfully. He has triumphed in his hour of temptation, he goes forward knowing that, for all its agony, it becomes a movement towards God and it is for the disciples to learn to follow in the same way.

Matthew again moves Mark in the direction of that pointed to by the Third Gospel. Encouraged by that version, he omits the Markan assessment of the significance of Jesus' prayer, 'that, if it were possible, the hour might pass from him'. Luke's version of course knows that 'the hour' must be entered into for it is that of the power of darkness through which Jesus must go. Mt. 26.55 also gives the arrest the significance of 'the hour'. By their common suggestion that Jesus' prayer was, 'If it was possible...' they both allow Jesus to express more clearly his openness in understanding of the will of God. There is enough of a move from Mark to justify Barbour's assertion that they 'make the prayer into an act of alignment with the Father's will rather than a plain submission to it' which it is in Mark.[10]

If the Gethsemane episode takes us to the beginning of the passion narrative proper and marks the point where there begins a fairly clear movement of Matthew in the direction of Luke, this same re-alignment can be seen in the later episodes of the narrative, though in a fairly clearly descending order of obvious links.

In his description of Jesus before the Sanhedrin, though following Mark closely, Matthew has a number of points which reveal the influence of the Lukan form of the narrative. In place of Mark's account of the high priest's direct question, 'Are you the Christ, the Son of the Blessed?' he has his questioner's use of an oath in the service of his demanding Jesus to 'Tell us' (plural as Luke) 'if you are the Christ'. It is a request not as in Mark for a revelation of his status, but rather for incriminating evidence the truth of which they have already rejected and which is to be used solely in the service of strengthening their already determined rejection of him. Luke also, in 22.67 and 70, has this same outlook. Both move in a different direction from Mark's direct rejection of what is presented as a revelation of Jesus to the Jews.

In place of the Markan 'I am', Matthew has 'You have said so', a form of answer which shows clear signs of the influence of Luke's 'You say that I am'. Jesus does not actually answer their question but turns it back upon themselves, so witnessing to the utter perversity that makes them ask it. They actually acknowledge his status but their determined hostility makes them move forward into a calculated rejection of him.

Finally in this episode, to Mark's reporting of Jesus' witness to his future appearance at the right hand of God, both Luke and Matthew (each in their own characteristic language) add the declaration that his exaltation is imminent. In Matthew, this appears to be influenced by Luke's narrative which makes this exaltation the outcome of the movement of Jesus to it by way of his crucifixion. The First Evangelist does not express the significance of the cross in these terms and is, indeed, unable to do so for he is constrained by his following of Mark. When he is released from this control for the resurrection narrative, however, he does move in this direction which has been

10. R.S. Barbour, 'Gethsemane in the Passion Tradition', *NTS* 16 (1969–70), p. 250.

suggested to him by the form of Luke's story.

With the end of the trial before the Sanhedrin, so-called minor agreements between Matthew and Luke against Mark come virtually to an end. Both, however, emphasize the reluctance of Pilate to condemn Jesus and both emphasize the perversity of the Jews. While Luke conveys this by the overall structure of the narrative, Matthew does so by adding to the Markan outline the episodes of Pilate's wife's anxiety and the hand-washing. The Markan stance is being shifted in a fairly heavy-handed way and it may well have been because of the Lukan form of the story that he had before him.

Luke's and Matthew's stories of the actual crucifixion have little in common for the Markan and Lukan frameworks are quite distinctive and far removed from each other. It would not make for an improper claim, however, to suggest that the Matthaean resurrection appearance owes something of its outlook to the Third Gospel's account of Jesus' glorification by way of his cross.

It would seem then that from the episode in Gethsemane to the actual point of the death of Jesus on the cross, Matthew and Luke have enough points in common to suggest that they either have a direct relationship or are dependent upon a source or traditions common to them both. Other common material in the two Gospels is, by the advocates of Q, accounted for by maintaining that they both followed that. There seems then at least the makings of a case for the extension of that document to include a passion narrative. It is true of course that both Evangelists would be using it in ways other than those found in their Gospels as a whole. Matthew uses it selectively and as a supplement to Mark: Luke takes it over to such an extent that his use of Mark at this point is minimal if, indeed, it can be said to exist at all. Matthew remains in the control of Mark whilst Luke deserts that source entirely.

However, such attitudes on the part of the two Evangelists are not unprepared for by their earlier practice, more especially by their actions in the passages where Q and Mark are alleged to overlap. Of their handling of the parable of the Mustard Seed (Mt. 13.31-2; Lk. 13.18-9) there appears 'broad agreement'[11] that Luke reproduced Q whilst Matthew has conflated this with Mark. Much the same strategy would seem to be apparent in their handling of Jesus' missionary

11. J. Nolland, *Luke 9.21–18.34* (WBC, 35b; Dallas: Word Books, 1993), p. 727.

charges. Matthew has conflated Q and Mark whilst Luke in general presents an edited version of Mark in 9.1-6 and does the same with Q for his mission of the Seventy in 10.1-16.[12] Even though Catchpole voices the suspicion that 'Luke may have created more and Matthew preserved more than tends to be supposed by some exponents of Q', to suggest that Q contained a saying represented in Mt. 10.5b and did not include Lk. 10.8b does not call into question the general assumption that Luke represents Q more exactly than Matthew.[13] He used it overall as a control in a way that Matthew did not, and tended to use it less as a supplement to Mark than the First Evangelist did.

There is less agreement over their use of the Beelzebul pericope. Matthew is often thought to be expressing Q in his claiming of Spirit inspiration for Jesus[14] whilst it is suggested that Luke's version of the parable of the Strong Man is a radical redaction of that found in Q which actually resembled the version found in Mark and Matthew.[15] This solution, however, is in the end far less likely than one which suggests that Luke is following Q and that Matthew follows Mark though expanding it with ideas taken from Q.[16] Mark has a straight-forward defence of Jesus against the charge of his being in the employ of Beelzebul. Luke's version is very different. The significance of the deeds is actually disputed. Though the crowds as a whole marvel, some accuse him of demon-possession whilst others, far less hostile, actually want him to prove himself by a sign. The answer deals with the overall significance of the events: the focus is upon what is happening rather than upon Jesus himself. The strong man is being overpowered, thus witnessing to the casting out of Satan and the arrival of the kingdom of God. There is no mention of blasphemy against the Holy Spirit and no actual direct defence of Jesus: it is rather the presence of the kingdom which is being discussed. Matthew first follows Q because it is less clumsy than Mark even though he follows Mark's agenda rather than Q's double-pronged defence. He has Mark's version of the parable for this better fits his single

12. H.T. Fleddermann, *Mark and Q* (BETL, 122; Leuven: Leuven University Press, 1995), pp. 101-25.

13. D. Catchpole, *The Quest for Q* (Edinburgh: T. & T. Clark), pp. 151-52.

14. C.S. Rodd, 'Spirit or Finger', *ExpTim* 72 (1960–61), pp. 157-58.

15. Fleddermann, *Mark and Q*, p. 55.

16. F.G. Downing, 'Towards the Rehabilitation of Q', *NTS* 11–12 (1964–65), pp. 169-81.

christological line, adds the Q v. 30 which is not entirely relevant to
the single complaint and then takes up the Markan theme of blasphemy
against the Holy Spirit, its presence most likely being responsible for
his description in v. 28 of Jesus as Spirit-empowered (cf. Mk 3.30).

Even here therefore, where there seems to be more interchange
between the three Gospels, Luke seems to be expressing Q's outlook
and words whilst Matthew has allowed his control to be the Gospel of
Mark. The Beelzebul episode gains in importance as being one of the
few Q narrative episodes.

Other narrative is of course found in the temptation episode. Both
Matthew and Luke use Q though both reveal knowledge of Mark. Of
some importance for our argument is a decision about which of our
two Evangelists retains the Q order of the temptations. Usually
Matthew is considered to have done so because his first two temptations are introduced by 'If you are the Son of God...', and because his
story allows the Deuteronomy quotations to appear in a neat reverse
order.[17] Yet the originality of Matthew should not be so quickly
assumed.[18] Luke's usual conservative use of Q should make us open to
the possibility that here too he is following that source with but minimal change. It is true of Matthew no less than of him that the final
temptation which they describe closely prefigures the conclusions of
their particular Gospels. Each could have re-ordered in the service of
that. What we have in Luke is a less self-contained episode than that
found in the First Gospel. It is not such a decisive, one-off, once for
all event, concentrated into a moment at the end of forty days, as it is
in Matthew. It rather describes temptations that are typical of those
that he must face continually and which, as Feuillet maintains, represent 'surtout les souffrances et les épreuves de toutes sortes endurées
par l'église'.[19] For Matthew Jesus, already like Israel called God's son,
has that status attacked but, whereas Israel failed, he remained firm,
his victory being acknowledged by angels. Luke, by contrast, has that
sonship actually to be worked out. He is challenged to test himself and
take a way of self-gratification, to test the devil and to follow a way
alien to God, and, finally and climactically, to test God in an act of
self-assertiveness. Testing God is the natural climax of the series and

    17. J.A. Fitzmyer, *The Gospel according to Luke* (Garden City, NY: Doubleday,
1981), pp. 505-508.

    18. C.F. Evans, *Saint Luke* (London: SCM Press, 1990), pp. 255-56.

    19. A. Feuillet, 'Le recit lucanien de la tentation', *Bib* 40 (1959), pp. 613-31.

makes for the starkest contrast to the way God wills him to follow. He wins through but the devil will return to continue the testing. It will not cease until Gethsemane when the final victory will be won and the events leading to the cross and glorification will be set on an inevitable course.

Jesus remains vulnerable, but it is just that vulnerability which gives significance and value to his teaching. Matthew has actually reversed the Q order in the service of his Christology. Luke gives the order of Q. It sets Jesus out on a way by which the validity of his teaching and the eschatological perspective from which it is given are authenticated by the life of the one who gives it. The temptation narrative points forward to the passion narrative and virtually demands it as its seal.[20]

Luke's is a distinctive passion narrative. As compared with Mark, the atmosphere of tragedy, of total darkness is missing. Evil is real and is arraigned against Jesus in the form not only of Judas and of Pilate, but of the devil's hold over the disciples and his release at the agony in the garden. But Jesus is confident through it all. The narrative to be found in the Third Gospel moves away from the stance of Mark to go in the direction of that later to be taken by John. Jesus moves forward with a confidence born out of the knowledge that the sufferings he is enduring are actually the means of his exaltation. His answer to the high priest forms the control in the light of which the whole narrative is to be understood: 'From now on shall the Son of Man be seated at the right hand of the power of God'.

The crucifixion itself enables that confidence to be realized. Jewish and Roman perversity continues but Jesus progresses confidently through it. He is one with God's will, still responding wholly to him and acknowledged by the one whom he acknowledges in return. His plea for forgiveness for the Jews and his acceptance of the outsider confirm his oneness with God and so enable him to commend himself into the Father's hands. In that confidence he can then expire—his total surrender of his life has enabled his entry into paradise which, by virtue of its mention as a positive response to the dying thief's request to share in his kingdom, is to be seen as entry into that kingdom which is now his and which, reflected on earth, awaits its final manifestation.

---

20. Though see C.M. Tuckett, 'The Temptation Narrative in Q', in F. Van Segbroek *et al.* (eds.), *The Four Gospels* (BETL, 100; Leuven: Leuven University Press, 1992), pp. 479-507.

The Third Gospel does not have the Markan cry of desolation and it places the reference to the rending of the temple veil and the darkening of the sun before the moment of the death of Jesus. The centurion believes, not because of the death, but because of 'what had taken place'. Likewise, it is these things which make the crowds return home beating their breasts. The death itself is not salvific. The outlaw receives his promise of being with Jesus, not by virtue of the latter's death but because of his obedience and surrender to the will of God. The centurion declares that Jesus is 'righteous'. Though having overtones of the Septuagint's description of the Suffering Servant of Isaiah, it avoids any reference to a vicarious death that such a description might contain. To the fore is the description of the righteous man that is found for instance in Wisdom 1–5 and taken up in Psalm 31 which Jesus actually quotes. Jesus' movement to the cross and his manner of accepting its suffering marks him out as a Son of God and ensures his movement into the presence of his Father. His obedience, his surrender and his gentle response before his accusers enable his outreach and his confidence on the cross and ensure both his adoption by God, his vindication and the ultimate revelation of that.

It is important to give the passion narrative of the Third Gospel its own space and not to read it in terms of Mark/Matthew or of the 'cross kerygma'. In particular its own distinctive treatment of the death of Jesus must be acknowledged. That death is not itself the point of disclosure as it is in Mark where it alone makes sense of the significance of what has gone before. As we have seen, in Luke the centurion witnesses to something wider than the death: it is to the whole crucifixion scene which is itself described in terms called out by the entire movement of Jesus to it. 'What had taken place' of course includes the death, though it gives it no great significance, for Luke does not use ἐξέπνευσεν as the climax of that movement into nothingness which it is in Mark. In the Third Gospel it is simply a statement of decease. The work of Jesus is completed for he has fulfilled his Father's will so completely that he can now let go. Death becomes simply the movement to that future which the suffering has itself enabled.

Fitzmyer, whilst recognizing the Third Gospel's distinctive presentation of the cross, has attempted to bring it within the orbit of a more common New Testament understanding of the theologia crucis by seeing the episode of the penitent thief as the first-fruits of the achievement of the cross and therefore as something of a paradigm of that salvation achieved by way of it. 'That scene', he writes, 'certainly conveys to the reader of the Lucan gospel in a highly literary way something about the salvific character of Jesus' death.'[21] That interpretation, however, certainly goes beyond Luke's meaning. The episode of the 'penitent' thief is expressly separated by v. 44 from the events encompassing the final movement towards Jesus' death. At that stage Jesus is still in control and acting in a manner which is wholly at one with that which directed his whole ministry. Earlier, he had received the woman who was a sinner, proclaiming forgiveness as both a condition of and a response to her love, and had taken the initiative in bringing salvation to Zacchaeus. The episode with the robber is of the same order: it does not depend on the death of Jesus nor even on the cross seen as an event in itself. The difference in the terms in which the gift is described depends upon the fact that both Jesus and the robber are quickly to die. The cross enables the exaltation but it is itself simply the climax of that continuing dedication to the will of God that has marked out Jesus' whole life and which as a whole has enabled his exaltation to God's right hand, thus achieving the entry into his kingdom. The cross climaxes and focuses the saving work of God through Jesus but it does not itself achieve it.

Jesus dies as the righteous man who is God's son and whose death betokens, not his rejection by God nor the refusal of the Father's help, but his reception by God for his soul has been found pleasing to him (Wis. 2.12, 18-20, 8-9; 4.13-15). Jesus' death enables the eschatological event (which is the exaltation of Jesus to God's right hand) but it is not separated out from what led up to it, with which it is of one piece, and from that to which it leads. It is the climax of what went before and the enabler of what follows. But as a climax it is of no value in isolation and as an enabler is of use only for that which it enables.

The Third Gospel presents a story of Jesus' passion which is different in a number of significant ways from that presented by Mark and Matthew. It is this distinctiveness which must be acknowledged and given due weight in any consideration of whether it can be understood

---

21. Fitzmyer, *Luke*, p. 23; cf. *Luke the Theologian* (London: Geoffrey Chapman, 1989), pp. 203-22.

as the passion narrative of Q.[22] It does result in a different understanding of the cross. That is not a salvific event in itself. It does not
see that as reversed in a resurrection event but actually understands
the cross as enabling Jesus' movement into life. It puts forward Jesus
as one to be imitated, as the example of the righteous man whose life
is to be emulated and whose way of surrender is put forward as the
way to life for all. This movement into life validates his teaching as it
authenticates him. By enabling his entry into glory, it makes him a
living presence, gives life to his words and enthrones him as Son of
Man.

Here there is some tension with Luke's narrative as it now stands in
the Third Gospel. In that Gospel, the death of Jesus makes for a time
of waiting. The resurrection enables a series of appearances which
reveals him as alive, explains and justifies his sufferings, and points
forward to the life of the church. The appearances are brought to an
end by his ascension which achieves his exaltation to the right hand of
God.

The crucifixion narrative itself, however, does not really allow for
this extension but rather witnesses to the death itself as the point of
Jesus' entry into his kingdom. It is that which effects the realization of
the penitent thief's request. In Luke's own narrative, the teaching of
the risen Jesus actually witnesses to this understanding (Lk. 24.26). It
hints that Luke is reworking an idea which a source has suggested and
which has not been fuly worked out by him. He is using a source
which sees the death of Jesus primarily in terms of his acceptance by
the Father, his entry into Sonship and his example to those who would
respond to his teaching and so follow in his way.

That this narrative of the passion is consistent with Q's outlook is
clear, first in its presentation of the cross and, second, in its understanding of it as the means of enabling the eschatological entry of
Jesus into his kingdom.[23] Q begins with narrative, if not of a baptism
of Jesus then at least with that of his temptation. I have argued that
that temptation climaxes with the movement to Jerusalem and the
rejection of the challenge to jump down from the pinnacle of the
temple. Jesus refuses to test God and instead sets out by way of

22. J.S. Kloppenborg, 'Theological Stakes in the Synoptic Problem', in
Segbroek *et al.* (eds.), *The Four Gospels 1992*, pp. 108-19.

23. I rely heavily on C.M. Tuckett, *Q and the History of Early Christianity*
(Edinburgh: T. & T. Clark, 1996).

surrender to the real exaltation which awaits him. The expectation of a future return of the devil at an opportune time is certainly fulfilled at the agony in Gethsemane. The angel's appearance accomplishes then what is achieved already in the Markan and Matthaean versions of the temptation.

The Third Gospel's passion narrative as the expression of Q's is that to which the Q form of the temptation pointed. Kloppenborg has maintained that 'the reason why Q has a different view of the passion than that of the kerygma (or even the Markan passion story) is that it derives from a different orbit of tradition'.[24] For him, that different view entails an omission of any passion narrative. Nevertheless, he maintains that Q refers several times to the murder of Sophia's envoys and that Jesus is undoubtedly the most prominent of them (6.23; 11.47-51; 13.34-35; 7.31-35). He accepts Jacobsen's view that this motive derives from the deuteronomistic view of Israel's history.[25] Q apparently conceived of the death of Jesus in accordance with the deuteronomistic pattern: it was the expected fate of a messenger of Sophia. Yet Q shows no influence of 'either the passion kerygma of the Crucified and Risen Messiah or of the narratives of the passion with their apologetic use of the Old Testament and the motif of the suffering Just One'. For Kloppenborg, 'Q moves in an entirely different direction'. He would here seem to be expecting Q to point to something like a passion narrative. His unwillingness to contemplate the possibility that it might actually have contained one is his belief that Q moved 'in an entirely different direction'. If we are right to see the Third Gospel's passion narrative as coming from Q this would by no means underplay Q's distinctiveness. It would not give Q what is usually meant by a 'cross kerygma' which would necessarily line it up with that outlook from which Kloppenborg wishes to dissociate it. It would retain its distinctiveness though it would put a brake on that move 'in an entirely different direction' which he ascribes to it.

That it would be appropriate for even the early strand of Q seems to be the implication of Seely's 1991 and 1992 articles on the death of Jesus in Q.[26] For him, 14.27 contains Q's earliest interpretation of

24. J.S. Kloppenborg, *The Formation of Q* (Philadelphia: Fortress Press, 1987), pp. 85-87.

25. 'The Literary Unity of Q', *JBL* 101 (1982), pp. 365-89.

26. D. Seely, 'Blessings and Boundaries: Interpretations of Jesus' Death in Q', *Semeia* 55 (1991), pp. 131-46; 'Jesus' Death in Q', *NTS* 38 (1992), pp. 222-34.

Jesus' death since it has no part in framing the boundaries of the Q community which other passages aim to do. For Seely, the basic meaning of 14.27 is that 'to associate with Jesus in an authentic way, one must carry the cross and travel the path he walked'. As expressing something of a Cynic attitude which only Q exhibited, it would encourage disciples to enter imaginatively into the death of Jesus and so to gain the strength to re-enact it literally. Though his later article talks of Q's being 'uninterested' in Jesus' death, he nevertheless maintains that 'that death is being held up as an example in so far as it is focused on as a criterion of discipleship'. Willingness to follow a teacher in suffering and even death is in Q 'so central to the tradition that it could be used, as in 14.27, to separate that individual who is a follower of Jesus from one who is not'.

Again, as with Kloppenborg, there seems to be a certain inconsistency. Q would seem to demand some attention to the death, and thus to the passion, of Jesus. The disciple is one who follows in his footsteps and who is enabled by meditating upon his manner to enter upon a life of self-surrender that might even lead literally to a cross. Yet, at the same time, it is maintained that Q does not encourage interest in Jesus' passion. One has to suspect that this latter position is largely motivated by the strong desire to keep Q from any possibility of proclaiming a 'cross kerygma' which gives some form of salvific value to Jesus' death and separates that out as a means of atonement. In their denial of this, the Q exponents are no doubt right. Their weakness it seems is their refusal to see the significance of the Third Gospel's distinctive portrayal of the cross and thus to acknowledge that it could well complete that to which Q itself seems to point.

If the passion narrative of the Third Gospel can be accepted as being at one with even the early stream or form of Q, it is even more in harmony with the outlook of redactional Q or Q in its final form. As Tuckett maintains, '[i]n trying to identify specific concerns of Q, we should perhaps take seriously the whole of Q, no doubt part-tradition part-redaction, as making a contribution to this'.[27]

Tuckett himself has stressed that 'underlying much if not all of the Christological language is the idea of rejection, hostility, suffering and violence experienced by Jesus and/or his fellows'.[28] Jesus as Wisdom's envoy, as one of the prophets portrayed in a deuteronomistic mould,

27. *History of Early Christianity*, p. 81.
28. *History of Early Christianity*, p. 281.

and even as son of Man is cast in the form of a suffering agent of God whose attackers bring about his vindication by God. Dominant motifs are those of the righteous man of Wisdom 1–5, the prophetic fulfilment of Isaiah 61 and the son of Man who arouses opposition and hostility. It is the idea of suffering as well as that of vindication which the son of Man figure suggests.

Moreover, Q itself suggests that the members of its community see themselves as facing opposition and hostility. Though this may not be official persecution, it certainly points to a situation of rejection and isolation. They are, however, to love those who despise them, to offer the other cheek when they are attacked, and to give not expecting any return. Only so will they become children of God (6.29-35). They are to follow in the way of Jesus who is himself the true emissary of Wisdom and whose style they therefore are to share (11.49-51). Jesus' movement to the cross and his manner upon it would be both an example to be imitated and would show a stance which will actually inspire.

The passion narrative of the Third Gospel also accords with the eschatological outlook of Q. It is true of course that it does not of itself see the exaltation of Jesus by way of the cross as a preliminary to his return (22.69) but it does, as we have seen, present it as the entry into his kingdom and so pictures him as ready for that return to which Q itself looks forward (12.39-46; 17.22-37). Yet that future kingdom is already anticipated in Q. It is a present heavenly reality into which Jesus enters and which casts its light already on those who respond to the preaching whilst threatening those who refuse (10.9, 11). The answer to John the Baptist and the reply to the Beelzebul charge show that this world already reflects its presence (7.22-23; 11.20) whilst the linking of the parable of the Leaven to that of the Mustard Seed means that its future dimension is brought, at least in part, into the here and now (13.18-21). Vaage, though seeing a Cynic interpretation of early Q, allows for this dimension when he writes, '[a] way of life that might seem to others to be poor and insignificant was here proposed as being instead quite satisfying, salutary, self-sufficient, free of worry, full of possibility'.[29]

The passion narrative of the Third Gospel is in keeping with the theology of Q. But it also adds something to it, not new it is true, but

29. L.E. Vaage, *Galilean Upstarts: Jesus' First Followers according to Q* (Valley Forge: TPI, 1994), p. 65.

giving a depth to what is there expressed and making explicit what in
Q is as a whole only implied. First, it clearly sets forth Jesus as an
example of the kind of stance that his teaching commends and that
discipleship entails. The life that the Q community leads becomes a
response, not merely to his teaching, but to him. Its members live
their lives in response to his own as they witnessed to his surrender to
God both at the beginning of his public ministry and at its end. Moreover, as that stance so clearly enabled his exaltation, it guaranteed that
their following in his footsteps would ensure their own.

The passion narrative meant that Jesus really became their contemporary and that they were embraced by the eschatological event which
his entry into his kingdom had realized. He became more than a figure
from the past. As far as we can tell, the passion narrative of Q did not
lead into a story of the resurrection. Goulder has seen signs of what
could have been a Mark/Q overlap in the story of the empty tomb.[30]
The resurrection narratives in Matthew and Luke however are so different that it could not have extended to them unless these Evangelists
acted at this point in ways very different from their earlier usage.
That Q contained an empty tomb narrative is unlikely for it would
have meant that the movement to exaltation would have ended in
something like bathos. Mark can find meaning in such an ending but Q
is wholly unlikely to have followed his path. The lack of resurrection
appearances presents no problems for it is the exaltation to which the
passion narrative bears witness and which forms the basis of its
confidence for both the present and the future. It presents a Christology very much akin to that of the Epistle to the Hebrews where Jesus'
suffering again leads to and enables his exaltation to the right hand of
God and where the resurrection is made virtually redundant. But Jesus
lives: Q comes from a truly eschatological community.

Tuckett has written recently that the 'burden of proof must
inevitably lie with those who would claim that Matthaean or Lucan
traditions did belong to Q'.[31] Nevertheless he himself responds to his
own challenge to make some part of the Third Gospel's narrative of
the rejection at Nazareth come from that document, whilst Catchpole
and others have set themselves the task of determining its beginning.[32]
Plainly there are a number of possibilities and this essay, written by

30. *Luke*, pp. 774-79.
31. *History of Early Christianity*, p. 227.
32. Catchpole, *Quest*, pp. 60-78.

one who is not himself convinced of the necessity to advocate the use of a Q at all, is simply an attempt to investigate one of them. It clearly falls far short of proof but it does, nevertheless, set forth what would appear to be a reasonable possibility which, in the light of the reasons put forward for belief in Q, deserves consideration. It discusses Q as a hypothesis for that is all it is or can be. It may be a very good hypothesis and, in the hands at least of some of its advocates, that is what it is. But the best of those discussions have been mindful of the necessarily tentative nature of their conclusions. I began by referring to Neirynck's article in which he expressed some concern that Q was now talked of as a gospel. We might end by returning to that article and to his rejoinder that the advantage of calling Q a 'sayings source' is that it 'reminds us of the fact that we have no direct access to the text of Q: it remains a hypothetical source text that we are to reconstruct from Matthew and Luke'. If my argument carries any weight it will strengthen Neirynck's conclusion. Indeed it may even strengthen only to confuse it, for 'sayings source' then itself becomes a somewhat inadequate description of Q. 'Gospel' may even become a more useful term provided that it is used of something which is very different from Mark to express an outlook which is very much its own, as it takes its own view of the cross and resurrection to eschew the seemingly dominant Pauline understanding of the kerygma.

It is a pleasure to offer this small contribution to John Ashton even though it makes a very inadequate token of the gratitude, respect and affection which he evokes. In his study *The Interpretation of John* he endorses de Jonge's scepticism about attempts to delineate the literary sources of that Gospel and in an aside to me at the New Testament seminar he confessed his inability to be enthused by matters of Gospel sources. I cannot therefore look forward to his endorsement of this essay or even of its intention but at least I can hope that it might occasion one of his pungent ripostes which, always discerning, are even by their disconcerting nature inevitably challenging and ultimately positive.

THE GOSPEL THIEF SAYING
(LUKE 12.39-40 AND MATTHEW 24.43-44) RECONSIDERED

Crispin H.T. Fletcher-Louis

The brief Gospel saying which likens the future judgment and the coming of the son of Man to the activity of a thief (Lk. 12.39-40 and Mt. 24.43-44, par. 1 Thess. 5.2, 4; Rev. 3.3; 16.15; 2 Pet. 3.10; Gos. *Thom* 21, 103) is riddled with interpretative difficulties. These extend beyond the immediate application of the image to its place within the wider literary context and the relation of the Gospel text to other early Christian witnesses to the saying. Any attempt to solve those interpretative questions would be a lengthy study. In this context I offer the outlines of a new approach, which, I believe, promises to unlock some of the hidden treasures of the saying. Since some of the inspiration for my proposal is due to some masterful detective work by John Ashton (to which we will come later) it is a great pleasure to offer him this study.

First, let us reflect on some of the problems posed by the saying. The first, and most pressing, is to explain the positive appropriation of the thief image. The correlation between a burglary and the coming of the Son of Man is implicit in Luke's transition from v. 39 to v. 40 and is made explicit by Matthew's διὰ τοῦτο in v. 44. With the possible exception of the two instances of the theft parable in the *Gospel of Thomas*, the image is always regarded a worthy analogy to describe God's future judgment. How can God's action or that of his principal agent (the son of Man) be compared to that of a thief? Suffice to say that, for this reader, no attempt to deal with this problem has done sufficient justice to the theft image and its extant literary context.[1]

---

1. Two are worth noting. J. Jeremias (*The Parables of Jesus* [trans. S.H. Hooke; London: SCM Press, rev. edn, 1963], pp. 48-49) tries to avoid the problem by reconstructing an earlier de-allegorised version in which there is no christological application. Whether or not this reconstruction is legitimate, the meaning of the extant

Secondly, it is striking that Jesus speaks as if the coming of the thief is a well-known (past) event (Lk. 12.39 τοῦτο δὲ γινώσκετε ὅτι...; Mt. 24.43 ἐκεῖνο δὲ γινώσκετε ὅτι, cf. 1 Thess. 5.2). Several scholars have wondered whether the thief simile is not in fact derived from Jewish tradition; specifically an eschatological, and in that sense 'apocalyptic' tradition.[2] That the saying is so widespread in early Christian tradition would lend support to this assumption. However, no such Jewish tradition has been found.[3]

Thirdly, there is the widespread impression among commentators that, particularly in the Lukan version, which may otherwise be regarded as closer to Q, the saying is poorly integrated into its context. Thematic connections between thievery (Lk. 12.33-34), the importance of watching (Mt. 24.42; Lk. 12.37-38, cf. 1 Thess. 5.2-10; Rev. 3.3 and 16.5) and preparedness (Lk. 12.35-36) are self-evident. But at a cursory reading the reader can be forgiven for failing to see any clear connection between dressing ready for a journey (Lk. 12.35); the image of a newly wed husband returning from his wedding feast (Lk. 12.36); a master taking up the position of a slave (Lk. 12.37) and the uncertainty of the number of the nightly watches (Lk. 12.38). This might suggest that the Evangelists have simply resorted to catchword bonding.

Yet on the other hand, closer inspection of the various versions of the thief tradition reveal an uncanny repetition of similar themes, which suggest that at least for the early church there were some

texts is not hereby avoided. J.D.M. Derrett (*New Resolutions to Old Conundrums: A Fresh Insight into Luke's Gospel* [Shipston-on-Stour: Drinkwater, 1986], pp. 50-60) senses the difficulty and concludes that the thief is demonic, which strains the clear sense of the text.

2. W. Brückner, *Entstehung der paulinischen Christologie* (Strasburg, 1903), pp. 179-80; G. Harnisch, *Eschatologisch Existenz. Ein exegetischer Beitrag zum Sachanliegen von 1 Thess. 4, 13-5, 11* (FRLANT, 110; Göttingen: Vandenhoeck & Rurecht, 1973), pp. 89-95; C.P. März, 'Das Gleichnis vom Dieb. Überlegungen zur Verbindung von Lk. 12,39 par Mt. 24,43 und 1 Thess. 5,2.4', in F. van Segbroeck, C.M. Tuckett, G. van Belle and J. Verheyden (eds.), *The Four Gospels 1992: Festschrift Frans Neirynck* (3 vols.; Leuven: Leuven University Press), I, pp. 634-36.

3. Recent work on the son of Man sayings has demonstrated the way in which such sayings are related to very specific Jewish traditions. See C.H.T. Fletcher-Louis, *Luke–Acts: Angels, Christology and Soteriology* (WUNT, 2; Tübingen: Mohr [Paul Siebeck], 1997), pp. 225-50, on Lk. 7.34; 12.8-9; 17.24 and Acts 7.56.

important relationships amongst the constellation of images around the thief saying. The watching and preparedness theme could of course be considered essential to the thief saying, yet it is noteworty that it is a dominant theme in 1 Thess. 5.1-10 (cf. Rev. 3.3; 16.15). In all three of the Gospel versions, that is including the *Gospel of Thomas*, the thief saying is related to a wedding (Lk. 12.36; Mt. 25.1-13 and *Gos. Thom.* 103-104): the parable which immediately follows *Gos. Thom.* 103 (our thief saying) is Thomas's version of the wedding parable of Mk 2.18-20 (par. Mt. 9.14-15 and Lk. 5.33-35). Since Thomas does not repeat Lk. 12.36 or Mt. 25.13 at this point it is clear that he is not slavishly dependent on Matthew or Luke, but was himself conscious of a traditional association between wedding and thief. But what was that association?

So we are left with an ambivalence. On the one hand, there appears to be only a loose connection between the thief saying and its Gospel contexts. On the other hand, the way the tradition has been handled implies that first-century Christians saw a pattern in the beads on the string. Any fresh light on the saying in its context would be extremely welcome.

Exodus as the Controlling Intertextual Context

I propose that the controlling literary and conceptual context for the Gospel saying and its immediate environment is the exodus narrative and the contemporary Passover haggadah.[4] The most explicit clue that this is the appropriate conceptual matrix of this material is provided by the Lukan context established at Lk. 12.35. In Lk. 12.35 Jesus calls the disciples to stand with their 'waists girded and lamps burning'. There is no biblical parallel for the precise combination of these two. The girding of the waist is common but the exact wording ὑμῶν αἱ ὀσφύες περιεζωσμέναι is found only at LXX Exod. 12.11 which prescribes the preparations on the night of Nisan 15th for the Israelites' flight from Egypt. Since the LXX reads αἱ ὀσφύες ὑμῶν περιεζ-ωσμέναι the only difference from the Lukan text is the order of the

---

4. My proposal is partially anticipated by A. Strobel, *Untersuchungen zum eschatologischen Verzögerungsproblem auf Grund der spätjüdisch-urchristlichen Geschichte von Habakuk 2,2ff* (NovTSup, 2; Leiden: Brill, 1961), pp. 203-98. Strobel recognized the importance of Passover themes, though he failed to place the thief image itself in that context.

first three words.[5] Though there is no mention of the lighting of lights in Exodus 12, the fact that the exodus took place at night means that the second part of Lk. 12.35 may also be supplied from the intertextual context of Exod. 12.11. Since Lk. 12.37b—the description of the Lord's coming to his servants and reversing roles by serving them—is related to the Lukan version of Jesus' last Passover meal in Jerusalem, that verse would also suit very well an exodus context.

The exodus narrative also supplies a precedent for theft viewed as a positive command of God. In Exod. 3.21-22 Moses is promised at the burning bush that when he leads the people out of Egypt they shall ask their neighbours for 'jewellery of silver and gold, and clothing... and so they shall plunder the Egyptians'. In Exod. 11.2, prior to the last plague against the Egyptians and the release of the Israelites, Moses is told to tell the Israelites to ask their neighbours for objects of silver and gold. Finally in Exod. 12.35-36 it is reported that the Israelites fulfilled God's word through Moses 'and so they plundered the Egyptians'. It is not difficult to imagine that, if Pharaoh or the demonic power standing behind Pharaoh is regarded as a householder, a story about a householder being burgled at an unknown hour could very well allude to this Old Testament event.

Exod. 12.42 describes the night of the Passover as a night of vigil (προφυλακή LXX) or in the MT a night of watchings (לֵיל שִׁמֻּרִים). This would then explain the presence of the watching theme so prominently in the Gospel context and 1 Thessalonians 5. The three watches of Lk. 12.38 would therefore be derived, not from the singular Greek noun, but from the plural שִׁמֻּרִים. If ever there was a theft in the night (Paul's phrase) it took place at the exodus from Egypt. As far as I am aware this is the only Old Testament case of theft, burglary or plundering being viewed as a positive fulfilment of God's command.

If the exodus plundering is in mind here then we would expect

5. For the Lukan conformity to Exodus at this point see esp. Strobel, *Unter-suchungen*, p. 209. Of the other Old Testament texts cited as parallels (e.g. 1 Kgs 18.46; 20.31-32; 2 Kgs 4.29; 9.1; Job 38.3; 40.7; Prov. 31.17; Isa. 32.11) none in the LXX version is as close as Exod. 12.11. Isa. 32.11 reads περιζώσασθε τὰς ὀσφύας. The lack of a ὑμῶν, the entirely negative sense of this warning in the literary context of Isa. 32 and the comparative insignificance of this prophetic text in Jewish liturgical life in the first century render this text a poor alternative to the Exod. 12.11 allusion.

other indications within Q 12.39-40,[6] its literary context and contemporary Jewish religious and social history that that is so. With the working hypothesis that it is the exodus narrative which provides the intertextual substructure of this Synoptic material we will examine in turn each of the three details of the tradition: the theft image, the son of Man title and wedding banquet.

Plundering the Egyptians and the Pattern of Eschatological Zelotic Theft

The plundering of the Egyptians is mentioned in two of the three references to the Israelites asking for the possessions of their neighbours (Exod. 3.22 and 12.36; cf. Exod. 11.2; Gen. 15.14 and Ps. 105.37). It is of sufficient importance within the exodus narrative for us to suspect that the thief parable might bring to the mind of any Jewish Christian that Old Testament model of God's judgment of the wicked and redemption of the righteous. This is the more likely given that the exodus narrative is *the* defining story of Jewish identity and Passover one of Judaism's greatest festivals. The exodus was not only a past event constitutive of Israel's present identity, it was also the model of subsequent salvation.[7]

Within the Bible itself there is evidence that the plundering theme influenced other narratives, both those which recount the formation of the Israelite nation and those which prophesy a future new exodus on the pattern of the old. Two particularly striking examples are noteworthy. The first, the account of Jacob's leaving his father-in-law Laban's house in Paddan-aram (Gen. 31), exemplifies the importance of exodus in general, and the plundering theme in particular. This is the account of how, after twenty years with his father-in-law Laban, first as a guest, then, as time progressed, as a hostage in Laban's service, Jacob is rescued in order to be able to return to the promised land. David Daube has demonstrated an over-arching exodus pattern evident in numerous details of this story.[8] The plundering-of-the-Egyptians motif is conspicuously present in Rachel's theft of her

6. I use the Q abbreviation, following the Lukan text, without prejudice to any particular source-critical solution to the presence of double tradition in Matthew and Luke.

7. D. Daube, *The Exodus Pattern in the Bible* (All Souls Studies, 2; London: Faber & Faber, 1963), pp. 13-14.

8. Daube, *Exodus Pattern*, pp. 62-72.

father's household gods (Gen. 31.19, 30-42). The parallels between Genesis 31 and Exodus are impressive and were well discerned by later rabbinic interpretation.[9]

The theft by Rachel of her father's gods is never treated as a positive command by God, as in the exodus narrative; it takes place without Jacob knowing and receives no value judgment by the narrator. Daube argues that a positive value judgment is implicit in the fact that this feature of the exodus pattern is rooted in the Old Testament law for the freeing of a slave. According to Deut. 15.13 when a slave is sent away a free person he should not be sent out empty-handed.[10] Certainly, as we shall see, this legal framework was important for later interpretation. For our purposes it is important to note that in Genesis 31 the plundering theme has been understood not only with reference to the dispossession of ordinary material wealth (viz. Laban's livestock and daughters), but also with specific reference to *foreign gods or idols*. This, we shall discover, was an important element in subsequent interpretation of Exodus 11–12.

The second example of inner-biblical interpretation of the exodus and plundering motif is provided by the prophecy of a future king and his deliverance in Isaiah 11. After the description of the king in Isa. 11.1-9, vv. 10-19 proceed to describe how through this king 'the Lord will extend his hand yet a second time to recover a remnant that is left of his people, from Assyria, from Egypt, from Pathros, from Ethiopia, from Elam, from Shinnar, from Hamath, and from the coastlands of the sea'. From what follows the 'first time' is clearly the Egyptian exodus. Verses 15-16 describes an exodus from Assyria and Babylonia in which God's action in drying up the Red Sea is repeated for the people of God at the river Euphrates. The comparison with the Egyptian exodus is made explicit at Isa. 11.16b and so when in v. 14 Israel is said 'to plunder the people of the East', the influence of the exodus plundering motif cannot be mistaken.[11] The description of the king in Isa. 11.1-9 provides important raw materials for messianic expectation in the postbiblical period and we should expect that a similar weight was placed on the plundering theme within Isa. 11.10-16.

The importance of the exodus for the identity of the Jewish people and their understanding of their future redemption cannot be

9. Daube, *Exodus Pattern*, pp. 71-72.
10. Daube, *Exodus Pattern*, p. 70.
11. A different verb (בזז) is used.

underestimated and these two texts point to the importance of the theft or plundering motif within that narrative. However, it could be objected that, though the importance of the exodus narrative in the postbiblical period is well known and well documented,[12] there is no evidence that the plundering/theft motif was particularly important. I have already noted the history-of-religions question raised by the eschatological theft in Q 12.39 and those scholars who have wondered whether this was not a well-known figure of eschatological speech. An examination of Jewish sources reveals a sizeable body of evidence to suggest that this plundering played an important role in Jewish eschatological expectations and would lead to concrete socio-political action in conformity to the exodus pattern. Thus, Jesus' reference to the thief may well have tapped into an established 'apocalyptic' use of the image.

Plundering the Egyptians: A Just Recompense for Slavery

An assessment of the place of the plundering motif in late Second Temple Judaism begins with the literary interpretation of the biblical text. Whilst the plundering motif has caused modern commentators embarrassment, the predominant Jewish understanding seems to have been that it was an entirely justifiable recompense for the Egyptian treatment of the Jews.

This interpretation is found already in two texts which are no later than the second century BC. So, for example, in the dramatic retelling of the exodus narrative provided by Ezekiel the Tragedian, we read, at lines 162-66;

> But ere you go I'll grant the people favour;
> one woman from another shall receive
> fine vessels, jewels of silver and of gold
> and clothing, things which one may carry off,
> so as to compensate them for their deeds.

---

12. See, e.g., T.H. Gaster, *Passover: Its History and Traditions* (London and New York: Abelard-Schuman, 1958); J.B. Segal, *The Hebrew Passover: From the Earliest Times to AD 70* (London Oriental Series, 12; London: Oxford University Press, 1963), pp. 1-41. For the influence of the exodus pattern on later expectation see, e.g., 1QM 3.12–4.11; 11.8; 1QS 6.2 (cf. Ezek. 20.38); 8.12-14 (cf. Isa. 40); Josephus, *War* 2.259; *Ant.* 20.97-98.

A similar explanation is found at *Jub.* 48.18. In both texts the biblical understanding of the Israelite action as a 'spoiling' (MT נצל; LXX σκυλεύω), which is tantamount to robbery, has been understood in terms of compensation. The precise understanding of that compensation is ambiguous. The ambiguity is well laid out by Philo in his *Vit. Mos.* 1.140-42;

> And they did this not in avarice, or, as their accusers might say, in covetousness of what belonged to others. No, indeed. In the first place, they were but receiving a bare wage for all their time of service; secondly, they were retaliating, not on an equal but on a lesser scale, for their enslavement...
>
> In either case, their action was right, whether one regard it as an act of peace, the acceptance of payment long kept back through reluctance to pay what was due, or as an act of war, the claim under the law of the victors to take their enemies' goods. For the Egyptians began the wrongdoing by reducing guests and suppliants to slavery like captives, as I said before. The Hebrews, when the opportunity came, avenged themselves without warlike preparations, shielded by justices whose arm was extended to defend them.

This explanation of the biblical text is repeated in early Christian interpretation (e.g. Tertullian, *Adversus Marcionem* 2.20). It then appears in a talmudic tradition in which representatives of various nations appear before Alexander the Great to sue for redress against past Israelite injustices. The Jewish defendant has the Egyptians depart in shame when he calculates the wages due for the Israelites' time of slavery.[13]

The wide spread of texts across time and socio-religious context which carry this interpretation means it was *the* dominant one in our period.[14] There are, however, various alternative interpretative strategies which exhibit a certain embarrassment with the literal sense of the text. To these we now turn.

---

13. *Gen. R.* 61.7, cf. *b. Sanh.* 91 and the scholium on the twenty-fifth day of Sivan in ch. 3 of *Megillath Ta'anith.*

14. An alternative interpretation which justifies the plundering is found at *b. Pes.* 87b and *ARN* A 41.12. There the wealth taken by the Israelites was that which had originally been accumulated by Joseph (Gen. 47.14).

Plundering Replaced by the Receipt of Gifts

In Josephus *Ant.* 2.314 the plundering theme is transfigured into the bestowal of gifts upon Israelites;

> And he [Pharaoh], summoning Moses, ordered him to depart...They even honoured the Hebrews with gifts, some to speed their departure, others from neighbourly feelings towards old acquaintances.

Josephus has removed the language of theft and thinks that some Egyptians, being friendly towards the Israelites, gave them gifts willingly. This is hardly a natural reading of the biblical text where the Egyptians are anxious to do anything to be rid of a rebellious body of underlings who are causing them so much trouble. Earlier in the narrative some Egyptian midwives *had* demonstrated affection for the Jewish plight (Exod. 1.15-16). However, there is no sign that Josephus has these Egyptians in mind. The progression of a considerable time period since Moses' birth, when there were Egyptians who would act to save Jews, and the intensification of the narrative of conflict between the Israelites and their Egyptian overlords mean that Josephus's interpretation is hardly a natural one based on the biblical text alone. This suggests that he had his own reasons to suppress the normal interpretation which was to justify the Israelite action.

A similar explanation is provided by the *Mekilta deRabbi Ishmael* (tractate *Pisha* 13.129-40 to Exod. 12.36). Commenting on the expression 'And the Lord gave the people favour', the midrash records various traditions which intend to place the Israelites above reproach. For example:

> ...R. Eliezer the son of Jacob says: The Holy Spirit rested upon the Israelites. And every one of them could say to the Egyptians: 'Lend me your article which you have put away in such and such a place'. The Egyptians would then bring it forth and give it to him. The word 'favour' here only means, 'the Holy Spirit', as in the passage: 'And I will pour upon the house of David, and upon the inhabitants of Jerusalem, the spirit of grace' etc. (Zech. 12.10). R. Nathan says: There would be no need of saying: 'So they let them have' except to indicate that they let them have even what they did not ask for. The Israelite would say to an Egyptian: 'Let me have such and such a thing'. And the Egyptian would say to him: 'Take it, and here is another one like it.'

Again any notion of theft is removed by the insistence that the Egyptians gave willingly. On the second half of Exod. 12.36, 'And they despoiled the Egyptians', the *Mekilta* comments that 'This means that their idols melted, thus ceasing to be idols and returning to their former state (*Pisha* 12.142-43)'. This is an unequivocal avoidance of the literal reading of the text according to which it is the action of the Israelites in taking from the Egyptians that is described as a plundering.

Before Josephus and the *Mekilta* the dominant tradition was a justification of the plundering motif as an expression of divine justice. With these two texts a certain embarrassment at that literal interpretation is evident. The fact that after the tannaitic period (whence the *Mekilta*) the older justifying tradition resurfaces in the Talmud, midrash Rabbah and the scholion to the *Megilath Ta'anith*, suggests that this was always the dominant interpretation, which, only towards the end of the first and the beginnning of the second century, had to be modified.[15] Why was this so? Why did Josephus and the *Mekilta*, the one writing for a Gentile audience and the other for a Jewish one, adopt a different and new interpretation?

There is yet a third set of rabbinic texts which, though less clearly dated to the end of the first century or the beginning of the second, also reveal embarrassment at the plundering episode. In these texts we also find an interpretation which is of direct import for our examination of the New Testament thief saying. Of three texts carrying a similar tradition *PRE* 48, is perhaps the earliest:[16]

> The Holy One, blessed be He, said: If I bring forth the Israelites by night, they[17] will say, He has done His deeds like a thief. Therefore, behold, I will bring them forth when the sun is in his zenith at midday...
>
> In the unity of (God's) Name Israel went forth from Egypt full of all good things, comprising (all) blessings, because He remembered the word which He spake to our father Abraham, as it is said, 'And also that nation, whom they shall serve, will I judge, and afterwards shall they come out with great substance' (Gen. 15.14).

This is an extremely important text since it recognizes that it could be said of the flight from Egypt that God acted as a thief. More than that, the expression 'they will say' could be taken to mean that the author

15. For the interpretation in Josephus and the *Mekilta* compare also *b. Pes.* 118b.

16. Cf *ARN* A 29.7 and *Mid. Teh.* 113.2.

17. G. Friedlander, *Pirque de Rabbi Eliezar* (trans. Sepherhermon Press, 1916), p. 386 n. 15, 'The first editions read: "The Egyptians will say: Now has He done His deeds according to the way of thieves".'

knew that this is precisely what some (Jews, Christians or pagans) *did* say. It could even mean that the author knew that it was, or had been, a saying amongst some Jews that God comes as a thief.[18]

At any rate, the author of this discussion in *PRE* 48 is evidently unhappy with the possible implication that God could act as a thief. He states that God brought Israel out in broad daylight; the implication being that God did not act as a thief because the Israelites took from the Egyptians with their full knowledge and in public view.

Pirque de Rabbi Eliezar is, as it stands, a late (ninth century) rabbinic text. However, it frequently carries very early traditions which are notable for their affinities with traditions found in the pseudepigrapha. This interpretation could well date from the second or third century AD. However, since there is not an earlier text which appeals to the daylight flight in order to suppress the danger of the plundering interpretation,[19] there is the suspicion that here *Pirque de Rabbi Eliezar*, like Josephus and the *Mekilta*, is wanting to avoid an older and better established interpretation. This would suggest that here *Pirque de Rabbi Eliezar* should be dated to a similar period to the interpretation offered by Josephus and the *Mekilta*.

The impression that the interpretation in *Pirque de Rabbi Eliezar* was created at a similar time and in similar circumstance to that in Josephus and the *Mekilta* is reinforced by the fact that in itself the midrash is not very convincing. First, it obviously involves a suppression on the literal meaning of the biblical text of Exod. 3.22 and 12.36. Secondly, there *is* such a thing as 'daylight robbery'. Just because the Israelites left at midday does not mean that either side in the conflict could not interpret the Egyptian loss of wealth as a circumstance forced upon them by the exigencies of the situation, and hence as a theft.

Finally, the interpretation of the midrash is not an entirely natural reading of Exodus 12. In Exod. 12.29ff. the firstborn are killed at midnight. There is a loud cry in all Egypt and Pharaoh and his household

18. The textual variant cited by Friedlander (previous note) reveals a knowledge in some witnesses of the pagan tradition discussed below. It is difficult to decide which of the two versions is earlier, since both make sense in a late first-, mid-second- century *Sitz im Leben*.

19. Philo's comments in *De Vita Mosis* to the effect that the Israelite plundering was justified as the despoliation of the defeated by the victors would actually go some way to justifying the 'theft' interpretation.

arise '*in the night*'. 'Then he summoned Moses and Aaron *in the night*, and said, "Rise up, go away from my people, both you and the Israelites!" (v. 31). The Egyptians then urge the Israelites to hasten their departure and the people of God leave in haste. We would be forgiven for thinking that the Israelites left whilst it was still dark. In Deut. 16.1 the Israelites are said to have been brought out of Egypt at night (לְיְלָה). Exod. 12.22 stipulates that the Israelites would not leave their houses 'until morning (בֹקֶר)'. This is probably in the mind of Ezekiel the Tragedian when he says that the Egyptians came out ἠώς (line 168). But both Exod. 12.22 and Ezekiel most naturally have in mind the early hours of the morning. Certainly Exod. 12.22 and Ezekiel's Exagoge 168 are a long way from the noonday of *PRE* 48. Before the rabbinic literature there is no evidence that the Israelites were thought to have come out 'when the sun [was] at its zenith at midday'.

This survey of the Jewish interpretation of the biblical text has produced two important conclusions. First, there was a significant shift in interpretation away from an unashamed justification of the literal text to various attempts to apologise for or remove the literal meaning. These later texts can be dated with some confidence to the end of the first century onwards, though in later Amoraic texts the older tradition re-emerges. How is this development to be explained? The second contribution to our study of the Gospel saying is the importance of the discovery of *PRE* 48, which can make a strong claim to supply, at least indirect, evidence for a Jewish eschatological thief saying. Some Jews or Christians were saying that at exodus God came as a thief in the night. Both groups might reasonably expect that in the future God would again come as a thief in the night.

In order to clarify the nature of the expectation to which *PRE* 48 witnesses and in an attempt to answer the former question we turn to evidence which suggests that the plundering motif influenced the contemporary expectation and behaviour of Second Temple Jews. Here there are principally three sets of data: pagan polemic, evidence from the Jewish revolt under Trajan and Christian texts.

The Plundering of the Egyptians in Pagan Polemic

Remarkably, there are three pagan authors, Manetho, Lysimachus and Pompeius Trogus, who draw on the exodus narrative (in however distorted a form) and the plundering activity of the Israelites in their description of and polemic against Judaism. Pompeius Trogus's account in his *Historicae Philippicae* is exemplary:[20]

> ... the Egyptians, being troubled with scabies and leprosy and warned by an oracle, expelled him, with those who had the disease, out of Eygpt, that the distemper might not spread among a greater number. (13) Becoming leader, accordingly, of the exiles, he carrried off by stealth the sacred utensils of the Egyptians, who, trying to recover them by force of arms, were compelled by tempests to return (2.12-13).

Pompeius's account is exemplary of all three, in one important respect: that which is stolen is Egyptian religious property. In the other two idols are stolen. It is not entirely clear whence this development arose, though Genesis 31 and the comment in the *Mekilta* on Exod. 12.36 provide important corroboration for its place within the Jewish history of interpretation.

In itself the recurrence of this issue in pagan polemic confirms the importance of that part of the exodus narrative for Second Temple Judaism. Combined with two other sources of information the place of this pagan tradition in a larger picture becomes clear.

The Trajanic Revolt and the Plundering of the Egyptians

Despite the paucity of our knowledge of the Trajanic revolt, one thing is clear: the Jewish motivation was strongly religious and violence was directed at pagan temples.

There is abundant evidence, particularly from the area of Cyrene, that pagan temples, among them the sanctuary of Apollo, the temples of Hecate, Zeus, the Dioscuri, Pluto, Artemis and Isis, were destroyed.[21] In the papyri dating from the period of the revolt there is a repeated reference to the Jews as impious ἀνόσιοι.[22] The epithet has

20. Recorded in *Pseudo-Justin* Epitome 1.9–3.9. See M. Stern (ed.), *Greek and Latin Authors on Jews and Judaism. Edited with Introductions, Translations and Commentary* (Jerusalem: Israel Academy of Sciences and Humanities, 1974), I, pp. 332-43. For Manetho (third century BC) and Lysimachus see Josephus, *Ap.* 1.228-52 and *Ap.* 1.304-11 respectively.

21. See generally A. Fuks, 'Aspects of the Jewish Revolt in AD 115–117', *JRS* 51 (1961), pp. 98-104; S. Applebaum, *Jews and Greeks in Ancient Cyrene* (SJLA, 28; Leiden: Brill, 1979), pp. 258-60, 271-333, 355.

22. See *Corpus Papyrorum Judaicarum* (CPJ) no. 438 l. 4; no. 443 col. II, ll. 4-5;

evidently become a semi-technical term, which since Alexander Fuks has been interpreted in the light of the widespread desecration of pagan temples.[23] This feature of the revolt is further confirmed by Appian's comment in his *Bellum Civium* that Pompey's burial ground at a site dedicated to Nemesis was devastated by the Jews during the revolt under Trajan (2.90).

In the absence of any earlier use of the word ἀνόσιοι by pagans of Jews, Fuks argued that this epithet came into use for the first time as a result of the Jewish action during the revolt.[24] However, Applebaum compares other incidents of Jewish iconoclasm in the Second Temple period[25] and the expression should probably be related specifically to the pagan tradition of polemic against Jewish impiety rooted in the exodus narrative. Manetho says that the Israelites acted in a particularly sacrilegious manner (ἀνοσίως).[26] This might mean that the action of the Jewish revolutionaries under Trajan was a particularly intensive and devastating example of a Jewish attitude and course of action which had occurred in the past. Though there is no explicit mention in the sources of the exodus plundering, the overlap in language between the papyri and Manetho might also suggest that the exodus pattern was determinative on the ground.

Applebaum and Fuks both argue that the development of the revolt in North Africa—Cyrenian Jews adopting a scorched earth policy and moving *en masse* to Alexandria—suggests that the revolt was conceived of as a return of the diaspora from exile to the promised land.[27] In the death-throes of the first Jewish revolt the sicarii leader Jonathan the Weaver had led Jews of North Africa into the wilderness in the expectation of demonstrating various signs and wonders; tokens

cf. *Acta Pauli et Antonini* in CPJ no. 158a col. vi, 14; in the *Acta Hermaisci* CPJ. no. 157, col. iii, 49-50, cf. iii, 42-43.

23. *Aspects*, pp. 103-104.

24. *Aspects*, pp. 103-104. Fuks's insistence on the novelty of the Jewish behaviour has recently been echoed by M. Goodman in his essay, 'Diaspora Reactions to the Destruction of the Temple', in J.D.G. Dunn (ed.), *Jews and Christians: The Partings of the Ways AD 70–135* (The Second Durham-Tübingen Research Symposium on Earliest Christianity and Judaism; Tübingen: Mohr [Paul Siebeck], 1992), pp. 34-35 (27-38).

25. *Jews and Greeks*, pp. 258-60, 333. See esp. 1 Macc. 2.45; 5.68; *Ant.* 17.149; *War* 1. 648; *Vit. Mos.* 65-67.

26. Josephus, *Ap.* 1.248.

27. Fuks, *Aspects*, p. 104; Applebaum, *Jews and Greeks*, pp. 335-36.

of salvation (Josephus, *War* 7.438-39).[28] Unsurprisingly the exodus pattern was clearly important for Jews living in Egypt and the environs and so the influence of the plundering theme on Jewish iconoclasm would be natural.

Romans 2.22b: 'You that Abhor Idols, Do You Rob Temples?'

Without entering the exegetical intricacies of a difficult Pauline text, the interpretation of which has no scholarly consensus, we may cautiously draw on Rom. 2.22b as further evidence for the importance of the exodus plundering. A significant body of commentators interpret Paul's words through the tradition of pagan polemic which we have outlined.[29] The same language of temple robbery (ἱεροσυλεῖν) is used by Manetho (*Ap.* 1.249) and Lysimachus (*Ap.* 1.310-11). For this verse to have any force in Paul's argument then his allegation against his Jewish readers has to have some truth. That is, it must be the case that some Jews have in the past engaged in theft from pagan temples. If the pagan tradition is in view then that suggests that before AD 70 there was an established hermeneutic which relied on Exod. 12.35-36 as a basis for contemporary plundering of pagan temples.

An assessment of the last three pieces of evidence leads to a possible synthesis of our discussion thus far. The interpretation of the exodus plundering by Jews at times led to a re-enactment of that behaviour, with a particular focus on pagan idols. Though that activity may have had a long history, it was a particular feature of the second revolt (AD 115–117). It may therefore have also been characteristic of zelotic behaviour during the first (AD 66–73) and third (AD 132–135) revolts. The views of Josephus, the *Mekilta* and *PRE* 48 make sense as embarrassed attempts to avoid a hermeneutic which had in recent history led to disastrous results for the Jewish people.

At any rate there is here a wealth of evidence to suggest that the plundering of the Egyptians had led to the expectation that similar activity would be characteristic of the eschatological redemption. That, I believe, is the appropriate history-of-religions context for the Gospel thief saying.

---

28. Josephus calls this an ἔξοδος in *War* 7.439.

29. For a review of this position and its assentors see D.B. Garlington, '*Hierosylein* and the Idolatry of Israel (Romans 2.22)', *NTS* 36 (1990), p. 143.

The Angelomorphic Son of Man and the Redemption from Egypt

What place then does the son of Man have in this exodus pattern? In the Old Testament it is the *Israelites* who do the plundering, so why the reference to a son of Man of whom there is no mention in the Old Testament exodus material? In all the postbiblical discussion of the exodus plundering it is the Israelites who are the thieves, with the exception of the one text in *Pirque de Rabbi Eliezar*. In that text, which, I have argued, betrays knowledge of a much wider tradition and well-known Jewish(-Christian) saying, it is *God* who acts as the thief. That is not an unreasonable extension of the Israelite plundering since their action is, in a sense, his action. If the plundering is considered (with *Jubilees*, Ezekiel the Tragedian, Philo and later rabbinic tradition) as an expression of biblical justice, then it is ultimately God's justice at work in the plundering. If God could be thought of as the cause of the theft, then that would explain those New Testament texts where it is the Day of the Lord that comes as a thief. But, once again, we are left with a puzzle as to the place of the son of Man title in the Gospel saying.

A comprehensive explanation of the presence of the Son of Man title would require an engagement with a complex history-of-religions background for which there is no space at this juncture.[30] Instead I offer some suggestions which, I think, point in an illuminating direction.

In the first place the presence of the son of Man title is intelligible as a movement from God to God's principal agent. In the *Similitudes*, *4 Ezra* and arguably already in Daniel 7 the son of Man figure performs a plenipotentiary function as God's agent in matters of salvation and judgment.

This recognition leads us to reflect on the role of the angel of the LORD, who, in the Old Testament, plays a similar role as principal agent. The role of the angel of the LORD in the redemption from exodus is, as so often, difficult to pin down. The angel of the LORD

---

30. I have outlined what I consider to be a significantly new approach to the son of Man problem in my *Luke–Acts*. Unfortunately, that approach, which attempts to tie together messianic (human) and angelic (divine) characteristics in the one figure, makes a thoroughgoing explanation of the son of Man thief saying *more* complicated than the predominant view of scholarship during this century, according to which the son of Man figure is a heavenly angelic redeemer.

does not appear explicitly in Exodus 12. However, by 13.21 the people journeying through the wilderness are led by the LORD's presence in a cloud by day and in a pillar of fire by night. At 14.19 this pillar of cloud is somehow connected to the presence of the angel of God which was going before them and, at this point, moves behind them in order to protect them from the oncoming Egyptians. After some progression in the journey narrative (Exod. 14.25–18.27) and the giving of laws at Sinai (Exod. 19–22.19) it is now, once more, the angel of the LORD who bears God's name who is to go before the people as they enter the promised land.

The oscillation in the exodus narrative between the LORD and the LORD in angelomorphic form is typical of the early books of the Pentateuch (cf. e.g. Gen. 16-19, 22). The fluidity between God and his angel begins at Exodus 3, the episode at the burning bush. Despite a lack of specific reference in Exodus 12 to the angel of the LORD it is not surprising that already at Num. 20.16 and Judg. 2.1-4 it is the angel of the LORD who is responsible for bringing the people out of Egypt.

Whilst there is no explicit reference to the angel of the LORD in Exodus 12 there is in any case an implicit one in the mention of the 'destroyer' (המשחית) who is to kill the first-born (v. 23). In 1 Chronicles 21 we encounter a destroying angel (מלאך־משחית) who punishes Israel after David's sin in taking a census.[31] It is not surprising then that Ezekiel the Tragedian calls the destroyer of Exodus 12 the 'fearsome angel' (δεινὸς ἄγγελος, line 159, cf. 187 'death'). In the Wisdom of Solomon the destroyer becomes the 'all-powerful word' who leaps forth from heaven and stands, as did the angel of the LORD in 1 Chron. 21.16, between heaven and earth. The Wisdom of Solomon is particularly important because here the destroying angel—the Word[32]—is identified with Wisdom (Wis. 9.1-2), who is given the responsibility of leading the people out of Egypt in the pillar of cloud and fire (10.15-20). Clearly then there was a significant postbiblical tradition according to which God uses an angelic agent to rescue the Israelites and to destroy the Egyptians. This was a tradition which

31. Cf. the expression 'company of destroying angels' used of the plagues sent against Egypt in Ps. 78.49.

32. For the Word of God as the angel of the LORD see already Ezekiel the Tragedian, *Exagoge*, line 99.

developed the natural reading of Exodus itself and various other texts associated with it.

The extent and significance of this tradition is, however, problematic because in rabbinic interpretation, well known from the Passover haggadah, there is the opinion that God brought Israel out of Egypt, 'not by the hand of an angel, and not by the hand of a seraph, and not by the hand of a messenger', but that rather he brought them out himself. The wording of this formula, which appears in a number of rabbinic texts, is similar to that of LXX for Isa. 63.9, which, at variance with the MT, denies the role of an angelic presence in the exodus narrative: οὐ πρέσβυς, οὐδὲ ἄγγελος, ἀλλ᾽ αὐτὸς ἔσωσεν αὐτούς. In the Hebrew version of this verse the saving role of the angel of the presence is specifically affirmed. The Greek version explicitly contradicts Judg. 2.1-4 and Num. 20.16. This is surprising because it is only in Greek postbiblical Jewish literature (viz. Wisdom of Solomon) that we find any clear reference to the angel of the LORD rescuing Israel from Egypt. And yet it is the rabbis, who read the MT, who follow the tradition present in the LXX.

The reason for the vehement rabbinic denial of an angelic mediation is puzzling and has not yet been satisfactorily explained,[33] though John Ashton has made an attractive contribution to the problem which, we will see, suggests an important connection with the Son of Man figure.

In a clever piece of detective work Ashton has drawn our attention to the use of the denial clause 'Not by the hand of an angel', in an attempt to suppress the role of the name-bearing angel of Exod. 23.20-21:

> The *Mekilta of R. Ishmael* handles the problematic text with some subtlety. It concludes the Tractate Kaspa with a discussion of Exod. 23.19 ('You shall not boil a kid in its mother's milk'). The next Tractate, Shabbata, which is also the last, takes up the midrash at Exod. 31.12 ('And the Lord spoke to Moses'): 'Directly and not through an angel (מלאך) nor through the emissary (השליח)'. Thus the midrash breaks off just before the offending verse that describes the liberating role of the מלאך יהוה, and

---

33. J. Goldin ('Not by Means of an Angel and Not by Means of a Messenger', in J. Neusner [ed.], *Religions in Antiquity: Essays in Memory of Erwin Ramsdell Goodenough* [Leiden: Brill, 1968], pp. 412-24), has tried to explain the presence of this formula in a number of rabbinic texts, including the Passover haggadah, on the grounds of sensitivity to the intrinsic logic of the biblical text. However, he has not successfully explained the impetus for its insertion where it is not demanded, nor, in the case of the *Mekilta*, where it contradicts the biblical text.

when the commentary is resumed, some eight chapters further on, it indirectly repudiates this role with a remark ostensibly addressed to the nature
of God's communication with Moses. Since there is nothing in 31.12 to
make one suspect the presence of an intermediary (and why would God
need one when addressing Moses?), we can only suppose that it is the
threateningly intractable Exod. 23.20 that has provoked the vehement
denial with which the new tractate, Shabbata, commences.[34]

Ashton thinks the reason for the suppression has something to do with
the threat to monotheism that this name-bearing angel was believed to
pose. In the context of tannaitic Two Powers debates that is highly
likely.

For our purpose it is worth reflecting on the possibility that this
text, which implicitly connects the name-bearing angel of Exod.
23.20-21 to the angel censored from any activity at the Passover,
provides indirect evidence that it was the angel(ormorph)ic Son of
Man to whom the rabbis were objecting. In any study of Jewish apocalyptic and mysticism it quickly becomes apparent that this name-
bearing angel looms large in mediatorial speculation. Its foundational
impact in the formation of Samaritan and gnostic mediatorial theology
has been demonstrated by Jarl Fossum.[35] It is of particular importance
that the transformed Enoch(/Metatron), who in the *Similitudes* is
identified with the Son of Man, is closely bound up with this name-
bearing angel (*b. Sanh.* 38b; *3 En.* 12.5; 48c).[36] Given that already in
1 En. 69 the Enochic Son of Man is associated with the secret name of
God, it is possible that this was an early, pre-AD 70 tradition. In which
case the presence of the son of Man in the Gospel thief saying, which
itself is anchored in the exodus narrative, is no surprise. The son of
Man therefore performs a function akin to that of the angel who led
the Israelites out from Egypt.

Given the brevity of our discussion these connections may appear
tenuous. They at least have the advantage that they offer another
factor in an explanation of the denial clause in the Passover haggadah.

34. *Studying John: Approaches to the Fourth Gospel* (Oxford: Clarendon Press,
1994), p. 79.
35. *The Name of God and the Angel of the Lord* (WUNT, 36; Tübingen: Mohr
[Paul Siebeck], 1985).
36. For the broader stream of name-bearing angelomorphic mediatorial speculation within Second Temple Judaism see my *Luke–Acts*, pp. 109-215. In particular
the impact of Exod. 23.20-21 on messianic expectation at Zech. 12.8 should be
noted.

If an angel(omorph)ic redeemer, otherwise associated with the son of
Man, was expected to lead Israel through its new exodus—participating or initiating in some way an eschatological plundering—then, in
the light of the disastrous events of AD 66–73, 115–117 and 132–135,
that figure would quite likely be *persona non grata* amongst Jews who
regretted these revolts. In the same way that Josephus, *Mekilta* and
PRE 48 suppress the plundering motif, we can expect the rabbis to
have suppressed the role of this angelic figure in the pattern of
redemption.

We have now sketched the broad outlines of the history-of-religions
context of the essential elements in the Gospel thief saying itself (Lk.
12.49-40 and Mt. 24.43-44). We have already seen that many of the
individual details in the immediate context (esp. Lk. 12.35-40) also
make sense in the light of the exodus narrative. One remaining feature
which we have not explained is the recurrence of the wedding parable.

Song of Songs and the Passover Haggadah

The key to the presence of the wedding parable, which in the Gospels
is clearly meant to be an allegory of the people of God and Christ,
God's representative, is the strong association between the Song of
Songs and Passover. This was perceptively recognized by Anton
Strobel in his 1973 study of the eschatological material in the
Gospels.[37] The Song of Songs is the scroll set for the feast of Passover. There is no other unequivocal evidence that the two were
already associated in the first century. However, throughout rabbinic
literature the Songs are interpreted allegorically of God's relationship
with his people and the exodus narrative figures prominently as an
example of the salvation-historical interpretation of individual verses.[38]
This would imply that the association with Passover was an earlier

37. *Untersuchungen*, pp. 233-54
38. For the dominance of the allegorical interpretation of the Songs among the
rabbinic corpus and the three principal midrashim to the Songs see e.g. E.E. Urbach,
'The Homiletical Interpretations of the Sages and the Expositions of Origen on Can-
ticles, and the Jewish-Christian Disputation', in J. Heinemann and D. Noy (eds.),
Studies in Aggadah and Folk Literature (SH, 22; Jerusalem: Magnes/Hebrew University, 1971), pp. 247-75.

one.[39] Strobel has collected a number of specific points of connection between the Gospel wedding material and the interpretation of the Songs, which need not be repeated here. Those connections would merit further investigation, though I think the case has been adequately made. It is now secured by the fuller examination of the thief saying against the exodus background, which Strobel was not able to supply.

We have now made at least a preliminary response to the problems which I laid out at the beginning of this study. All the individual elements in the thief tradition make very good sense in the context of the exodus pattern. In particular the difficulty of the thief saying is greatly eased when it is placed in a specific biblical context and post-biblical expectation of eschatological theft. Jesus speaks of the theft as if it were a well-known event precisely because it was one of the best-known events in salvation history and contemporary Jewish eschatological expectation.

39. The importance of Ezek. 16, which also provides an allegory of Israel's espousals with her God, should also be mentioned. The opening verses of Ezek. 16 were also widely interpreted in relation to the exodus narrative.

THE BELOVED DISCIPLE AND NATHANAEL

David Catchpole

Talk of 'a riddle wrapped in a mystery wrapped in an enigma' would be more than justified among those who reflect on the tantalizing figure of the beloved disciple in the passion narrative of the Gospel of John. The theological problem posed by the presence of that passion narrative (however defined) within the Gospel has been addressed with characteristic sensitivity and subtlety in John Ashton's magisterial volume *Understanding the Fourth Gospel*,[1] but what are we to make of that shadowy presence, 'the recipient of Jesus' most intimate confidences',[2] who appears and reappears in the passion narrative— and appears yet again in the appendix to the Gospel? How may we ease the perplexity produced by this person whom we see, whom we hear, and yet whom in a sense we do not know? And why does he apparently appear in the passion narrative and the passion narrative alone (13.23-26; 18.15-17; 19.25-27; 20.1-10; 21.7, 20-23)?

Let us just pause, however, to consider whether the passion narrative is where the beloved disciple (the BD) exclusively appears, and specifically whether 13.23-26 is where he first appears. An alternative suggestion is that he has already come on stage in the guise of the unnamed disciple of the Baptist, who was not Andrew and who heard about 'the lamb of God' and followed Jesus (1.35-40).[3] This suggestion, it must be said, has very little to commend it. Andrew's companion does nothing that Andrew does not, and rather less than Andrew does, in leaving the Baptist and finding the Messiah. His is a 'bit part' which is more than a bit paltry. Yet it is only fair to add that one of

---

1. J. Ashton, *Understanding the Fourth Gospel* (Oxford: Clarendon Press, 1991), pp. 485-514.
2. Ashton, *Understanding*, p. 5.
3. For example, K. Quast, *Peter and the Beloved Disciple* (JSNTSup, 32; Sheffield: JSOT Press, 1989), pp. 30-31.

the main arguments mounted by Franz Neirynck[4] against the equation of this shadowy figure with the BD is less than overwhelming. An insistence that the formulation in 13.23, 'one of the disciples—the one whom Jesus loved', is a first time introduction, and therefore that the BD cannot have appeared before in the narrative of the Fourth Gospel, is weakened by examples of reintroductions of known persons elsewhere in the Gospel. Thus, Andrew is 'introduced' in 6.8 as 'one of his disciples... Simon Peter's brother' in spite of our having met him already in 1.40. Similarly, Judas Iscariot is 'introduced' as 'one of his disciples' in 12.4 in spite of an earlier full introduction as 'one of the twelve' in 6.71. It is therefore not absolutely impossible that readers of this Gospel, who in any case soon have to learn to take aporias in their stride, might have met the BD prior to 13.23. And, we may then ask, if the BD is not the Baptist's unnamed disciple, could he be one of the other *dramatis personae*?

In order to test a hypothesis which responds to this question I would like to move forward in three stages. The first is a brief review of the status and function of the BD in some of the well-known passages where he explicitly appears. The second is a critical examination of the 'signs source' (SQ) hypothesis, and the affirmation of the dependence of the Fourth Gospel on the Synoptic Gospels in general and (for our present purposes) Matthew in particular as a better alternative. The third is a redaction-critical study of Jn 1.35-51 in the light of Matthaean source material, and the unexpected discovery of a quite uncanny resemblance between the BD and Nathanael!

I

Let us begin our series of studies of BD passages at the end, that is with Jn 21.1-14. This tradition, some form of which was available within the Johannine community, was probably added to the Fourth Gospel as part of a second edition. A well-nigh irresistible case can be made for Lk. 5.1-11 as the underlying tradition, and also for reminiscences of Lk. 24.13-35, 36-43 as formative factors.[5] But leaving

4.   'John 21', *NTS* 36 (1990), pp. 321-36 (332), repr. in F. van Segboeck (ed.), *Evangelica II* (Leuven: Peeters, 1991), pp. 601-16 (612); cf. also 'The Anonymous Disciple in John 1', *ETL* 66 (1990), pp. 5-37, repr. in *Evangelica II*, pp. 617-49.

5.   Neirynck, 'John 21', pp. 321-29, repr. in *Evangelica II*, pp. 601-609.

that aside for the moment and concentrating on the internal Johannine connections, it is evident that the Evangelist has been concerned to achieve substantial links with other Johannine material. On the one hand, v. 13 contrives to recall Jn 6.11 and all the rich christological and sacramental tapestry of that chapter. On the other hand, v. 14 with its reference to the third appearance of Jesus to the disciples contrives to unify the three traditions in 20.19-23, 24-29; 21.1-13, and to separate them from the preceding tradition of an appearance to Mary Magdalene, 20.11-18. This has already been done by two other means: first, the contrast between permissible (vv. 20, 25b, 27) and impermissible (v. 17a) touching; second, the announcement, 'I am ascending...' (v. 17b), which needs to be read in the light of Tob. 12.20b as the immediate prelude to an ascent.[6] So the appearance in 20.11-18 is an episode *on the way to* heaven, and the three which follow are, like the majority of appearance traditions in the Synoptic Gospels, appearances *from* heaven. All these carefully achieved editorial connections serve to show how massively important 21.1-14 is as the grand finale of the final edition of the Fourth Gospel. But that only makes it all the more significant that within the story multiple disruption turns out to be a price worth paying for another of its dominant motifs, the presence of the BD. Four dislocations call for notice.

First, Jesus knows the problem of fishing failure (v. 5) and introduces a solution from a distance of approximately 100 metres, no less (v. 8)! It has to be said that he belongs in the boat, not on the shore. But if he had been in the boat he would not have needed to be recognized—by the BD!—nor would he have been able to provide on the beach the carefully prepared 'sacramental' meal (vv. 9, 12a, 13), itself the climax of the story.

Secondly, the disciples are said not to know the identity of the stranger on the shore (v. 4b; in spite of 20.19-29!). That enables the BD, having at first shared their ignorance, to be the person who first recognizes him (v. 7a). But the disciples' ignorance fits ill with their earlier acceptance of his astonishing and authoritative alteration of the fishing strategy, which was to produce such signal success (v. 6).

Thirdly, the BD recognizes the Lord (v. 7: ὁ κύριός ἐστιν), just as

---

6. This reading would be all the easier in the light of John's christological use of angelic patterns, cf. Ashton, *Understanding*, pp. 141-47; *idem*, *Studying John* (Oxford: Clarendon Press, 1994), pp. 71-89.

the remaining disciples will somehow do later (v. 12: εἰδότες ὅτι ὁ κύριός ἐστιν). This recognition is not evidence of an underlying tradition of the first appearance of the risen one, but belongs on the level of redaction. On that level, recognition is doubtless for the BD provoked by the catch itself (v. 7 after v. 6), but the evidence of the catch does not of itself trigger immediate recognition in others. Thus, Peter has the same evidence available, but he reaches the correct conclusion only on the basis of hearing (v. 7b: ἀκούσας ὅτι ὁ κύριός ἐστιν), and specifically hearing the BD. The distinction between him and the BD on the one hand, and between him and the other disciples on the other, cannot be missed.

Fourthly, the disciples minus Peter bring the catch ashore after having been 'not far from the land' (v. 8), but Peter later at the request of Jesus brings some of that total catch of fish ashore (v. 11). This can only happen because he has been separated from the other disciples. The fish which he brings are, moreover, in some competition with the ὀψάριον provided and eventually shared out by Jesus (vv. 9, 13).

If the BD had not been in the story, there would have been no dialectic between recognition and non-recognition, no private conversation between him and Peter, no premature separation of Peter from the remaining disciples, no special journey by Peter to obtain the freshly caught fish, and no dislocation between the fish specially obtained by Peter and the fish provided by Jesus for a 'sacramental' reunion. In short, the BD's presence is responsible for rather a lot! A story about how Jesus in the boat brought success to Peter's fishing from the boat has suffered severely but also, from the Evangelist's point of view, in a very splendid cause. The primacy of Peter has given ground in the face of the super-primacy of the BD. If Peter is a model of belief because he accepts without reserve the word of the BD, then it is above all important that it is the word of the BD which is the ground of that belief.

I wind the tape back, as it were, to Jn 20.1-10. Once again acting in tandem with Peter, his super-primacy again imposed on Peter's primacy, the BD complicates what should be a straightforward story.

The double preposition in v. 2, ἔρχεται πρὸς Σίμωνα Πέτρον καὶ πρὸς τὸν ἄλλον μαθητήν..., and the singular/plural discrepancy in v. 3, ἐξῆλθεν οὖν ὁ Πέτρος καὶ ὁ ἄλλος μαθητής καὶ ἤρχοντο εἰς τὸ μνημεῖον, get the story off to an awkward start. A third oddity is the BD's stuttering movement to the tomb and only later, after an interval and following Peter's entry, into the tomb. A fourth is the doubling of the very precise description of the wrappings, visible apparently inside the tomb (vv. 6b, 7) but equally (so it seems) from outside the tomb (v. 5). More pregnant with meaning than any of these is the explanation of unbelief, which will only later become belief (cf. οὐδέπω 7.39; 19.41), and the low-key return home (vv. 9, 10), which serve to highlight the secondariness of the BD's believing (v. 8b: εἶδεν καὶ ἐπίστευσεν). The silence concerning Peter's belief is as heavy and loaded as the silence of Paul about who won the debate in Antioch (Gal. 2.11-14): Paul lost—and Peter doubted, at least in the pre-Johannine version of the tradition whose approximate contents can be reconstructed with relative ease on the basis of all this internal evidence.

Of course, that process of reconstruction can progress in leaps and bounds once non-Johannine tradition in the form of Lk. 24.12 is invoked. Franz Neirynck is surely right that the two versions of Peter's visit to the tomb are 'so strikingly similar that a literary-critical explanation is needed'.[7] Moreover, within that literary-critical explanation the priority of the Lukan over the Johannine version in every detail without exception can be affirmed with some confidence. Arguments to the contrary have proved unavailing. As others have remarked, Lk. 24.24, τινες τῶν σὺν ἡμῖν, is a Lukan generalizing plural and not a hint of the presence of a companion with Peter in Lk. 24.12.[8] Moreover, while the verb θαυμάζειν is capable of implying a response of belief, that is not how it is understood within the continuity of the Lukan narrative, for the scepticism of the apostles (v. 11) has been in no way reduced for the Emmaus travellers (v. 24) and appears to have been dispelled later and for the first time by the appearance of the risen one (v. 34). So the tradition-historical sequence leads from Lk. 24.12 as it stands to Jn 20.2-10 as it stands, and the dislocations listed above emerge, like those in Jn 21.1-14, as the price worth paying by the Evangelist in order to facilitate his

7. 'John and the Synoptics: The Empty Tomb Stories', *NTS* 30 (1984), pp. 161-87 (174), repr. in *Evangelica II*, pp. 571-600 (590).
8. See Neirynck, 'Empty Tomb Stories', p. 173, *Evangelica II*, p. 589; contra R.E. Brown, *The Gospel according to John XIII–XXI* (London: Chapman, 1971), pp. 1001-1002; Quast, *Peter*, pp. 104-105.

grand design—the emergence of the BD as the prototypical resurrection believer. He is the model of 'seeing and believing'. He is the
person through whose belief the evidence of the tomb is incorporated
into the testimony of faith. And, given the ease with which v. 8 could
have been formulated to read 'and they saw and believed', the fact that
the singular form was chosen must surely confirm that he is the
person to whom the community of the Fourth Gospel looks for the
authentication of its Gospel. Given the immense interest shown
throughout the resurrection traditions in who had this or that experience first, this can only mean that while Peter may be important the
BD is super-important.

I wind the tape back a little further to Jn 19.25-27. Here is the BD
again, once more associated with a prominent person, this time the
mother of Jesus. His appearance is startling and, in my view, can mean
only one thing: that it has to do, not with encouragement of Mario-
logical excesses articulated in such terms as 'the symbol of the New
Israel', or 'an evocation of Lady Zion' or 'the new Eve',[9] nor with
exemplary filial compassion, but with the completion of the mission of
Jesus and the establishing of the succession to him. May we note the
following important points, some of which I owe to the extremely
insightful 1962 article by Michel de Goedt entitled 'Un Schème de
Révélation dans le Quatrième Evangile'?[10]
    First, the importance of what Jesus says to Mary and to the BD is
signalled by the women's being set *near* the cross (v. 25), contrary to
the unanimous Synoptic presentation of their watching from afar (Mt.
27.55; Mk 15.40; Lk. 23.49), and by their being introduced into the
story *before* Jesus' death (v. 30), again contrary to the unanimous
Synoptic presentation. The importance is underscored even more by
what happens immediately afterwards in v. 28, μετὰ τοῦτο εἰδὼς ὁ
Ἰησοῦς ὅτι ἤδη πάντα τετέλεσται, ἵνα τελειωθῇ ἡ γραφή, λέγει,
Διψῶ. This second fulfilment of Scripture forms an *inclusio* with the
first (v. 24), to make the two actions of the four-man execution squad
(dealing with Jesus' clothing, and easing Jesus' thirst) frame the BD
incident in vv. 25-27. A linkage between the squad's first action and
the BD incident has already been established by the μὲν...δέ of
vv. 24b, 25, but it is the linkage between the BD incident and the

9.   Brown, *John XIII–XXI*, pp. 913, 925-26.
10.   *NTS* 8 (1962), pp. 142-50.

squad's second action which is more important still. What draws forth the final τετέλεσται (vv. 28, 30), which frames that second action, is pinpointed by the single word τοῦτο (v. 28). It is nothing more and nothing less than the provision made by the dying Jesus.

Secondly, the mother of Jesus appears for the first time in the passion setting (contrast Mk 15.40), taking precedence over even Mary Magdalene. The reader knows her already as someone whose conduct in 2.1-11 becomes precisely meaningful by virtue of the parallel with the conduct of the brothers in 7.1-9, that is, they all accept Jesus as a miracle worker and try to force his hand as such (cf. 7.6), and they are pious as Judaism defines piety (cf. 7.3-5, 10), but they are neither believers (7.5) nor disciples (7.3). Unsurprisingly, the physical relationship, which could so easily be used as an obstacle to the recognition of Jesus' heavenly origin (6.41-42), had provoked in the mother's case the formula of separation τί ἐμοὶ καὶ σοί, γύναι; (cf. Judg. 11.12; 2 Sam. 16.10; 1 Kgs 17.18; 2 Kgs 3.13; 2 Chron. 35.21; Mk 5.7). Now, however, things are different, and by deliberate use of symmetry the Evangelist causes the incident at the cross, the τέλος, to be the obverse of the incident in Cana, the quintessential sign, the ἀρχὴ τῶν σημείων (2.11). The mother of Jesus makes her second, her last, personal appearance, taking precedence with another family representative over even Mary Magdalene. But more can be said even than that. After the trio of women has been listed, the words Ἰησοῦς οὖν ἰδὼν τὴν μητέρα αὐτοῦ (v. 26) refer back and draw attention to all three by singling out the first and therefore most important member of the group. And in referring back, the reader is encouraged to view it as a complete inventory of those who were there. But then she or he has a surprise: without warning, without preparation, the BD turns out to be there as well.

Thirdly, Michel de Goedt drew attention to the use of a formal three-stage scheme in vv. 26-27: ἰδών...λέγει...ἴδε. The Evangelist employed this formal scheme on just two previous occasions, that is, in 1.29, 36 with the Baptist as subject and Jesus as object, and in 1.47 with Jesus as subject and Nathanael as object. While ἴδε statements occur here and there in the narrative, always with considerable Johannine intensity, even when on the lips of that formidable partner in Johannine theological dialogue, Pontius Pilate (19.5, 14), the use of this 'disclosure formula' ἰδών...λέγει...ἴδε...by Jesus himself is bound to resonate with special formality and authority. That being so,

Jesus' formal designation of the BD should be evaluated with another crucial thought in mind. Here in vv. 25-27, the one and only occasion when the BD appears without Peter, he has been chosen in preference to Peter (who remains, as it were, locally available, cf. 20.2), and chosen also in preference to the brothers of Jesus (who are inclined to travel to Jerusalem for festivals, cf. 7.10). The absence of Peter, and the transfer of Jesus' mother not to the brothers but to the BD, cannot be ignored when his towering status is being so boldly affirmed. This is a status which the community of the Fourth Gospel would recognize, for the BD is in a real and unique sense the successor of Jesus: 19.25-27 puts him in Jesus' own position!

The three studies of Jn 19.25-27; 20.1-10; 21.1-14 serve to spell out the implications of 13.23-26, the passage in which the BD comes on stage for the first time—at least, explicitly! That he is brought on stage at all is, in the light of a comparison with the Synoptic Gospels, doubtless the fruit of Johannine redaction. Here, as elsewhere, he has been imposed artificially upon the tradition. But specifically here in 13.23-26 something is said of him which, according to 21.20, the Johannine community continued to regard as definitive. He reclined ἐν τῷ κόλπῳ τοῦ Ἰησοῦ (v. 23) or ἐπὶ τὸ στῆθος τοῦ Ἰησοῦ (v. 25). For the reader such language could not but resonate with what had been affirmed editorially when the poem about the Word was attached at the beginning of the Gospel's second edition: 'The only begotten Son, who is close to the Father's heart (εἰς τὸν κόλπον τοῦ πατρός), has made him known'. In other words, that which the Son is in relation to the Father, i.e. the revealer, the BD is in relation to the Son.[11] The chain of revelation stretches from Father to Son, from Son to BD, from BD to the community. In the context of Jn 13.18-19, 21-30 the BD is in prime position, and even Peter, if he is to gain access to the truth, must do so by asking the BD!

For the beleaguered Johannine community it was doubtless not possible to exaggerate the importance of all this. Needing legitimation, as it surely did after the cutting of the umbilical cord which connected it to its Jewish parent, the synagogue community, and damaged also by defections from its own ranks, it found that legitimation embodied and established in the person and the role of the BD.

11. Cf. Brown, *John XIII–XXI*, p. 577; P.S. Minear, 'The Beloved Disciple in the Gospel of John', *NovT* 19 (1977), pp. 105-23 (117).

II

Before we venture into the minefield of Johannine source criticism it may be as well to make some preliminary observations about principles, procedures and criteria in order to try to clear the ground. This is particularly *ad rem* because it is hard to rebut the comment that advocates of rival hypotheses tend to engage in a dialogue of the deaf.[12]

First, a qualified movement towards Johannine dependence upon the Synoptic Gospels is discernible in John Ashton's statement that 'although John almost certainly knew Mark, and possibly Matthew and Luke as well, his differences from the Synoptics are so great that they cannot be satisfactorily explained by a simple theory of literary dependence'.[13] But does not that tend to presuppose, indeed to require as a *sine qua non* of literary dependence, that the way John used the Synoptics must be like the way any one of them used any other? Surely it must be possible in principle to allow that, within a setting of literary dependence, the Fourth Gospel used any one of the other Gospels with greater freedom and less restraint.

Secondly, where there is an overlap between the Fourth Gospel and a Synoptic Gospel, there ought to be some features of the Fourth Gospel which appear to be earlier, as well as others which appear to be later, than those in the parallel Synoptic version if we are to posit the existence of a version of the tradition which is prior to both. That much ought to be apparent from the debate about the Q hypothesis, focusing as it does (and indeed must) on the fact that in an extended series of so-called double traditions the earlier version is sometimes and indeed very often found in Matthew and at other times and also very often found in Luke.[14] Of course, we can argue in particular cases about 'earlier' and 'later', but the principle ought to be agreed.

Thirdly, Johannine inclusion of features which are clearly redactional in one of the Synoptic Gospels ought by and large to be sufficient to prove the dependence of the Fourth Gospel, not on pre-Synoptic tradition but on that Synoptic Gospel.

12. Ashton, *Studying John*, p. 90.
13. Ashton, *Understanding*, p. 81.
14. C.M. Tuckett, *Q and the History of Early Christianity* (Edinburgh: T. & T. Clark, 1996), p. 10.

Fourthly, if the hypothetical SQ were to survive it would need not to become so inflated by non-sign material that its classification as a signs source became inappropriate—a consideration which must surely restrain the inclusion within it of a passion narrative. Equally, it would need not to be deflated by the unavailability of too many of the already very limited number of sign traditions in which the Fourth Gospel itself invests. This where, I believe, the hypothesis of a signs source antedating the first edition of the Fourth Gospel sits uneasily with the hypothesis, adopted by John Ashton[15] and others, that the signs in John 6 and 11 (not to mention 21) were added for the first time in the second edition. And, to pose the question even more sharply, what brief could we hold for the survival of SQ if, let us say, the traditions of the officer's servant (4.46-54) and the paralytic (5.1-18) became unavailable along with those of the feeding (6.1-14) and the walking on the water (6.16-21)?[16]

Fifthly, while the Johannine aporias are, as John Ashton has insisted,[17] a major resource for advocates of SQ, they manifestly fascinate and even frustrate us much more than they did the Evangelist. He quite clearly was not bothered. Literary roughness worried him not! And if he was not bothered or worried, we cannot expect the aporias always to denote seams between tradition and redaction. They may do sometimes, indeed many times, but at other times they may belong within the redaction. At the same time, it is worth adding a further balancing point. It is hard to believe that so sophisticated a writer as the Fourth Evangelist would permit his theological-schematic design to be skewed by an aporia which was not only allowed to survive but was also liable to plant a misleading seed thought in the minds of his readers. This applies specially to 20.30-31: how can this statement of purpose, allegedly inappropriate to the Fourth Gospel itself, have been allowed to stand at the close of the first edition of the Gospel? That the Evangelist should show such self-defeating deference to a tradition which his own work had supposedly set out to correct is indeed hard to believe.

This last point perhaps deserves elaboration. When Rudolf

---

15. Ashton, *Understanding*, p. 81.

16. The dependence of Jn 5.1-18 on Mk 2.1-12, 23-28; 3.1-6 has been argued—in my view, quite irresistibly—by F. Neirynck, 'John 5,1-18 and the Gospel of Mark', *BETL* 95 (1990), pp. 438-50, repr. in *Evangelica II*, pp. 699-712.

17. Ashton, *Studying John*, pp. 90-113.

Schnackenburg declared, quite rightly, that 'if 20.30 already formed the conclusion of a signs-source used by the evangelist, he certainly made the thought his own when he ended his Gospel with these words',[18] he at a stroke removed the discrepancy between the outlooks of the alleged source and the Evangelist upon which the hypothesis in part depended. Such a discrepancy becomes all the more will-o'-the-wisp in the light of the match between 20.30-31 and several other statements about signs which the Evangelist has placed at the conclusion of various episodes (cf. 10.41; 11.47-48; 12.37), all of them indicating the fundamental function of signs in the generation of belief. In isolation, they might not—indeed, in a Jewish context (cf. Deut. 13.1-11), could not—sustain belief, but they could certainly create an impression on grounds of sheer quantity (7.31; 12.37) or lack of precedent (9.32) and they unquestionably served a revelatory purpose.[19] Finally, if Jesus' total mission is an ἔργον (4.34), which manifests itself in microcosm in each of a series of ἔργα (9.4); and if again and again the terms ἔργον and σημεῖον are used synonymously (7.3 and 7.31; 9.4 and 9.16; 10.25, 32, 37-38 and 10.41; 12.37 and 15.24); then the story of that total mission in the Fourth Gospel can be characterized entirely naturally as a book of signs. As to an SQ-type inference from 20.30-31, as was said once in a different connection, we have no need of this hypothesis.

We are now in a position to assemble a set of four exhibits, each of them supporting either one or both of the conclusions that the SQ hypothesis is unsustainably fragile and that the direct dependence of the Fourth Gospel upon one of the Synoptic Gospels is impressively more probable. The first exhibit does not bear directly on the SQ hypothesis; the remaining three do.

The first exhibit is Jesus' meeting with Mary Magdalene (Jn 20.11-18). Introduced with typical Johannine imperturbability about aporias (v. 11, cf. vv. 1-2), displaying the typical Johannine device of misunderstanding (v. 15; cf. vv. 2, 13), and illustrating the way in which 'the good shepherd calls his own sheep by name... and they follow him because they know his voice' (10.3, 4), this little story otherwise stays

---

18. *The Gospel according to John* (London: Burns & Oates, 1968), I, p. 19.

19. Cf. F. Neirynck, 'The Signs Source in the Fourth Gospel', *Academiae Analecta* 45 (1983), pp. 3-28 (26), repr. in *Evangelica II*, pp. 651-77 (674), appealing to 6.14; 7.31; 9.16b; 10.41; 12.18, 37.

close to its Matthaean counterpart (Mt. 28.9-10). The two versions of
this story not only match formally, the one (Mt.) has, by all the
normal canons, not a single detail which is less primitive than anything in the other (Jn). For our purpose, particular interest attaches to
the message for the 'brothers' about the journey.

First, it is somewhat artificial to have a message conveyed to the
brothers (Jn 20.17) when he will shortly appear to them (Jn 20.19),
and when no action is required of them in order to see him—contrast
the Mt. 28.7, 10/Mk 16.7 instruction to go to Galilee to meet him
there. The notion of a message from Jesus appears therefore to be a
relic—as a matter of fact, a relic of MtR. Secondly, the saying about
the journey (from Jerusalem to Galilee) in Mt. 28.10 reiterates the
saying in Mt. 28.7/Mk 16.7. This saying is widely recognized as the
product of MkR (cf. 14.28): it was not part of the pre-Markan tradition of the visit of the women to the tomb. Hence MtR is responsible
for placing on the lips of Jesus a saying which would not exist but for
MkR. And the writer of the Fourth Gospel is aware of such a journey
saying: he simply and wholly unsurprisingly adjusts it so that it
describes a journey in the vertical rather than the horizontal plane.
That upward journey, described in terms reminiscent (as we have
already seen) of the famous last words, the Johannine-sounding words,
of the angel Raphael in Tob. 12.20, is a natural element in the Fourth
Gospel's scheme of the descending and ascending emissary with its
angelic overtones. Thirdly, without the message there is no significant
content remaining within Mt. 28.9-10, apart, of course, from Jesus
himself and Mary Magdalene herself. Mary is made available (as it
were) by Mk 16.1-8. Her seeing Jesus, prior to the eleven's seeing him
in Galilee, makes the occasion a preliminary epiphany to a woman,
and for that there is biblical precedent (cf. Judg. 13.2-7, prior to
13.9-23). So the appearance of Jesus is a MtR construction, and the
Fourth Gospel is influenced by that redaction. Fourthly, the intended
recipients of the message ('the disciples and Peter', Mk 16.7; 'his disciples', Mt. 28.7) have, under the influence of MtR, become the
'brothers' (Mt. 28.10). Such language is easily interpreted on the
Matthaean level by reference to Mt. 12.46-50; 23.8, but on the
Johannine level it is new, unprecedented and unusual (cf. Jn 21.23).
Again, the Fourth Gospel seems to be aware of the effects of MtR. So
the Fourth Evangelist appears to have no source other than Matthew
for his story of an appearance by Jesus to Mary Magdalene. Indeed,

for an appearance of Jesus, a message from Jesus, a journey by Jesus, he is directly dependent upon MtR. That means that he knew and used the Gospel of Matthew.[20]

The second exhibit is, to borrow John Ashton's definition, 'the testimony' (Jn 1.6-7, 19-34),[21] within which he and Robert Fortna in their different ways discover the beginning of SQ. Fortna[22] assigns to SQ Jn 1.6-7 and (i) the four-part interrogation of the Baptist, climaxed in the Isa. 40.3 quotation; (ii) the two-baptisms saying, with the witness to 'the one who comes after me' sandwiched between its two halves; (iii) the witness to 'the lamb of God' and (iv) the Baptist's declaration of purpose, 'that he might be revealed to Israel', and his personal vision of the descent of the dove-like Spirit upon the one who has been disclosed as the Son of God. Everything else in Jn 1.19-34, and I would regard this as quite significant, is assigned to Johannine redaction (JnR).

There is not much to say about item (iii), the 'lamb of God' saying, but items (i), (ii) and (iv) repay scrutiny. On (i), the interrogation, we must recall how highly artificial it is even to check whether the Baptist is the Messiah or, come to that, the Mosaic prophet. Nothing he said or did in any nook or cranny of the Synoptic tradition suggests either. This is manifestly artificial Christian schematizing. It also happens to match the small artificial addition in Lk. 3.15 ('all were questioning in their hearts concerning John, whether he might be the Messiah'), which, as in Fortna's reconstruction of SQ, introduces the two-baptisms saying, and which is almost unanimously credited to Lukan redaction (LkR). On (ii), the two-baptisms saying, a good deal of evidence suggests that the intervening announcement of 'the one who comes after me' reflects Q theological concern and derives from Q editorial creativity.[23] If so, the Fourth Gospel would be dependent either on Q redaction (QR) or on at least one of the Synoptic Gospels which was influenced by that redaction. One could actually go further than that in order to meet the concerns of a Q unbeliever: On the basis of Mk 1.7-8 it is clear that the saying about 'the one who comes after

20. Neirynck, 'Empty Tomb Stories', pp. 166-71; *Evangelica II*, pp. 579-86.

21. Ashton, *Understanding*, pp. 284-85.

22. *The Fourth Gospel and its Predecessor* (Edinburgh: T. & T. Clark, 1988), pp. 15-34.

23. D.R. Catchpole, *The Quest for Q* (Edinburgh: T. & T. Clark, 1993), p. 160.

me' does not have to be the filling in the two-baptisms sandwich, as it were, and therefore that redaction—if not QR, then either MtR or LkR—is responsible for that sandwich. That means that the Fourth Gospel is dependent on Synoptic redaction. On (iv), the baptism complex, the MtR changing of the heavenly announcement after Jesus' baptism from 'you are...' to 'this is...' does not revise the essentially personal and dream-like character of Jesus' experience, for even in dreams things can be said to persons other than the dreamer! But the point is that MtR is responsible for making the heavenly voice speak to a person or persons other than Jesus. That is exactly what happens in Jn 1.32, 34.

Pulling all of (i), (ii) and (iv) together, and noting in addition that the way in which the different items are arranged in sequence is also a matter of Fourth Gospel/Synoptic matching, it is (I submit) hard to resist the conclusion that the writer of the Fourth Gospel knew not just Synoptic tradition but also Synoptic redaction. He therefore used the Synoptics.

Would this conclusion be harder to reach if the hypothesis under scrutiny were John Ashton's more Boismardian separation of strands within Jn 1.6-7, 19-34, as a result of which SQ contains (i) the interrogation, doubled but lacking the Isa. 40.3 quotation—and therefore, incidentally, lacking any answer by the Baptist to the question set by the examining priests and levites; (ii) the declaration about the unknown one, whom it is his task to reveal to Israel; (iii) the Baptist's vision of, and witness to, the descent of the Spirit upon the one whom he discloses as the Son of God?[24] I do not think so. The discussion of the two-baptisms saying, with the announcement of 'the one who comes after me' sandwiched in between, is removed from the agenda along with the witness to the 'lamb of God', but the other items remain.

The third exhibit is the healing of the officer's son (Jn 4.46-54). There are two keys to the understanding of what this story contributes to our present investigation, namely the geographical data and the 'signs and wonders' (v. 48).

A survey of geographical data must begin with Jn 2.12a. After the archetypal sign (cf. v. 11a) Jesus, we are told, 'went down to Capernaum with his mother, his brothers, and his disciples...' This report,

24. Ashton, *Understanding*, pp. 284-91.

however, leads nowhere, for Jesus, having gone to Capernaum, immediately goes somewhere else (v. 13)! The apparent oddity of this is
matched by the *prima facie* pointlessness of the subsequent report that
'Jesus went again to Cana of Galilee, where he made the water wine'
(4.46a). It turns out, however, that the pointlessness of this report is
more apparent then real. Cana is in two respects serviceable: first, it is
the place where Jesus' glory has been revealed in the definitive sign
(2.12), and secondly it is not Capernaum! The overt link with the
archetypal sign enables the recollection of that amazing act of Jesus to
condition and colour what is about to be told. And the space between
Cana and Capernaum enables Jesus to be near, but not at, the scene of
the problem of the officer's critically ill child (cf. v. 51). That will
enable the officer eventually to travel from Jesus to his home, to meet
a group of servants who give him good news about his son, to enquire
about the timing, and to believe on the basis of an exact checking of
the evidence.

The geographical data are easily explained in view of the correspondence between the journey to Capernaum in Jn 2.12a and the
introductory scene setting of the Q tradition of this miracle: 'Jesus
came to Capernaum' (Mt. 8.5/Lk. 7.1).[25] The writer of the Fourth
Gospel seems to have substituted a journey to Cana for a journey to
Capernaum, while leaving traces of the original footprints of Jesus in
the sand, as it were. But his substitute journey by Jesus to Cana begins
in Jerusalem (4.43-45, 54), in spite of the creation of a further tension
with the story of Jesus' prior spell of activity in Samaria. The idea of
a journey from Judea to Galilee is not part of the subsequent miracle
story, but by superimposing it upon his material the Evangelist doubtless wished to paint a picture of Jesus' rejection in Jerusalem (v. 44)
and reception in Galilee (v. 45). Jerusalem, the home of οἱ Ἰουδαῖοι
(= the Jews? yes! the Judeans? yes!), has become his πατρίς, his own
community to whom he came and by whom he was not received
(1.11), but Galilee is different. The people there epitomize the pattern
of 1.12—they 'receive' (4.45) and, in the guise of the officer, they
'believe' (4.48, 50, 53). So the Evangelist's editorial work is sustained
and subtle. This is why the healing of the officer's child takes place
against the background of a journey from Jerusalem to Cana near

25. On the original Q version, which approximates most closely to Mt. 8.5-10,
13, cf. U. Wegner, *Der Hauptmann von Kafarnaum* (WUNT, 2.14; Tübingen: Mohr
[Paul Siebeck], 1985); Catchpole, *Quest*, pp. 280-308.

Capernaum instead of a journey from elsewhere to Capernaum.

Talk of the Evangelist's editorial work can now be expanded to take in the totality of his reworking of the tradition, and in the process to pause over the concern with 'signs and wonders'. First, v. 46a, 'Then he came again to Cana in Galilee where he had changed the water into wine', must, as already noted, be redactional. Secondly, v. 47a, 'when he heard that Jesus had come from Judea to Galilee', must be redactional, a knock-on effect of introducing the artificial section vv. 43-45. Thirdly, it has long been recognized that v. 48 is intrusive and owes its position to JnR. The familiar reasons are (i) that Jesus abruptly addresses a plural audience instead of a singular petitioner; (ii) that he criticizes a request for a miracle, but proceeds immediately to meet that request (cf. 2.4); (iii) that the criticism is unjustified, because the officer has not laid down any conditions for belief—he just wanted his dangerously ill son to be made healthy; (iv) that the officer's 'second' plea (v. 49) would read better as an initial request and not, as here, a doublet of the reported earlier request (v. 47b). Plainly, the intrusive v. 48 is designed to speak to those who remember Moses as the worker of signs and wonders par excellence (cf. Deut. 34.10-12) and require the 'prophet like Moses' (Deut. 18.15) to go and do likewise.[26] It is designed to do a little more than that as well, for its formulation is precisely that of Thomas's demand in Jn 20.25. The parallel between the alleged attitude of the officer and the actual attitude of Thomas is doubtless connected to the fact that the first reference to the officer's belief (v. 50), for all that it is said to be belief in Jesus' word, has been totally overpowered and overshadowed by the second such reference (v. 53). And that (second) dominant act of belief was based on a careful checking of what had happened (vv. 52-53a). By putting in the redactional layer (vv. 48, 51-53) John was acting consistently and downgrading reliance on firsthand experience of, or direct evidence demonstrating, an act of God through Jesus.

---

26. In addition to what Deut. 34.10-12 says about Moses, the performance of 'signs and wonders' is highlighted elsewhere in Deuteronomy as belonging to the great acts of God in salvation, specifically the great acts of Moses which were indeed the acts of God at the time of the exodus; cf. Deut. 4.34; 6.22; 7.19; 11.3; 26.8; 29.3. This becomes a standard motif in other biblical passages; cf. Exod. 7.3, 9; 11.9, 10; Neh. 9.10; Pss. 78.43; 105.27; 135.9; Jer. 32.20, 21; Wis. 10.16 (as acts of Wisdom); Bar. 2.11.

Fourthly, the officer's 'second' plea (v. 49) would read better as an initial request and not, as here, a doublet of the earlier request reported in indirect speech (v. 47b). The sole reason for the doubling of a single request by the officer is to permit v. 48 to be woven into the fabric of the story. Fifthly, vv. 50c-53, the story of the officer's journey and his conversation with his servants, must be (as already suggested) redactional, a spin-off of the opening up of a distance between the healer and the healed boy, v. 50b. In this light we can solve the problem of the officer's believing twice (vv. 50b, 53b). The first reference to his belief—v. 50b, 'the man believed the word that Jesus spoke to him'—can now function as the sole climax. Moreover, and this is very important, the three-part combination of distance between the healer and the healed child, the journey by the officer, and the conversation with the servants, is a Luke/John agreement against Matthew/Q, given that the Q version of this tradition has arguably been preserved much more intact by Matthew than by Luke. To put it more precisely, it can now be recognized as an agreement between JnR and LkR. Sixthly, we note that within the JnR section, vv. 50c-53, there is in v. 52 the observation that 'yesterday at one in the afternoon the fever left him (ἀφῆκεν αὐτὸν ὁ πυρετός)'. Up to that point the reader was unaware that the invalid had a fever! In fact, very few people get feverish in the Gospels, indeed only this young person and Peter's mother-in-law, of whom it is said almost identically that ἀφῆκεν αὐτὴν ὁ πυρετός (Mk 1.31/Mt. 8.15).[27] How, one may ask, did the officer's child contract a fever? Answer: through MtR, which put the healing of the soldier's servant/son (Mt. 8.5-13) immediately before the healing of Peter's mother-in-law (Mt. 8.14-15)! Plainly this time JnR was influenced by MtR.[28] Seventhly, v. 54 depends upon the JnR remodelling of the geographical setting of the story.

It is now possible to see just how massive the Evangelist's own contribution was to Jn 4.46-54. The underlying tradition spoke of Jesus' having come to Capernaum and there being asked to heal the critically ill son of an officer. In response, he spoke an authoritative word announcing healing, and on the basis of that word the officer believed. This is in fact the essence of the Q/Matthew version of the tradition.

27. The only other instance in the New Testament is in Acts 28.8.

28. Cf. F. Neirynck, 'John 4,46-54: Signs Source and/or Synoptic Gospels', *ETL* 60 (1984), pp. 367-75 (373), repr. in *Evangelica II*, pp. 679-87 (685).

What has been added is a heady literary/theological cocktail of the LkR scheme, MtR detail, and JnR theologizing. Advocates of SQ tend to assign vv. 46b-47, 50-54a to that source. The above, rather different, analysis of the history of tradition points to another conclusion, one in which direct use of two Synoptic Gospels renders the SQ explanation of the data unnecessary.

The fourth and last exhibit is Peter's confession (Jn 6.60-71), a story which needs to be set in its extended sequence in John 6 as a whole and then analysed formally in its own right.

The starting point must be the remarkable agreement between the Fourth Gospel and Matthew/Mark in the sequence involving the feeding of the thousands of hungry people in Jn 6.1-15 (cf. Mt. 14.13-21, 32-39; Mk 6.30-44; 8.1-10), the walking on the water in Jn 6.16-21 (cf. Mt. 14.22-33; Mk 6.45-52), the refusal of a sign in Jn 6.22-30 (cf. Mt. 16.1-4; Mk 8.11-13), the discourse about food in Jn 6.31-59 (cf. Mt. 16.5-12; Mk 8.14-21), and Peter's confession in Jn 6.60-71 (cf. Mt. 16.13-23; Mk 8.27-33). What must be remembered here is that the Markan order is the *Markan* order, not something that goes back to pre-Markan tradition. Pre-Markan collections have some schematic or form-critical affinities,[29] but the items in this particular sequence have nothing of that sort in common. So the John/ Matthew/Mark correspondence in order suggests dependence by the Fourth Gospel on one or other of those two Synoptic Gospels.

The Caesarea Philippi-type episode at the end of the sequence shows John corresponding very closely indeed to Matthew/Mark, less so to Luke. The Fourth Gospel shares eight features with Matthew/Mark: (i) an acknowledgment of Jesus' status, (ii) in direct speech (iii) by Peter, who (iv) speaks on behalf of the whole disciple group (v) in a context where the prospect of passion and death casts a shadow, and (vi) the presence of the devil (vii) in the life of a disciple is (viii) acknowledged by Jesus. The list is shorter in respect of Luke since that Gospel does not at this juncture envisage the passion as a problem, nor is the presence of the devil in the life of a disciple acknowledged by Jesus. From whom did John get this episode? Nothing in the Fourth Gospel looks independent of, or earlier than, Matthew/Mark. Moreover, direct dependence would be all the more

29. Cf. H.-W. Kuhn, *Ältere Sammlungen im Markusevangelium* (SUNT, 8; Göttingen: Vandenhoeck & Ruprecht, 1971), pp. 11-52.

probable if we were to assign to MkR the whole of Mk 8.27-33! I have argued that elsewhere, and I stand by that argument.[30] The Fourth Gospel would then be dependent, either on MkR or on Matthew, who himself depended wholly on MkR.

We can go on to observe how very clear is the theological capital which the Fourth Evangelist has made out of revising the Synoptic material at his disposal. The redaction-critical coherence of an interpretation of the Fourth Gospel on the basis of the Evangelist's use of Matthew/Mark itself serves to strengthen the source-critical premise. Essentially he has remodelled Peter's confession of Jesus and set it in a new context. The sermon on Exod. 16.4, 15 in Jn 6.31-58[31] had caused consternation among 'the Jews' and also division among 'the disciples'. Jesus had spoken of himself in extremely strong and realistic terms as God's gift in word and sacrament. This has proved just too much. Jesus' question, 'Do you also wish to go away?' (v. 67) enables Peter's answer to be the confession of the continuing loyalists. Note in this connection four points:

First, Jesus has spoken about some disciples who do not believe (v. 64), and he explains their position by an appeal to predestination (v. 65, cf. v. 44)! This predestinarian comment on them is a quotation of the main argument he used to answer criticism from 'the Jews' (vv. 41-42). Now an appeal to predestination is, of course, a sectarian reflex. So the loyalists whom Peter represents, the sectarian breakaway group from the Jewish community, have the problem that some of their own number peel off and go back to where they came from.

Secondly, the devil is not speaking through Peter, as was the case in Mt. 16.23/Mk 8.33. He is at work in Judas (v. 70) and in those former Christian Jews who have now gone back to the non-Christian community. To associate the former members of the Christian group with Judas (v. 64) is bad enough—to associate them with Satan is ferocious indeed. Such graceless polemic, in which there is an either/or–light/darkness–in/out view of reality, is again typically sectarian and for us wonderfully revealing. Some *cause célèbre* must have produced such

---

30. 'The "Triumphal" Entry', in E. Bammel and C.F.D. Moule (eds.), *Jesus and the Politics of his Day* (Cambridge: Cambridge University Press, 1984), pp. 319-34 (326-28).

31. See P. Borgen, *Bread from Heaven* (NovTSup, 10; Leiden: Brill, 1963); *Philo, John and Paul* (Atlanta, GA: Scholars Press, 1987), pp. 121-44.

aggression, and it is not hard to discover what it was. The high-powered sacramental teaching in vv. 51-58, grounded in the claim that Jesus is not only giver but also, in the form of his 'flesh', the divine gift (v. 51), has deeply offended both 'the Jews' (v. 52) and also 'the disciples' (vv. 60-61). Those disciples are represented by Judas who will later, in an impressively extended discussion in Jn. 13.18-31, be implicitly reconnected up to the John 6 narrative (τρώγειν, 6.54, 56, 58; 13.18, introduced redactionally in the quotation of Ps. 41.10[32]) and explicitly made to share Jesus' bread before defecting and disappearing into the darkness. All this suggests that after the first trauma of the expulsion of the Christian Jews from the synagogue on christological grounds, there was a second trauma as some of the Jewish Christians baulked at the developing interpretation of the separated community's eucharistic 'boundary marker'.

Thirdly, not 'You are the Messiah', says Peter, but 'We have come to believe and know that you are the Holy One of God' (v. 69). Why the change of terminology? Answer: The language of holiness is the language of heavenliness and of Sonship. It presents Jesus as a person who belongs essentially to the divine world, the world of the angels in which he is unique (cf. Jn 10.36). But the echo of Mt. 16.16 diff Mk 8.29 is deafening.

Fourthly, with the problem of defection from the Johannine community in mind it would be good to take seriously the internal connection between ἡμεῖς πεπιστεύκαμεν...(v. 69) and the reading πιστεύητε (20.31). The writer is concerned to keep the Jewish Christians from lapsing back into becoming Christian Jews (i.e. members of the Jewish synagogue community who hold a low view of Jesus) or, worse still, non-Christian Jews (who regard Jesus as someone who led Israel astray).

III

On what is, I hope, a suitably secure foundation a further proposal can now be constructed, namely that the Caesarea Philippi tradition in Mt. 16.13-23/Mk 8.27-33 is not only known to and used by the Fourth Evangelist but also very specifically one of the sources of Jn 1.35-51. It would be no surprise that this should be the case, for there are at least two other complexes in the Fourth Gospel where the influence of

32. Cf. Borgen, *Bread from Heaven*, pp. 92-93.

that tradition is discernible. The first of these is Jn 3.14-15 where the Evangelist declares that 'just as Moses lifted up the serpent in the wilderness, so must the Son of Man be lifted up, that whoever believes in him may have eternal life'. The implicit allusion to Num. 21.8-9, 'And the Lord said to Moses, "Make a poisonous serpent, and set it on a pole; and everyone who is bitten shall look at it and live"' demands that Jesus' crucifixion shall be in mind, and if we paraphrase the saying to read 'the Son of Man must be crucified...', then it is clear that Mk 8.31/Mt. 16.21/Lk. 9.22 is the Synoptic stimulus for this saying.[33] The second Johannine complex documenting the influence of the Caesarea Philippi tradition is Jn 12.23-34. After (i) a saying about the glorification of the Son of Man (v. 23, cf. Mk 8.31), there follows (ii) a saying about loving/hating and losing/guarding one's life (v. 25, cf. Mk 8.35-37); then (iii) a saying about 'following' Jesus (v. 26, cf. Mk 8.34); then (iv) a saying about the confrontation between Jesus and 'the ruler of this world' (v. 31, cf. Mk 8.33), who is Satan (Jn 13.27; 14.30); and then finally and particularly interestingly (v) a query voiced by the crowd which assumes (a) the identity of the Messiah and the Son of Man, and (b) that the idea of the death of the Messiah is odd (v. 34, cf. Mk 8.29, 31-32, drawing on Ps. 89.36-37, 'His line shall continue for ever, and his throne endure before me like the sun'). This overall schematic correspondence suggests, as Rudolf Schnackenburg rightly observed,[34] the Evangelist's awareness of the collection of sayings in Mk 8.29-37/Mt. 16.16-26. Such a suggestion is not, I think, ruled out of court by the thought that Jn 12.24-26 may be an editorial insertion:[35] quite the contrary, the redaction would in that case be conditioned by awareness of a Markan combination of originally disparate sayings.

Against this background the narrative in Jn 1.35-51 can be evaluated. The introductory story of how links were established between Jesus and disciples recalls Mt. 4.18-22/Mk 1.16-20, though with the Andrew/Peter and Philip/Nathanael pairings replacing Peter/Andrew and James/John. It also has an unmistakable ring of Mt. 16.13-16, 17-19 diff Mk 8.27-29. First, from Nathanael we hear a full-blooded christological acclamation, 'You are the Son of God! You are the

---

33. Passion sayings using δεῖ occur uniquely in Mk 8.31, and in Jn 3.14; 12.34.

34. *The Gospel according to St John* (London: Burns & Oates, 1980), pp. 384-85.

35. Ashton, *Understanding*, p. 494.

King of Israel!' (v. 49, cf. Mt. 16.16 diff Mk 8.29). Secondly, there is
not simply an acclamation *of* Jesus (vv. 41, 45, 49) but also an acclamation *by* Jesus: thus, Simon Peter is to be called Cephas/Peter as well
as Simon (v. 42, cf. Mt. 16.18), and in similar vein, Nathanael is
hailed as a truly representative Israelite (v. 47). This all suggests a
correspondence between John 1 and Matthew 16.

What is very striking is that the partnership of Andrew and Philip,
who quite normally act as middlemen in the Fourth Gospel (cf. Jn 6.5-
8; 12.21-22), swings into action so as to put in touch with Jesus the
duo Peter and Nathanael. But in addition to the parallelism between
Peter and Nathanael a tendency to subordinate Peter to Nathanael is
detectable. First, the confession of Jesus is not voiced by Peter (diff
Mt. 16.16) but in a preliminary way voiced by Andrew (v. 41) and
then, in its fullest form, transferred to Nathanael (v. 49). Certainly,
Peter will in due time voice the view of the twelve that Jesus is 'the
Holy One of God' (6.69), but Nathanael gets in first. Secondly, the
Fourth Gospel knows about, but makes singularly little of, the 'twelve'
(mentioned only in 6.67, 70, 71; 20.24). In fact from within the
Fourth Gospel we only know about Peter, Judas and Thomas as members of that inner group. However, if we may allow ourselves to
recall what we know from the Synoptics, Nathanael is not a member,
and all the others in 1.35-51 are (cf. Mk 3.16-19). Arguably, a non-
member must be vitally important to the Johannine community to be
permitted to voice the great confession. Thirdly, the encounter with
Nathanael, not that with Peter, is the climax of the sequence of
encounters. Moreover, it is structured in terms of de Goedt's
'disclosure formula' ἰδών...λέγει...ἴδε..., used (let us recall) only
twice with Jesus as subject here in v. 47 and later in 19.26-27, so that
those two episodes form an *inclusio* for the whole mission of Jesus.
Fourthly, the interpretation of Simon's new name is not developed in
terms of community (diff Mt. 16.18), whereas Nathanael is the person
to whom community ideas are rather clearly attached (v. 47). Fifthly,
it is not Peter who is the recipient of the divine revelation (diff Mt.
16.17) but Nathanael, who is made to represent those who see the
ultimate and transcendent vision of the truth about Jesus (vv. 50, 51).
Sixthly, the fact that Nathanael is ἀληθῶς Ἰσραηλίτης in a document
which uses Ἰσραήλ/Ἰσραηλίτης language so rarely (only 1.31, 47, 49;
3.10; 12.13) is extremely important. Adolf Schlatter's observation,
invoked by John Ashton, comes to mind here: 'When a Greek speaks

of a Jew with his religious practice in mind he calls him Ἰουδαῖος, (but) when a Jew speaks of a Jew with his relationship to God in mind, he calls him Ἰσραήλ'.[36] For the terms in which Jesus acclaims Nathanael belong squarely within Jewish consciousness, point up and authenticate his relationship with God, and make him the representative of the community towards which the witness of John the Baptist was directed (1.31). In his acknowledgment of Jesus, therefore, this model Israelite becomes the model believing Christian Jew.

All these considerations seem to point up a new and rather unexpected idea. The role of Nathanael here, in and of itself and also in relation to Peter, is quite extraordinarily like the role of the BD in John 13–21, in and of itself and also in relation to Peter! That is certainly worth pondering. Now, if the position of Nathanael is comparable to the position of the BD, then he must indeed be representative of the community of the Fourth Gospel. Something like that is plainly needed to explain the extraordinary boldness of the Evangelist's activity in Jn 1.35-51. But what wonderful sense it all makes of this early part of the Gospel in both its first and its second editions!

We reach back to the first edition of the Fourth Gospel by, as it were, excising the famous Son of Man saying in v. 51. That this saying is an addition at some stage is evident from the switch from singular to plural forms as v. 50 leads into v. 51, as well as the new introduction in v. 51a. In the first edition, taking our cue from 2.1, 'on the third day there was a wedding in Cana of Galilee…', we count back and find that the first and second days must be those mentioned in vv. 35, 43. Of course, in the overall sequence the third day of 2.1 is the fifth day (cf. also 1.29), but it becomes clear that the sequence that really matters is the initial three days of the disciples' experience of Jesus. The prologue of the first edition of the Gospel therefore ended in v. 34, and the decisive action began in v. 35. Those initial three days reached their climax in the event in Cana which, carrying all the theological freight of the Evangelist, is labelled ἡ ἀρχὴ τῶν σημείων in 2.11. Now, of the four disciples of Jesus who are introduced in 1.35-51 three have their home town defined, that is, Bethsaida (v. 44): the only exception is Nathanael! At this stage we do not know where he comes from. But in the Johannine community it is known: he is 'Nathanael of Cana in Galilee' (21.2). It is in *his* home setting that the ἀρχὴ τῶν σημείων, which is also ἡ φανέρωσις τῆς δόξης αὐτοῦ,

36. Ashton, *Understanding*, p. 153 n. 52.

occurs. Moreover, the very personal importance for Nathanael of the Cana incident is underscored by the personal directness and singularity of the undertaking given to him by Jesus in 1.50: 'you will see (ὄψη) greater things than these.' All four disciples were equal in witnessing the glory, but one was more equal than the others.

In the second edition of the Fourth Gospel the Son of Man saying in v. 51 was added. This did not diminish in any way the immensely high status given to Nathanael. For one thing, it was to him personally (cf. καὶ λέγει αὐτῷ) that the promise to the community (ʾΑμὴν ἀμὴν λέγω ὑμῖν) was conveyed. For another, anyone who was disposed to see in the words 'in whom there is no deceit' no more than an echo of the piety of the psalmist (Pss. 24.4; 32.2) without any hint of the duplicity of the patriarch (Gen. 27.35) must have been put right by the manifest allusion to Jacob in v. 51. Just as the vision of God 'face to face' led to the conferring of the name Israel (Gen. 33.22-32), so the vision of Son of Man linking heaven and earth confirms the status of Nathanael as the true embodiment of the tradition to which the community of the Fourth Gospel believed itself to be the sole legitimate heir. That community looked to the BD. That community looked to Nathanael. In the Fourth Gospel, that which the BD is in relation to all the disciples and Peter in particular, Nathanael is in relation to the initial quartet and Peter in particular. If the BD and Nathanael are separate persons, the relationship between Jesus and the leading disciple is, to use a now famous phrase, 'a bit crowded'. But there is one obvious way to 'uncrowd' the relationship and this is it: to see in Nathanael none other than the BD himself!

THE TEMPLE INCIDENT OF JOHN 2.13-25:
A PREVIEW OF WHAT IS TO COME

Larry J. Kreitzer

John Ashton's *Understanding the Fourth Gospel* (1991) is a book that will, I have little doubt, stand up to the analyses of other New Testament scholars and confirm his place as one of the more important interpreters of the Gospel of John in the second half of this century. It is entirely fitting, therefore, that this brief note about one of the better known passages from the Fourth Gospel be offered to John in recognition not only of his years of service to the Faculty of Theology in Oxford, but also to the contribution that he has made to the scholarly world at large through his written work, which is perhaps best represented by *Understanding the Fourth Gospel*.

John the Evangelist gives us his account of the so-called 'cleansing of the temple'[1] in Jerusalem by Jesus in 2.13-25. That is to say, he places the episode at the beginning of his account of the public ministry of the Lord, immediately following the inaugural 'sign' of the water being changed to wine at the wedding of Cana (2.1-11). This runs right in the face of the accounts provided by the Synoptic Gospels (Mt. 1.12-13; Mk 11.15-17; Lk. 19.45-46), all of which place the temple episode at the beginning of Passion Week. How do we account for such a mammoth discrepancy of chronology?

Several solutions have been put forward over the years. The first is simply to accept the chronologies implied by both John and the

---

1. E.P. Sanders (*Jesus and Judaism* [London: SCM Press, 1985], pp. 61-76) has rightly challenged the legitimacy of continuing to describe the incident related in Jn 2.13-21 (and parallels) as 'the *cleansing* of the temple' since this assumes a negative attitude to the temple cultus which Jesus does not appear to have. He prefers to describe the incident as a 'symbolic demonstration' (p. 69) and in this he is surely correct. However, see C.A. Evans, 'Jesus' Action in the Temple: Cleansing or Portent of Destruction?', *CBQ* 51 (1989), pp. 237-70, for a critique of Sanders's interpretation.

Synoptics and say that there were actually two 'cleansings' of the temple by Jesus: one at the beginning of his ministry (Jn 2.13-15), and one at the end of his ministry (the Synoptic accounts). This solution is the one adopted by both Calvin and Luther and a number of more recent commentators, including B.F. Westcott,[2] William Hendricksen,[3] R.V.G. Tasker,[4] Leon Morris,[5] and D.A. Carson.[6]

On the other hand, a host of other scholars, perhaps the majority of New Testament commentators on the Gospel, have argued that the 'two cleansings' approach is fundamentally wrong-headed and fails to take into account the essentially *theological* agenda that John is pursuing throughout the compilation of his Gospel. The general agreement here is that the Evangelist has abandoned chronology in the interests of his Christology. Included in this group are G.H.C. Macgregor,[7] C.H. Dodd,[8] Rudolf Bultmann,[9] Barnabas Lindars,[10] Raymond E. Brown,[11] Rudolf Schnackenburg,[12] J.N. Sanders and B.A. Mastin,[13] John Marsh,[14] C.K. Barrett,[15] G.R. Beasley-Murray,[16] and Gerard Sloyan.[17]

2.   *The Gospel according to St John* (London: John Murray, 1900), p. 40.

3.   *Exposition of the Gospel according to John* (Grand Rapids, MI: Baker, 1953), p. 120.

4.   *The Gospel according to St John* (Grand Rapids, MI: Eerdmans, 1960), p. 61.

5.   *The Gospel according to John* (NICNT; Grand Rapids, MI: Eerdmans, 1971), p. 196.

6.   *The Gospel according to John* (Leicester: IVP, 1991), p. 178.

7.   *The Gospel of John* (MNTC; London: Hodder & Stoughton, 1928), pp. xiv-xv.

8.   *Historical Tradition in the Fourth Gospel* (Cambridge: Cambridge University Press, 1963), p. 162.

9.   *The Gospel of John: A Commentary* (Oxford: Basil Blackwell, 1971), p. 122.

10.   *The Gospel of John* (NCB; London: Marshall, Morgan & Scott, 1972), pp. 135-37.

11.   *The Gospel according to St John I–XII* (Garden City, NY: Doubleday, 1966), pp. 116-20.

12.   *The Gospel according to St John* (Tunbridge Wells: Burns & Oates, 1968), I, p. 344.

13.   *A Commentary on the Gospel according to St John* (London: A. & C. Black, 1968), pp. 116-17.

14.   *Saint John* (PNTC; Harmondsworth: Penguin Books, 1968), p. 162.

15.   *The Gospel according to St John* (London: SPCK, 2nd edn, 1978), p. 195.

16.   *John* (WBC, 36; Waco, TX: Word Books, 1987), pp. 38-39.

17.   *John* (Interpretation; Atlanta: John Knox Press, 1988), p. 40.

One other theoretical possibility must be mentioned, for the sake of completeness, on this point. It is possible that John's account is chronologically placed at the correct point in Jesus's ministry and that it is misplaced in the Synoptic accounts. In short, there was only one 'cleansing' and John's Gospel got it right. This is the solution adopted by William Temple,[18] Vincent Taylor[19] and, most importantly, John A.T. Robinson,[20] but it has not received widespread support within the scholarly community. Even so, this third suggestion does permit us to acknowledge a larger issue involving what Schuyler Brown has described as a 'scholarly illogicality'[21] in how New Testament scholars tend to use and apply primary source material. It is certainly true that John's Gospel has at times been neglected as a source of historical information pertaining to the life of Jesus, even if most do not agree, as I have noted above, that this truth necessarily pertains to a historical study of 2.13-21.

Why then does John give us the story of the 'cleansing of the temple' at the beginning of the ministry of Jesus? The answer comes in part by closely examining what the temple episode means in terms of Jesus's ministry. That is to say, in the Synoptic Gospels the episode is closely related to the decision on the part of the Jewish authorities to have Jesus put to death. In fact, this is explicitly stated in Mk 11.18 (and the parallel in Lk. 19.47). It is significant that John does not include this comment in his relation of the story at all. The closest parallel to this is found in a completely different setting—the raising of Lazarus (11.53). In other words, in John's Gospel it is the 'sign' of Lazarus which sets the wheels in motion and prompts the political machinery which eventually calls for, and obtains, Jesus's death. In Mark (and Luke) it is the episode in the temple which does so. This is not to say that John's account of the incident in 2.13-25 fails to mention this desire for blood on the part of the Jewish authorities; in fact the cryptic reply in 2.19 given by Jesus to the temple authorities presupposes just that. But it is to say that the event of the cross is merely foreshadowed here at the outset of John's Gospel. In moving the

---

18. *Readings in St John's Gospel* (London: Macmillan, 1945), p. 39.

19. *The Gospel according to Saint Mark* (London: Macmillan, 1959), pp. 461-62.

20. *The Priority of John* (London: SCM Press, 1985), pp. 127-31.

21. *The Origins of Christianity: A Historical Introduction to the New Testament* (Oxford: Oxford University Press, rev. edn, 1993), p. 36.

temple episode to the beginning of the Gospel, John is in fact free to call attention to the Lazarus incident as the reason why the Jewish leaders wanted to put Jesus to death. In short, the emphasis in Mark (and parallels) and John is decidedly different in relation to the decisive action on the part of Jesus which resulted in his execution.

Might the reason for the displacement of the temple incident be explained as part of the editorial processes of the production of the Gospel of John? It is sometimes suggested that the *original* version of John's Gospel followed the same basic chronology as the Synoptics and that it did have the temple episode in its historically correct position at the commencement of Passion Week. The displacement of it to the beginning of the Gospel is then said to be due to a redactor's reworking of the Gospel account and the interjection of the Lazarus story in ch. 11 into the narrative. This is a suggestion with which John Ashton himself agrees, although he does differ with other proponents of it as far as some of the details are concerned (here he is interacting with the suggestions of J. Louis Martyn and Barnabas Lindars). Ashton summarizes the essential point:

> Thus, although the present position of the temple episode suits John's purposes quite well, one can scarcely believe that this is where he found it in his source.[22]

Ashton goes on to discuss the importance of the temple episode within the larger context of the Gospel as a whole. He does this primarily by focusing on v. 22 of the passage, with its cryptic reference to the 'destruction of the temple' and its rebuilding 'in three days' (a cipher for the resurrection). Ashton describes this as an instance where 'the evangelist transforms a prophecy into a riddle';[23] he stresses the way in which such riddle-like statements serve to illustrate the Evangelist's fondness for using phrases or expressions which have more than one meaning. The point of the use of such multivalent material is, as Ashton sees it, that it facilitates the Evangelist's apocalyptic perspective in which revelation takes place in two stages, involves two audiences and is set against the backdrop of the two ages. In short, passages like Jn 2.22 need to be read on two levels: not only as events which have an anchor in the historical life and ministry of

22. *Understanding the Fourth Gospel* (Oxford: Clarendon Press, 1991), p. 201.
23. Ashton, *Understanding*, p. 415.

Jesus, but also as events which need to be remembered and interpreted within the believing community in light of the resurrection of Jesus from the dead. Ashton describes 2.22 (along with 12.16) as 'a key which helps unlock the secret of the Gospel as a whole', while going on to hint that 'future commentators on the Gospel may well find find further applications, great and small'.[24]

It is against this very helpful approach to John's Gospel that I would wish to find one further application and draw attention to one seemingly insignificant feature of the story of the temple episode recorded in Jn 2.13-21. I refer to the quotation from the Old Testament found in 2.17, a verse which carries within it all the multiple meaning, the *double entendre*, which is an important feature of Johannine style and to which John Ashton so rightly calls our attention. The verse is never itself discussed within Ashton's *magnum opus* on the Fourth Gospel, a fact which is somewhat surprising since it helps to illustrate his essential point so well.[25] Nevertheless, in a book which represents such a rich feast for the reader, it is comforting to know that an occasional crumb falls from the table and can be picked up by those who follow.

In 2.17 John the Evangelist records Jesus as quoting a rather ambiguous passage from Ps. 69.9 (68.10 LXX). The verse is given by the RSV as: 'For zeal for thy house has consumed me, and the insults of those who insult thee have fallen on me.' It is the ambiguity of the crucial verb 'to consume' which is often missed when we read the story in English translation. Most of the time when we read the verse we remember the demonstration in the temple itself and we take the force of the verb to mean that Jesus is just so consumed by zealousness for the father's house that he cannot bear to see the moneychangers making a profit in the midst of it; and so he is *consumed* by rage, loses his temper, and throws the whole lot of them out. But the Hebrew expression אֲכָלָתְנִי) which lies at the heart of the quotation (for which the LXX's κατέφαγέν με is a fairly accurate rendering) is much more dynamic and allows us to have another angle on the matter. The Hebrew verb אָכַל can mean 'to consume' in the sense of 'to destroy', and by implication can be taken to mean 'to cause to be put to death'. In other words, it may have the same force as, say, the sentence, 'the

24. Ashton, *Understanding*, p. 418.
25. Neither is it discussed in the follow-up, *Studying John: Approaches to the Fourth Gospel* (Oxford: Clarendon Press, 1994).

fire *consumed* the house' (the implication that the house is thereby
destroyed and 'dead'). When 2.17 is read in this light the meaning of
the verse is shifted away from its being a justification for Jesus's anger
to its being a declaration of his impending death. This is borne out by
the way in which the Evangelist has changed the tense of the verb
from an aorist (κατέφαγέν) to a future (καταφάγεται).

Perhaps this is part of the reason why John has chosen to place the
episode of the demonstration in the temple at the beginning of his
Gospel. It is as if he is saying to his readers, 'If you can understand
what Jesus says in this story by citing a verse from Psalm 69, you will
have a good clue as to the meaning of my Gospel as a whole'. The
demonstration in the temple thus becomes a preview for much that is
to follow; or, in the words of C.H. Dodd, the citation of Ps. 69.9 is 'a
veiled forecast of the Passion'.[26] It is a highly effective way of alert-
ing the readership to the tremendous theological truths that are to
come as the story of Jesus of Nazareth, the long-promised Messiah, is
unfolded. This is how Raymond E. Brown understands the verse,
calling attention to the way in which it sets up the allusion to the resurrection contained in 2.22:

> John interprets the Psalm to mean that zeal for the Temple will destroy
> Jesus and bring his death. Thus, even though John does not place the
> cleansing of the temple precincts immediately before Jesus' death as do
> the Synoptics, his account still preserves the memory that the action led to
> his death. In the present sequence the interpretation of the cleansing in ref-
> erence to the death of Jesus prepares for the interpretation of the saying
> about the Temple in reference to his resurrection.[27]

This 'forward-viewing' should not surprise us since it is a technique
that we know from other contexts. We actually encounter it in a variety of familiar ways within our world, in novels and films perhaps
more frequently than anywhere else. The best examples that spring to
my mind come from the world of cinema. We have space to consider
two examples in particular, each of which contributes to our understanding of the 'forward-viewing' technique in its own way.

First, we note Richard Attenborough's film *Gandhi* (1982). At the
very beginning of the film we see the fateful events of the assassination of Gandhi in the gardens of Birla House, New Delhi in 1948.[28]

26. *Historical Tradition*, p. 160.
27. *St John*, p. 124.
28. R. Attenborough (*In Search of Gandhi* [London: The Bodley Head, 1982],

We watch Gandhi, guided by two faithful great-nieces, Abha and Manu, move through the crowds of people on his way to lead prayers. He eventually comes face to face with the Hindu fanatic Nathuram Godse who draws a revolver, fires three times at point-blank range, and kills him. Then, abruptly, the film takes a completely different tack and we find ourselves back with Mahatma Gandhi at the beginning of his public life in South Africa. The film proceeds through his career as a lawyer in South Africa, his move back to India and his involvement in the events leading up to the independence of the nation in 1948. Finally, we find ourselves watching the last scenes of the film and, quite suddenly, we know what is to happen! We have already seen the assassination and here it is before us again, repeated with even greater effect because we know precisely *what* will happen and *how* it will happen. Yet we are powerless and can do nothing about it but witness it again. In the interim we have all but forgotten about having already seen the assassination itself. In this instance the technique of 'forward-viewing' has been used to make a point, and make it very powerfully indeed.

The second example comes from Oliver Stone's powerful and provocative film *JFK* (1991) which takes as its subject matter the assassination of President John F. Kennedy in Dallas, Texas on 22 November 1963. The film really deals with the 'conspiracy theory' of the assassination and the efforts of New Orleans district attorney Jim Garrison to uncover the truth of the incident. The actual assassination itself is depicted very early on in the film, as if to place the central event of the story-line before the audience as a matter of priority. In fact, the rifle shot which signifies the President's assassination comes at the end of a six-minute long montage of film clips and images which show how President Kennedy came to the political position he did and how he had arrived in Dallas to begin a fateful ride in an open-top limousine through the downtown area of the city. The rest of the three-hour long film is an explication of the meaning of this rifle fire and there are many flashbacks to it, including some footage from the famous 'Zapruder film' taken by a member of the public who was standing alongside the road with an 8mm cine-camera. This is all a deliberate ploy on the part of Stone, who explains how he envisioned the film from its conception:

pp. 205-14) discusses the making of this scene within the film, which was filmed in the gardens on the very site of the assassination itself.

We would first see the assassination from a conventional point of view, and then throughout the movie, we would see it again and again and again, like peeling an onion skin, until we got to the final moment, when the motorcade makes that turn, and this time you would really see it for the first time, and you would get it...I wanted people to really feel that sense of dread.[29]

In some ways this film provides another helpful insight into the nature of the narrative style adopted within the Gospel of John in that images of the actual assassination appear throughout the film in precisely the same way that hints of the death of the messiah crop up throughout the Gospel account. The future crucifixion of Christ is clearly what is meant, for example, in 3.14 with the image of Moses lifting up the serpent in the wilderness, and in 12.31-32 where Jesus is made to allude to his being lifted up from the earth so as to draw all people to himself.

It is perhaps not too far-fetched to suggest that this is precisely what John is attempting to provide for us in the form of the demonstration in the temple incident. The episode thus becomes a proleptic vision of what is to come within the Gospel story. To return to the Gandhi illustration for a moment, it would be absurd for anyone to suggest on the basis of the film that the Mahatma was in fact assassinated *twice* (once at the beginning of the film and once at the end). In the same way, it would be ludicrous for someone to stand up in the middle of the film theatre and, as the film approaches its end, shout, 'Now we see that Gandhi is going to be assassinated for the second time!' To insist on such a literal view of the film's chronology is to miss the dramatic effect intended by the director, to misunderstand his technique. In the same way, it is, in my opinion, stretching the limits of credulity to suggest that John is relating for us the first 'cleansing' of the temple and the Synoptics the second (as is often assumed by many harmonizations of the four Gospels). We have to recognize what John is trying to do here and not get hung up on the chronological question alone. There is a much more important theological truth at stake and it is upon that that we must focus our attention when we examine the Gospel.

The film director Michel Cimino put the essential point well. At the Cannes film festival in 1981 he said: 'When the details of history no

29. Cited in N. Kagan, *The Cinema of Oliver Stone* (Oxford: Roundhouse, 1995), p. 195.

longer serve the function of the story—discard them.'[30] In 2.13-21 John the Evangelist seems to have recognized the need to discard the details of history in order to make his point, and the Gospel story which he relates is all the more powerful as a result.

30. Cited in T. Crawley, *Dictionary of Film Quotations* (Ware: Wordsworth, 1991), p. 137.

THE ENIGMA OF THE FOURTH GOSPEL: ANOTHER LOOK*

David Wenham

1. *A Scholarly Consensus regarding the Fourth Gospel*

The differences between the Synoptic Gospels and the Fourth Gospel are substantial, as is well known. The usual explanation for these differences, which still commands the assent of most scholars, is that the Fourth Gospel's account of Jesus is more theologically coloured and less historically traditional than that of the Synoptic Gospels. Modern scholars speak of the Fourth Gospel being preaching about Jesus,[1] as 'poetic' or 'charismatic history',[2] of a 'two-level drama'.[3] The Fourth Gospel, on this view, is a heavily reinterpreted account of Jesus, which reflects the situation and theology of its author(s) at least as much as the situation and theology of Jesus. The author justifies his stylized account implictly by his frequent references to the Spirit's inspiration of Jesus' disciples.

---

*   This article first appeared in *TynBul* 48 (May, 1997), and is reprinted here with permission. It has a dual dedication. First, to the memory of my father, John Wenham, who died on 13 February 1996, and who had hoped to follow his published works on the Synoptic Gospels with a study of the Fourth Gospel. Secondly, to John Ashton on the occasion of his 65th birthday. I hope it is appropriate to offer a paper on the Fourth Gospel to a volume in John's honour, even though it is a very light-weight contribution compared to those he has published in his years in Oxford.

1.   E.g. B. Lindars, *John* (Sheffield: JSOT Press, 1990), pp. 36-37 on the discourses in particular; also his commentary, *The Gospel of John* (Grand Rapids: Eerdmans; London: Marshall, Morgan & Scott, 1972), pp. 51-52.

2.   M. Stibbe, *John* (Sheffield: JSOT Press, 1993), pp. 18-19. J. Ashton in his magnum opus, *Understanding the Fourth Gospel* (Oxford: Oxford University Press, 1994), p. 432, speaks of the Fourth Gospel as more a creed than biography, let alone history.

3.   J.L. Martyn, *History and Theology in the Fourth Gospel* (Nashville: Abingdon Press, 2nd edn, 1979), pp. 24-36 and *passim*.

There was a time when scholars saw the Fourth Gospel as a hellenistic reinterpretation of the Jewish Jesus-tradition. Although that view does probably have an important grain of truth in it,[4] it has now largely been discarded, as scholars have come to appreciate the very Jewish and even Palestinian character of the Fourth Gospel. The discovery of the Dead Sea Scrolls not only helped persuade scholars that Palestinian Judaism was much more hellenized than had been thought, but also threw up some particularly interesting parallels with the Fourth Gospel.

In place of the old consensus that saw the Fourth Gospel as a hellenistic reinterpretation of traditions about Jesus, the new consensus sees the Fourth Gospel as arising out of a crisis that took place towards the end of the first century CE, after the Christian community out of which the Fourth Gospel came had split from Judaism. The Council of Jewish Rabbis which took place in Jamnia in Galilee about 85 CE is thought to have been responsible for the split, because the rabbis introduced into the synagogue liturgy (the Eighteen Benedictions) a public cursing of the 'heretics' (the *minim*) and perhaps of the 'Nazarenes'. This curse is thought to have been directed against the Christians, and its effect was finally to drive out the Christians, who until now had remained part of the Jewish community, from the synagogue and from Judaism.

This painful post-Jamnia situation is thought to be reflected in various of the distinctives of the Fourth Gospel. First, there is the animosity of the Fourth Gospel towards 'the Jews', and in particular the references to followers of Jesus being 'put out of the synagogue' (9.22; 16.2). Secondly, there is the dualistic flavour of the Fourth Gospel: its sharp differentiation between Jesus' followers and 'the world', between 'light' and 'darkness', between the disciples as people who have revelation and who 'know' and others (especially the Jews) who are blind and who face judgment. All these are thought to point to what sociologists describe as a 'sectarian' situation, in this case produced by the ruptured relationship between the synagogue and the Johannine community. Thirdly, and following on from this, John's Christology has been explained in terms of this situation, with the portrait of Jesus as a heavenly other-worldly figure explaining the

---

4. For example, it remains probable that the logos theology in Jn 1, though very Hebraic, is intended to make sense to those familiar with Greek ideas of the logos.

unhappy failure of the Jews to understand and believe. Fourthly, the distinctive ethical imperative in the Fourth Gospel 'to love one another' makes sense in such a situation since sectarian groups often have strong communal and inward-looking concerns.[5]

This view is attractive in explaining many of the most striking features of the Fourth Gospel, and it is not surprising that a large number of Johannine scholars have accepted it. However, it is the thesis of this article that, like many scholarly consensuses, it is less persuasive than it might at first appear, and that we should be looking in some rather different directions for an explanation of John's distinctiveness.

2. *Doubts about the Consensus*

The Jamnia Hypothesis
The first problem with the modern consensus is its dependence on a highly uncertain view about what happened in Jamnia. Various scholars have questioned whether Jamnia did mark a decisive break between church and synagogue: there are doubts about what exactly happened at the Council of Jamnia, about what was or was not put into the liturgy, about whether it was intended to exclude Christians from the synagogue, and about whether it had that effect.[6]

Historical Traditions in the Fourth Gospel
Although the scholarly consensus has tended to see the Fourth Gospel as theological rather than historical (more so than the Synoptic Gospels), there has also been widespread recognition in recent years that the Evangelist had access to his own traditions of Jesus, whether or not he knew the Synoptic Gospels. In some cases at least, those

5.   The most influential proponent of the Jamnia hypothesis has been Martyn (*History and Theology*). On the Fourth Gospel as sectarian, see especially W.A. Meeks, 'The Man from Heaven in Johannine Sectarianism', *JBL* 91 (1972), pp. 44-72, reprinted in J. Ashton (ed.), *The Interpretation of John* (London: SPCK; Philadelphia: Fortress Press, 1986), pp. 141-43.

6.   Cf. J.P. Lewis, who reviews the Jamnia hypothesis and suggests that it should 'be relegated to the limbo of unestablished hypotheses' (*ABD*, III, pp. 684-37). The eschatological traditions of the Gospels, especially of Mt. 24/Mk 13/Lk. 21, may indicate that the events of 66–70 CE themselves (rather than the Jamnian Council) were seen by Christians as marking the decisive break with Judaism.

traditions have a highly Palestinian flavour, and may be as historical as well-attested Synoptic traditions.[7]

3. *'Late' Features of the Fourth Gospel not Late?*

As we have seen, the Jamnian hypothesis offers a neat explanation for some of the distinctives of John. However, in no case does the evidence demand the Jamnian conclusion, and in each case there is strong evidence indicating that the relevant features of John at least have their roots very early in the history of Christianity and long before Jamnia.

The Johannine Thunderbolt in Q
In support of this claim, I note first the famously Johannine sayings found in Mt. 11.25-27 and Lk. 10.21-22:

> I thank you, father, Lord of heaven and earth, that you hid these things from the wise and understanding, and revealed them to babes. Yes, father, because such was your good pleasure. All things have been delivered to me by my father, and no one knows the son except the father, nor does anyone know the father except the son and anyone to whom the son wishes to reveal him.

'Q' sayings such as this are usually seen as relatively primitive tradition, going back to the 60s, 50s or earlier,[8] but this one is

---

7.   The description in 3.22-26 and 4.1-3 of Jesus baptizing in Judea, before his Galilean ministry, alongside John the Baptist is a case in point. See R.E. Brown, *The Gospel according to John I–XII* (London: Chapman, 1971), p. 155; Lindars, *Gospel of John*, p. 164. The scholar who in recent years has most strikingly argued for historical traditions in the Fourth Gospel is J.A.T. Robinson, and his book *The Priority of John* (London: SCM Press, 1985) accumulates important evidence which has not always been sufficiently recognized by other scholars. Robinson's weakness, arguably, is in his failure to account sufficiently for the Fourth Gospel's wide divergence from the Synoptics.

8.   Some scholars see these sayings as representing a late stratum in Q (e.g. J.S. Kloppenborg, *The Formation of Q* [Philadelphia: Fortress Press, 1987], pp. 198-203). But even if they are right, the sayings still presumably antedate Matthew, Luke and John. Other scholars recently have questioned the Q hypothesis and have argued for Lukan use of Matthew. I am personally unpersuaded of the existence of Q, but I am convinced that in 'Q' material Luke sometimes has the earlier form of wording, and that the proponents of Q are right to see 'Q' tradition as antedating Matthew and

outstandingly Johannine, with its father/son language, its emphasis on revelation and the knowledge of father and son, and its epistemological dualism, the truth being known to the disciples but concealed from others. What this shows is that these Johannine themes need not necessarily have come out of a Jamnian context; the most one could say is that the Fourth Evangelist has emphasized these themes because of his Jamnian context; what is an isolated saying in the Synoptic Gospel has become a very important stratum in the Fourth Gospel. And yet it is hard to believe that, in the traditions of the 'Q' community (i.e. the community that preserved the saying), there was just one 'thunderbolt' saying of this sort. It seems likely that the saying reflects a perspective on Jesus that was important in this early Christian community.

The Markan Saying about the Purpose of Parables
Another saying that reflects precisely this perspective is the saying about the purpose of parables found in Mk 4.11-12, Mt. 13.11, and Lk. 8.10. The Markan version is: 'To you the mystery has been given of the kingdom of heaven; but to those outside in parables everything happens...' Matthew and Luke differ slightly from Mark, but have a striking range of small agreements with each other in wording and word-order: 'To you has been given to know the mysteries of the kingdom...' The agreement of Matthew and Luke here probably points to their having a non-Markan tradition;[9] so the saying is doubly attested and quite likely primitive. Significantly, the same epistemological dualism and emphasis on revelation appears in this tradition as was found in the Q saying above (even the same Greek verb of knowing, if we follow Matthew and Luke). The saying in this case is not so richly Johannine, but it confirms that features of the Fourth Gospel that have been seen to be Jamnian actually go far back in the early history of the Jesus-tradition.

Two further observations with regard to this text are relevant. First, the Synoptic saying leads into an allusion to Isa. 6.10, a text echoed twice in the Fourth Gospel (9.39; 12.40). Secondly, the

Luke. If, however, Luke did get the material in question from Matthew, still the Fourth Gospel is seen to be less distinctive than has often been supposed.

9. See J. Nolland, *Luke 1–9.20* (Waco, TX: Word Books, 1989), p. 377; also my article 'The Synoptic Problem Revisited: Some New Suggestions about the Composition of Mark 4.1-34', *TynBul* 23 (1972), pp. 3-38, especially p. 27.

Synoptic saying about mysteries being revealed and about 'parables' is reminiscent of thinking found in the Dead Sea Scrolls, notably in 4QpHab 7. Interestingly, some recent scholars have postulated that the author of the Fourth Gospel was originally an Essene.[10] On this hypothesis, a strand of early Christianity may have been influenced by and reflect Essene features.[11] Whether or not this is the case, it may be good to be reminded that the Dead Sea Scrolls represent a dualistic 'sectarian' way of thinking that is in some ways paralleled in the Fourth Gospel but that has nothing to do with Jamnia. If, as various scholars have argued, the early Christians were in some way associated with the Essenes, then John's 'sectarianism' may well have derived from that association.

Baptism and Transfiguration

Scholars have discussed at length the absence from the Fourth Gospel of any account of Jesus' baptism or transfiguration. What makes the absences the more remarkable is the 'Johannine' flavour of the narratives, with Jesus being identified as the divine 'Son', as the one specially 'loved' by the Father, and (in the baptism narrative) as the bearer of the Father's Spirit.[12] In both stories, the boundary between the heavenly and the earthly realms is broken through.

For my purposes, it is not necessary to discuss the reasons for the Fourth Gospel's failure to reproduce the narratives. What is significant is the evidence provided by these Synoptic traditions of the existence and importance of what are often seen as Johannine christological themes in pre-Johannine Synoptic tradition. The baptism of Jesus by John is widely regarded as a historical event by modern scholars, and it seems to have been recognized in all ancient Christian tradition as the starting point of Jesus' ministry. It is not possible to prove at what point it came to be associated with ideas of divine sonship and Spirit-anointing, but it is arguable that these baptismal ideas,

10. E.g. Ashton, *Understanding*, pp. 232-37.

11. See further D. Sefa-Dapaah, 'An Investigation into the Relationship between John the Baptist and Jesus of Nazareth: A Socio-Historical Study' (PhD thesis for Coventry University in collaboration with Wycliffe Hall, 1995).

12. Also in the baptism narrative is the idea of Jesus as the one who conveys the Spirit to others (baptizing them with the Spirit).

like the 'Q' thunderbolt, are early.[13] Evidence from Paul also has some importance here.

The Evidence from Paul

Even more striking evidence that John's distinctives need not point to a post-Jamnian situation is provided by Paul.

1. *1 Thessalonians 2.13-16*. 1 Thessalonians is agreed to be Paul's earliest or second earliest extant letter, to be dated about 50 CE, and the way that Paul speaks there of 'the Jews, who killed the Lord Jesus and the prophets and also drove us out' is rightly noted by John Robinson and others as a striking parallel to the Johannine way of speaking of 'the Jews' and of the Jews putting Christians 'out of the synagogue'.[14] There is thus no need to look to the Jamnian situation to make sense of John's teaching.

Admittedly, scholars have tried to distinguish between the sort of expulsion described in 1 Thessalonians and that described in the Fourth Gospel, but it is doubtful if the distinction can be seriously maintained. It may be that there is no definite evidence of an agreed policy by 'the Jews' to expel Christians from the synagogue before Jamnia, but there is plenty of evidence of some very vicious attacks on the early Christian movement (Paul himself being involved before his conversion),[15] and it is highly likely that the campaign against the Christians included the relatively moderate measure of excommunicating Christians from the synagogue.[16] To say this is not necessarily to deny that the wording of a passage like John 9 could reflect late first-century AD tensions between Jews and Christians, but there is no reason why the Johannine references to 'the Jews' and to expulsions

13. The fact that Jesus' baptism by John was remembered at all and was given such prominence in the early church could suggest that it was seen as out of the ordinary and as charged with special significance from the beginning.

On the great importance of the transfiguration story in the early church, see D. Wenham and A.D.A. Moses, '"There are Some Standing Here"...', *NovT* 36 (1994), pp. 146-63.

14. So *Priority of John*, pp. 81-86.

15. On the possibility of ongoing persecution of Christians after the crucifixion during the time of Pilate, see R. Riesner, *Die Frühzeit des Apostels Paulus* (Tübingen: Mohr, 1994), pp. 55-56.

16. My basic argument stands, therefore, even if the scholarly questions about the authenticity of 1 Thess. 2.14-16 are taken seriously.

from the synagogue should not go back substantially to a far earlier date.

2. *1 Corinthians 1–4*. 1 Corinthians may be dated to about 55 CE, and what is most striking here is the emphasis on Christian revelation and knowledge. The Corinthian Christians were a strongly charismatic community, who were excited by their experiences of the Spirit and by what had been and was being revealed to them by the Spirit: they had 'words of wisdom' and 'words of knowledge'; they were keen on eloquence and wisdom (perhaps influenced by Apollos the Alexandrian); and they were proud of their 'knowledge', which, for example, enabled them to eat food offered to idols with a good conscience. Paul has an ambivalent attitude to the Corinthians on these matters: he rejects their arrogance, their boasting about human beings, and their failure to think of the weaker brother or sister. But he too can speak of the Christian 'knowing' God, and he agrees with them that Christians have a 'secret wisdom...that has been hidden' but which 'God has revealed to us' now by his Spirit—a wisdom that 'the spirit of the world' cannot understand (2.7, 10, 12).

Accordingly, already in Corinth in the 50s we find various emphases and ideas that are also important in the Fourth Gospel, including the emphasis on revelation, on knowing God, and also on the Spirit. We do not find much emphasis on 'wisdom' in the Fourth Gospel, but the concept of 'the word' in the Johannine prologue has regularly been linked with the Jewish wisdom concept; we do not find the Johannine notion of Jesus as 'the word' in 1 Corinthians, and yet 'words' of revelation are important.[17] It would be unwise to make too much of such parallels, but it is possible that the charismatic Corinthians are much more Johannine than we might at first suppose, with their highly realized eschatology and their emphasis on the great works of the Spirit that featured in their community.[18] The Johannine

17. It is not at all impossible that Apollos would have been familiar with the Philonic doctrine of 'the word'. For a possible link between the Johannine 'word' and Pauline tradition, see arguably Col. 1.25, where 'the word of God' is in apposition to 'the mystery hidden'; so J. Ashton, *Studying John* (Oxford: Oxford University Press, 1994), p. 22 (though he also notes differences between the Colossian hymn and the Johannine prologue).

18. Interestingly E. Käsemann (*The Testament of Jesus* [London: SCM Press, 1968], p. 24) suggests that the Fourth Gospel may have originated in circles in the

view of the Christian community as having special revelation that sets it apart from 'the world' need not point to a late first-century CE context, but would be just as much at home in a mid-first-century Corinthian context.

But we can take the argument a step forward by asking: from where did the Corinthians get their emphasis on knowledge and revelation? Apollos may have been influential, but Paul owns that emphasis for himself, even though he objects to some ways it has been used by the Corinthians. And it seems entirely probable that it was Paul himself who taught the Corinthians about the Spirit's power and revelation. If he did, where did he get the ideas from? There is good reason to think that in this, as in so many other matters, Paul was influenced by Jesus-traditions with which he was familiar.

In support of this proposal, the evidence of 1 Cor. 13.2 is relevant. Paul's words here about 'having all faith so as to move mountains' have often been linked to the Jesus-traditions of Mk 11.23 and parallels, and his words in the same verse about 'knowing all mysteries and all knowledge' are plausibly linked to the dominical saying about parables (Mk 4.11-12 and parallels).[19] In 1 Corinthians 13, Paul's point is that, without love, all the powers that Jesus promised his followers are worthless.

'enthusiastic' tradition opposed in 1 Cor. 15 and 2 Tim. 2.18, and that the Fourth Evangelist may be endeavouring to 'combat a development in the church which did not take christology sufficiently into account... the controversy dealt with the slogan *solus Christus*'. Ashton (*Understanding*, pp. 92-93) comments on the 'slender evidence' for Käsemann's view, but perhaps this article contributes some further evidence. I would not call Corinthian enthusiasm or Johannine Christianity 'gnostic', though they may very well represent tendencies that develop into gnosticism. See further below; also my *Paul, Follower of Jesus or Founder of Christianity* (Grand Rapids and Cambridge: Eerdmans, 1995), p. 286. R. Bultmann (*The Gospel of John* [Oxford: Blackwells, 1971], pp. 9-10) finds the Fourth Evangelist and Paul influenced by gnosticism. He denies that the former has been influenced by the latter, arguing that the differences are too great, noting, for example, the unimportance of 'righteousness' in the Fourth Gospel, and differences in eschatology. Even at these points, however, the Johannine and Pauline traditions do not seem so different if 1 John is brought into the discussion, since we find there a greater interest in 'Pauline' themes such as atonement, righteousness and the parousia (1.7–2.2; 2.18). In the Fourth Gospel 'righteousness' is only found in 16.8 and 16.10: the trio there, 'sin', 'righteousness' and 'judgment', is somewhat reminiscent of Paul. I am grateful to John Muddiman for this observation.

    19. See further Wenham, *Paul*, pp. 81-84.

Other relevant evidence is in 1 Corinthians 1–4. Various scholars have suggested that the Corinthians were influenced by the saying of Mt. 11.27 and Lk. 10.21-22. Echoes of those Synoptic passages might be heard in Paul's language of 'hiding', 'revealing', 'wise', 'foolish', and 'babes', and it may well be that the Corinthians were claiming to be in the privileged position described by the 'Q' saying. There are other possible echoes of the 'Q' saying in 1 Corinthians, including 2.11: 'No one knows the things of God except...'. The echoes are not such as to prove dependence on the dominical tradition, but, given the importance of such tradition in Paul's teaching to the Corinthians (e.g. 7.3-4; 11.23-25; 15.1-7), it is at least a plausible hypothesis.[20]

We conclude (a) that the Johannine emphasis on revelation and knowledge had important precedents in Christian traditions dating back to the 50s AD, and (b) that these traditions were already regarded as dominical. We may surmise that John and Paul and the Corinthians are drawing on a common strand of Jesus-tradition.[21]

3. *Christology*. If the polemic against the Jews in the Fourth Gospel and its emphasis on revelation have striking parallels in early Christian tradition, what of its distinctive Christology, including its emphasis on Jesus as the pre-existent son of the Father who came down from heaven? Is this not rightly recognized as the end-point in the development of christological thinking in the New Testament church, and as belonging in something like the Jamnian context?

20. See my *Paul*, pp. 129-36, referring to the work of J.M. Robinson, H. Koester, B. Fjärstedt and P. Richardson.

21. If this is the case, then it is interesting to speculate about what that Jesus-tradition might have contained. Did it perhaps simply contain the 'Q' saying of Mt. 11.27/Lk. 10.21, 22 and the Markan logion about parables (Mk 4.11-12)? Or did it more probably contain other traditions, which are in common to the Fourth Gospel and 1 Corinthians? Did it, for example, contain substantial teaching about the charismatic Spirit and his work? This is inevitably speculative, but I suggested before that it is not likely that the 'Johannine thunderbolt' was a totally isolated saying and that there probably was a wider body of material of which it was a part.

Teaching about baptism, associating it with the gift of the Spirit, may also have featured significantly (cf. 1 Cor. 12.13; Jn 3.5). The Fourth Gospel ascribes to Jesus teaching on the Paraclete-Spirit, being the Spirit of Jesus and the revealer of truth, and of the disciples doing great works (14.12). The ideas are not dissimilar to Pauline ideas: though Paul does not speak of the 'Paraclete', the noun *paraklesis* and the verb *parakaleo* are important to him, e.g. in 2 Cor. 1.

Paul's evidence tells against this conclusion. The Christ-hymn of Phil. 2.5-11, for instance, speaks of a pre-existent Christ, who humbled himself and who then was 'super-exalted' by God.[22] Jesus is not described as one who 'descended' and 'ascended' as in the Fourth Gospel, but the thought is similar and the language is also closely related, with Paul's 'super-exalt' being the same root as John's characteristic references to Jesus being 'lifted up'.[23] Of course, the Pauline passage is very widely seen as a hymn that antedates the letter to the Philippians, and, if that opinion is correct, then we are taken back even earlier into the history of Christian thought.

Another hymn in the Pauline letters is Col. 1.15-20, and the similarities here to the Fourth Gospel and especially to its prologue are manifest: Jesus is the pre-existent son, involved in creation (like the wisdom of God in Jewish tradition) and then indwelt by all the fullness of God. If those scholars are right who regard Colossians as genuinely Pauline and the hymn as possibly pre-Pauline, then again Johannine Christology is seen to have early precedent. In any case the Christology of Colossians is not a million miles away from what we find in the undisputed letters of Paul. Even in 1 Corinthians, as we saw, ideas of divine wisdom are in the air, and in 8.6 Paul can comment on the one God and Father and the 'one Lord, Jesus Christ, through whom all things are and through whom we live'.

Other significant Pauline texts include Gal. 4.4: 'When the time had fully come, God sent his son, born of a woman.' The 'sending' language and the 'son' language are both rather 'Johannine'. And similar 'son' language is found in Rom. 1.3-4, which speaks of 'his son, born of the seed of David according to the flesh, set apart as Son of God in power according to the Spirit of holiness by the resurrection of the dead, Jesus Christ our Lord'. The structure of the verses in Romans is reminiscent of the Christ hymn in Philippians 2 ('in the form of God...became man...was highly exalted...Jesus Christ as Lord'), and

22. Ashton finds no Pauline kenosis in the Fourth Gospel (*Understanding*, p. 93), but in a passage like 13.1-17 we are not far away from it (also perhaps by implication in 17.24).

23. There are, of course, plenty of exegetical questions raised by the Philippians hymn, and there are certainly different nuances in the Philippians hymn and Johannine thought. But the similarity is quite sufficient to put a question mark over any assumption that the Fourth Evangelist's way of looking at things must be particularly late.

it may well be that there is a hint of pre-existence in the opening 'his son' in Rom. 1.3. In any case there is significant 'son' language. Interestingly once again, scholars have seen both Gal. 4.4 and Rom. 1.3-4 as early Christian credal material.[24]

Such evidence from Paul's letters, then, shows that Johannine Christology has precedent in early Christian tradition, and it makes good sense to propose that much of this early tradition was seen as dominical. This proposal is supported not just by the claims of the Fourth Gospel, but also by the evidence of Mt. 11.27/Lk. 10.21, 22, mentioned above as possibly having been known by Paul, which speaks in a rather Johannine way of the father and the son.[25] That Jesus should have been called 'the son' from an early date is not at all unbelievable, given the hardly disputable fact that he addressed God as 'Abba' in a way that impressed people a great deal.[26] There is other evidence, too, of Jesus' filial consciousness, including his parable of the rebellious vineyard tenants, where the owner of the vineyard finally sends 'his son'; that parable could well be reflected in a saying such as Gal. 4.4, with its description of God sending his son.[27]

Finally, on the question of Christology, it is arguable that Paul knew the traditions of Jesus' baptism and transfiguration (in something like the Synoptic form).[28] The evidence for his knowing the baptism includes the similarity of Jesus' baptism as described by the Synoptic Gospels and Christian baptism as understood by Paul (with water, by and with the Spirit, leading to adoption as a 'son' of God). It seems quite likely that for Paul Christian baptism brings the believer 'into

24. See, for example, J.D.G. Dunn, *Romans 1–8* (Waco, TX: Word Books, 1988), pp. 5-6; F.F. Bruce, *Commentary on Galatians* (Grand Rapids: Eerdmans; Exeter: Paternoster Press, 1982), pp. 194-95.

25. It is possible to argue that the Christology of the 'Q' saying is not identical to the Johannine idea; certainly there is no explicit suggestion of pre-existence. Moreover, it is possible to speculate about an original form of the saying that was 'weaker' in its christological implications. But the fact remains that highly 'Johannine' christological language was extant and had been ascribed to Jesus at a rather early date.

26. Only this explains Paul's use of the Aramaic word in Rom. 8.15 and Gal. 4.6. On Son of God as Jewish, see Ashton, *Understanding*, pp. 260-62, citing 4Q246.

27. See Wenham, *Paul*, pp. 136-37; also Dunn, *Christology*, pp. 39-45.

28. On the transfiguration, see Wenham, *Paul*, pp. 357-63; also Wenham and Moses, 'Some Standing Here'.

Christ', including into Jesus' baptismal experience of anointing by the Spirit (Gal. 3.26-27; 1 Cor. 12.12-13; 2 Cor. 1.21-22).[29]

If the traditions of the baptism and transfiguration were among those 'received' by Paul, then this is further evidence that key 'Johannine' christological emphases (e.g. Jesus as 'son', 'loved by the father' and closely associated with the Spirit) were all familiar and indeed important at an early stage in the history of the Christian church.

I speak of them as important because, if the baptism and transfiguration traditions were well known, they would inevitably have been seen as highly significant.[30] For example, the baptism of Jesus will have been seen as a defining moment, being the dramatic moment of Jesus' ecstatic anointing with the powerful charismatic Spirit, the moment when Jesus was revealed as Son of God, and a moment of revelation and knowledge of the father ('Abba'). It is not difficult to see how such an understanding of his baptism might be related to the sort of teaching that is represented in the 'Q' saying of Mt. 11.25-27/Lk. 10.21-22, which speaks about Jesus' own knowledge of the father[31] and about his mediating that knowledge to his disciples. Nor is it difficult to see how these strands of thought might then have fed into a view of Christian baptism as a repetition of, or incorporation into, Jesus' Spirit-experience of revelation and sonship (typically being associated with charismatic experiences). Arguably such may have been Paul's view and the view of followers of his in a place like Corinth. This will be considered further below.

4. *'Love One Another'*. If even John's Christology is not a secure indication of the Jamnian context of the Fourth Gospel,[32] what finally

29. See further Wenham, *Paul*, pp. 346-48.

30. The supernatural nature of the events would have simply highlighted their importance to many ancient readers/hearers of the traditions.

31. Note Luke's opening: 'In that hour he rejoiced in the Holy Spirit'.

32. I do not deny differences between the Fourth Evangelist and Paul in their Christology, any more than in other ways. But I consider that there is much more in common than has often been appreciated: thus, for example, the stereotype of the Fourth Evangelist as a more Catholic incarnational thinker and Paul as a more Protestant justification-atonement focusing theologian is at best over-simple, and may reflect a failure to recognize that the Fourth Gospel does not represent the sum of all the Evangelist's theology (as is clear from a comparison with 1 John) and that Romans and Galatians do not represent the sum of Paul's thought. That Paul and the

of his sectarian-sounding 'Love one another', which seems to contrast with the much more open 'Love your neighbour' and 'Love your enemies' of the Synoptic tradition?

Here again Paul sheds important light on the question, since 'love one another' was an important part of his Christian ethic. Thus, for example, in 1 Thess. 4.9 he states: 'Concerning love of the brotherhood, you have no need to have anyone write to you. For you are all taught of God to love one another.' In Rom. 12.10 he urges his readers to be affectionate 'in brotherly love towards one another', while in Gal. 6.2 he urges the Galatians to bear 'each other's burdens' and so 'to fulfil the law of Christ'.

For Paul, this emphasis on love of fellow-Christians is not something introvertedly sectarian, but is combined with a strong missionary concern and an insistence that Christians should do 'good to all', as well as to the household of faith (Gal. 6.10; cf. 1 Thess. 5.15). Much the same may be said about John since, although there is a particularly strong stress on loving fellow-believers, the Fourth Gospel is fundamentally concerned with God sending his son to bring people to believe (3.16), a commission that is then transferred to the church (20.21).

Again, Pauline evidence makes it clear that an emphasis of the Fourth Gospel which could point to the Jamnian context could just as well fit into an earlier context. Moreover, Paul's evidence points to 'Johannine' emphases being found in early Jesus-tradition. And this is again the case with the emphasis on 'love one another'.

The most significant evidence in this case is Gal. 6.2, where Paul speaks of carrying each other's burdens and so fulfilling 'the law of Christ'.[33] This text has been a teasing puzzle to commentators. Why does Paul refer to a 'law' of Christ at all? In Galatians of all letters, he seeks sharply to differentiate the Judaizers' law-based religion and the gospel of Christ; he sharply rejects any attempt to impose the law on Gentile Christians, and when it comes to speaking of Christian conduct it is a matter of living by the Spirit, not of subjecting oneself to law. And yet, in Gal. 6.2 he urges the Galatians to 'fulfil the law of Christ'.

Fourth Evangelist may be closer than has often been thought may be seen in a comparison of the climactic story of Thomas coming to faith in the risen Christ as Lord and God in Jn 20.24-31 with the important Pauline explanation of salvation in Rom. 10.9.

33. See also Wenham, *Paul*, pp. 256-71.

Why does he suddenly reintroduce the category of law as a specifically Christian category? What does Paul have in mind when he uses the phrase? Is it just a slightly odd way of saying that this is the way of Christ? Does he have the teaching of Jesus in general in mind? Or does he specifically have the love command in mind, as attested in the Synoptic Gospels where Jesus affirms loving one's neighbour as a primary command (e.g. Mk 12.31)?

The last suggestion has merit: Paul speaks of 'the law of Christ' because he has in mind the specific teaching of Jesus about loving one's neighbour. Admittedly the law in question is a law of Moses (Lev. 19.18), not very distinctively the law 'of Christ', but it is possible that it came to be thought of by Christians as Christ's law. Moreover, only a few verses earlier Paul quoted the 'love your neighbour' command as summing up the whole law (5.13-14).

Paul's words in Gal. 5.13-14 are notable for two things. First, they are strikingly similar to the dominical saying of Mk 12.31 and especially to the version of the saying found in Mt. 22.39. Secondly, they are structurally and verbally similar to Gal. 6.2, as can be seen below:

5.13	Through love be slaves to one another. For all the law is fulfilled in one word, 'You shall love your neighbour as yourself'.	6.2	Bear the burdens of one another. And so you will fulfill the law of Christ.

Given these striking similarities, the conclusion may seem inevitable that the 'law of Christ' for Paul was indeed 'love your neighbour as yourself', since, as Paul presumably knew, Jesus had strongly endorsed that Old Testament command.

For all the plausibility of this interpretation, there is an alternative explanation that has rarely been considered but which has even greater plausibility, namely that what Paul has in mind when he speaks of the 'law of Christ' is the 'new commandment' of Jesus which is attested in the Johannine tradition.[34] In Jn 13.34 Jesus says: 'A new command-

34. R.Y.K. Fung (*The Epistle to the Galatians* [Grand Rapids: Eerdmans, 1988], pp. 288-89) does make the connection that I suggest, but identifies the Mosaic command to love one's neighbour with the command given by Jesus as a 'new commandment'. A different alternative is offered by O. Hofius in his significant article 'Das Gesetz des Mose und das Gesetz Christi', in his *Paulusstudien*

ment I give to you, that you love one another. As I have loved you that you also love one another. By this shall all know that you are my disciples, if you have love among one another.' The instruction is repeated both in 15.12, where Jesus speaks of 'my commandment', and in 15.17. The command to love one another is referred to also in 1 and 2 John, where it is specifically described as something that you 'heard from the beginning' (1 Jn 3.11, 23; 2 Jn 5). This special commandment of the Lord is evidently a well-known tradition in the Johannine community.

Why should it be this tradition that is in Paul's mind in Gal. 6.2? First, because Paul refers (surprisingly, as we saw) to 'the law of Christ' and John ascribes to Jesus a specific 'commandment', namely the command to 'love one another as I have loved you'. It is true that Paul could have in mind the command to 'love your neighbour' as endorsed by Jesus, but, although he probably knew that dominical tradition (and indeed was influenced by it in Gal. 5.14), it is not obvious that Jesus' endorsement of the ancient Mosaic law of Leviticus 5.14 would lead to it being designated 'Christ's law', whereas the Johannine love commandment is quite specifically described in John as new and as deriving from Jesus. Furthermore, Jesus in the Synoptic tradition highlights two Mosaic laws—love God and love your neighbour—so that the singular '*law* of Christ' is a little odd, if the reference is to 'love your neighbour'. The Johannine 'love one another' is a singular commandment, ascribed to Jesus, and so fits the case better.

Secondly, because Paul in Gal. 6.2 explains the law of Christ to entail 'bearing *one another's* burdens', which corresponds closely to the new commandment of John, which is 'to love *one another*'. In both cases the 'law/commandment' has to do specifically with love for other Christians. We may compare 1 Thess. 4.9, where Paul may be echoing the same tradition: 'Concerning love of the brotherhood, you have no need to have anyone write to you, for you are all taught of God to love one another.'

Against this second point, it may be argued that 'love one another' is a perfectly good paraphrastic translation of the Hebrew 'love your

(Tübingen: Mohr, 1989), pp. 50-74 (originally in *ZTK* 80 [1983], pp. 262-86). He argues that the law of Christ is the way of the cross, and that the phrase 'the law of Christ' is derived from Isa. 42.4, the Isaianic Servant passages being so vital in Paul's thinking about the cross. Riesner suggests a possible connection between 1 Thess. 4.9 and Jn 13.34 (*Die Frühzeit des Apostels Paulus*, p. 336).

neighbour', so that in Gal. 6.2 (and elsewhere) we do not need to postulate any background other than the Mosaic/Synoptic 'love your neighbour'. It might similarly be argued that John's 'new commandment' is a Johannine version of the Mosaic/Synoptic 'love your neighbour'. However, the Synoptic evidence suggests that the precise force of 'love your neighbour' was a matter of dispute, and that Jesus himself resisted an interpretation that limited its application to fellow Jews, advocating a broad interpretation (even to the inclusion of enemies; cf. Mt. 5.43-47; Lk. 10.25-37). There is no evidence that he interpreted the Mosaic command specifically of love for fellow disciples. It is therefore striking if Paul and John both give Jesus' endorsement of the 'love your neighbour' command that specific slant, and also if, as we have said, both designate this command of Moses as the law/command of Christ, in John's case claiming it be something 'new'. At least we should conclude that Paul and John have a tradition of interpreting Jesus' words in common. But most probably we should conclude that the 'command/law' of Christ is not 'love your neighbour' (important though that was to Jesus), but a more specific instruction about love among the disciples.[35]

The big problem with this proposal may seem to be that, while the Synoptists associate the love command with Jesus, it is love of God, of one's neighbour, even of one's enemy, not specifically Christians

35. Rom. 13.8, where Paul says 'Owe no one anything, except to love one another' could tell against our argument, since the application in the context is to love in society generally (not to love within the brotherhood). Also in 13.9-10 Paul goes on to speak of love fulfilling the law and of the whole law being summed up in 'Love your neighbour as yourself'. This might appear strongly to support the view that Paul derives his teaching about love of the brotherhood from the command to 'love your neighbour', not from the Johannine command. The more likely explanation, however, is that Paul mixes his Jesus-traditions. Thus he can quite appropriately bring together Jesus' teaching about love as the fulfilment of the law with Jesus' teaching about the need for Christians to be loving servants to each other (Gal. 5.13-14; see below for discussion of the servant-teaching); he can use the 'love your neighbour' command to teach Christians about their responsibility to each other (Rom. 15.2; note in 15.3 the appeal to Jesus' example, and compare the Johannnine 'as I have loved you'); and occasionally he can use the phrase 'love one another' not just of Christians loving each other (Rom. 13.8). This mixing of traditions is entirely natural, since Paul is not reproducing Jesus' traditions as such, but using them creatively within his own teaching. The evidence in no way undermines my conclusion that Paul knew that there were at least two strands in Jesus' teaching about love, one broader and one narrower: compare 1 Thess. 5.15, or Gal. 6.10.

loving one another. How could they fail to mention what Paul and John both portray as Jesus' characteristic command? This might seem to point in the opposite direction, suggesting that it was Paul's teaching that gave rise to the Johannine new commandment rather than the other way around.

However, three points are worth making by way of reply to this. First, there is evidence suggesting that so-called Johannine tradition has its roots very early; the Q sayings of Mt. 11.25-27 illustrate this. Secondly, there is evidence of Paul being familiar with and influenced by Jesus-traditions.[36] Thirdly, in this as other cases, it is simplest to explain Paul from the Jesus-tradition than *vice versa*. Thus, Paul's 'law of Christ' expression is explicable from the Johannine Jesus-tradition, whereas if John was influenced by Paul we are left without any equally plausible explanation of Paul's language.

As for the Synoptics and the new commandment, although they do not directly attest the command to love one another, they come very close to it, particularly in contexts where Jesus discusses relationships between the disciples. This is clear from Mk 9.33-50, where Jesus speaks of receiving other disciples and not causing offence, saying, 'Be at peace with one another'. So too, in Mk 10.41-45, Jesus tells the competitive disciples that they should be servants and slaves to each other, following his example.[37] Matthew similarly emphasizes good,

36. I argue this in detail in Wenham, *Paul*. I deliberately did not discuss the Fourth Gospel at any length in that book; but positions taken in this article draw on material found there.

37. The Synoptic thought of 'being servants of each other' following the example of Jesus and of his death has a strong claim to being something quite distinctive of Jesus (much more so than 'love your neighbour as yourself'), and is very close conceptually to the Johannine new commandment, where 'loving one another' is associated with service and the death of Jesus (e.g. Jn 13). 'Bearing one another's burdens' in Gal. 6.2 is clearly a similar thought (cf. Rom. 15.1-3). Scholars have claimed Paul's familiarity with Mk 10.45, including in 1 Cor. 9.19, a context where we find some sort of a parallel to the 'law of Christ' of Gal. 6.2, since Paul speaks of himself being 'in Christ's law' (9.21; see Wenham, *Paul*, pp. 266-71). It may also be significant that in Gal. 5.13 we find the idea of love and service combined: 'Through love be servants to one another': for Paul the ideas of loving one another, serving, and of love as fulfilment of the law all come together, and all arguably have a basis in Jesus-tradition.

The idea of Jesus' disciples being his family/brothers/sisters also has a basis in tradition (e.g. Mk 3.35; perhaps Mt. 25.40); there would logically be a special responsibility of 'brotherly' love and loyalty towards them.

forgiving relationships with the brethren, both in the opening anti-
thesis of the Sermon on the Mount (5.21-24) and most notably in
ch. 18.

The Johannine love command is a good example of a feature of
John that is regularly taken to derive from the Fourth Evangelist and
to reflect his context, that context often being seen as post-Jamnian. If
my argument is correct, however, it turns out that Paul knew the
'Johannine' command as a Jesus-tradition decades before Jamnia. Paul
indeed turns out to be an important witness to various Johannine
Jesus-traditions.

It is tempting, in view of this conclusion, to take the discussion
further, and to ask if there are other Johannine Jesus-traditions that
Paul may have known. For example, if Paul knew the Johannine 'love
one another', did he also know the Johannine story closely connected
with that command, namely the washing of the disciples' feet?
Although not in the Synoptic Gospels,[38] the story is historically plausible, being very much akin to Jesus' other acted parables (e.g. his
riding into Jerusalem on a donkey and his eucharistic actions) and in
keeping with Jesus' well-attested teaching about servanthood (e.g. Mk
10.45). The depiction of Jesus as the humble servant in Philippians 2
could be derived from the Synoptic servant-tradition, but could possibly reflect the Johannine story of Jesus taking the form of a servant
and giving his life to 'wash' the disciples.[39]

It would be tempting similarly to link Paul's 'in Christ' language
with the Johannine emphasis on 'abiding in Christ' and in particular
with parable of the vine (Jn 15), which describes the disciples as
branches 'in the vine'. Scholars have offered all sorts of suggestions as
to where the Pauline usage comes from: has it something to do with
the corporateness of the idea of the messiah, or with Gen. 12.3, where
Abraham is promised that 'in you all the nations shall be blessed', or
with the powerful ritual of baptism, when the immersed convert was
plunged 'into' the new reality of Christ? Or is it possible that the
Johannine parable of the vine, however much John may have

38. Unless Lk. 12.37 and 22.27 hint at Lukan knowledge of the story.
39. Cf. G.F. Hawthorne, *Philippians* (Waco, TX: Word Books, 1983), pp. 78-
79; also L. Hurtado, 'Jesus as Lordly Example in Philippians 2.5-11', in
P. Richardson and J.C. Hurd (eds.), *From Jesus to Paul* (Waterloo: Wilfrid Laurier,
1984), p. 124.

elaborated it, may have been known to Paul as Jesus-tradition, and that this was a catalyst to his thinking?[40]

The answer is, of course, that anything is possible. But the evidence that we have looked at earlier in this article suggests that these possibilities are not implausible. There may also be something of a cumulative argument emerging, with a whole variety of Johannine materials (not least those found in the farewell discourses) having some sort of Pauline parallels.[41] But space prohibits the development of these ideas here, and it is not necessary for the argument of this article to do so.

Irrespective of these last two suggestions, the evidence that we have noted earlier not only goes a long way to undermining the Jamnian hypothesis, but also points towards an alternative view—namely that the Johannine traditions of Jesus considered here originate from a time even before Paul, and that they deserve to be treated with as much respect, historically, as do the Synoptic Gospels.

4. Why is the Fourth Gospel so Different?

To argue as I have above is only to restate (and hopefully to reinforce with significant new evidence) the kind of view represented by John Robinson, and the weakness of his discussion, as we saw, was that he failed to explain the divergence of the Fourth Gospel from the Synoptic Gospels.

The issue has perhaps begun to be addressed in that I have shown that John is not as different from the Synoptic Gospels as has often been supposed. And that argument does not just depend on one or two

40. On the history of the Johannine parable of the vine, see R. Bauckham, 'The Parable of the Vine: Rediscovering a Lost Parable of Jesus', *NTS* 33 (1987), pp. 84-101. S.S. Smalley ('The Christ-Christian Relationship in Paul and John', in D.A. Hagner and M.J. Harris [eds.], *Pauline Studies* [Exeter: Paternoster Press; Grand Rapids: Eerdmans, 1980], pp. 97-98) finds the whole pattern of divine-human indwelling to be similar in Paul and the Fourth Evangelist: 'you in God... in Christ... in Spirit; God in you... Christ in you... Spirit in you'. Smalley also finds a similar sacramentalism; the Fourth Evangelist and Paul both have the idea of conversion as rebirth (Jn 3; 1 Cor. 4.15; Gal. 4.19). We do not find Paul's 'body' image in the Fourth Gospel, and yet Jn 2.21 may be significant.

41. As always, we must beware of parallelomania. Ashton (*Understanding*, p. 98) comments that 'Surely any self-respecting Christian syncretist of the period would have shown *some* Pauline influence'!

texts. In fact, there are many more points of convergence than scholars have tended to recognize. It is true, for example, that there are no
Johannine 'I am' sayings in the Synoptic Gospels, but there are still
highly significant 'I am' occurrences (e.g. Mk 6.50; 14.62) and things
that come very close to what we have in the Fourth Gospel.[42]

But that is not to deny the differences. The clue as to the Fourth
Evangelist's intentions is in Jn 20.31: 'These are written that you may
believe that Jesus is the Christ, the Son of God, and that believing you
may have life in his name.' This verse sums up almost everything
about the Fourth Gospel, and is an overt statement by the author that
his purpose is christological. That statement corresponds to what we
find in the Fourth Gospel, with its strong emphasis on the person of
Jesus and on the question of who he was. Of course, all the Gospels
focus on Jesus and are interested in Christology, but, whereas
Matthew, Mark and Luke give us a relatively broad picture of Jesus
(his ministry and his teaching concerning the kingdom, ethics, the
future, etc.), John homes in much more sharply on the question of the
identity of Jesus. Almost every chapter (at least up to ch. 13) is about
Jesus as the Messiah, the Son of God and the source of life; the miracles in John are signs of Jesus' divinity, not (in the first instance)
signs of the kingdom.

The probability must be that this sharp focus reflects the author's
situation. He is writing to a situation where there is controversy about
who Jesus is. But who particularly does he have in mind?

First, it is probably correct to postulate conflict with 'the Jews',
hence the polemical note in the Fourth Gospel and the attention it
gives to the question of Jesus' Messiahship. This, however, in no way
requires us to think primarily, or necessarily at all, in terms of the
post-Jamnia situation. There was sharp controversy with the Jews

42. E.g. compare Mt. 7.13-14 on the 'way' to life with Jn 14.6; Mt. 18.12 on the
caring shepherd with Jn 10; Mt. 11.28-30 with the sentiment of various of the 'I am'
sayings. Cf. G. Maier, 'Johannes und Matthäus—Zwiespalt oder Viergestalt des
Evangeliums?', in R.T. France and D. Wenham (eds.), *Studies of History and Tradition in the Four Gospels*, II (Gospel Perspectives, 2; Sheffield: JSOT Press,
1981), pp. 267-92.

Occasionally one gets the impression that scholars have tended to read Johannine
Christology in as 'high' a way as possible, when actually the Synoptic Evangelists
are much closer to the Fourth Evangelist and the later church fathers in their appreciation of Jesus as divine than has sometimes been supposed.

throughout much of the first century, including the earliest days of the church's life.

Secondly, there is probably controversy with the followers of John the Baptist in the mind of the author. This is suggested by the considerable attention that is given to the question of Jesus and the Baptist in John 1–4, and by the emphasis that the Baptist was not the Messiah, not the light, and that he came to bear witness to Jesus: 'He must increase, but I must decrease' (3.30). This emphasis is very probably in response to people who were pushing in the opposite direction, making John greater and Jesus less. It is 1.20 that most strongly points in this direction, since the Baptist is there described as follows: 'He confessed, he did not deny but confessed, "I am not the Christ"'. It is clear that the Evangelist is putting the denial of John in bold type and capital letters, to ensure that his readers get the message loudly and clearly.

There is direct evidence of people who regarded John the Baptist as the Messiah only in the third century CE. But there is indirect evidence within the New Testament that may point to a Baptist movement continuing after Jesus' death: thus Acts 18.24-19.6 describes people knowing the baptism of John only and needing to be brought into a full understanding of Christian faith (including Apollos and including people in Ephesus, the traditional location of the Fourth Gospel). And there are various oblique hints within the New Testament which may suggest that there were tensions between some followers of John and the early Christians: Mt. 3.13-15 may be Matthew's response to people who claimed that John as Jesus' baptizer was his superior. The silence of the Synoptists about many aspects of John's ministry (and of Jesus working for a time in tandem with John as his follower and colleague, as described in the Fourth Gospel) may be a reflection of the same thing. They focus on John's witness to Jesus, and tend to play down his wider significance.

The same is true of the Fourth Gospel, and the author's failure to mention the baptism of Jesus by John may possibly be for the same reason. Whether it is or not, it seems probable that the strong emphasis on the supreme, heavenly status of Jesus in the Fourth Gospel is in part a response to a rival Christology in relation to John the Baptist.[43]

43. Ashton (*Understanding*, p. 167) suspects that the dispute with disciples of John was past history when the Gospel was written. Lindars (*Gospel of John*, pp. 60-61) thinks that it was the Jews, not ongoing 'baptists', who were making

A third (possibly related) factor is suggested by the Johannine letters, and in particular 1 John. Scholars are uncertain if 1 John was
written by the same author as the Fourth Gospel. But the style and
theology of the letter and the Fourth Gospel are at least evidence that
they come from the same sort of context and circle. The significant
thing from the point of view of this article is that 1 John portrays a
split Christian church, the split being over the question of Christology, as depicted in 2.18 and 4.1-3.

The exact nature of the split is uncertain. Some scholars have seen
the 'antichrists' as early docetics, whose main fault was in failing to
take seriously the 'flesh' of Jesus. But it is not at all certain that they
were denying the fleshly humanity of Jesus so soon after his life, and
perhaps more likely that they were denying that the fleshly Jesus was
the Christ, the Son of God. Just conceivably they could have been preferring John the Baptist to Jesus, or more likely separating 'the heavenly Christ' from the man Jesus. The early church tradition which
identifies the 'heresy' as a form of Cerinthianism, which claimed that
the Spirit descended on Jesus at his baptism and departed before his
death, still deserves to be taken seriously. It certainly looks as though
the heretics were interested in baptism and the Spirit, but not in the
death of Jesus—hence the emphasis in 1 John on the water and the
blood, indeed on the water, the Spirit and the blood. It may be that
they associated their own baptismal 'anointing' (*chrisma*) by the Spirit
with Jesus' baptismal experience, and saw Jesus as the prototype
Christian, on whom the anointing, 'Christ-making', Spirit came and in
whom the Spirit dwelt, rather than as one who was the incarnate
Christ and the eternal Son of God throughout his life, including in his
death.[44]

It is not difficult to see how such ideas could have been derived
from the story of Jesus' baptism, and I suspect that that story spawned
a whole variety of 'heretical' ideas, which are responded to in the

John out to be greater than Jesus. I think it is entirely possible that there were continuing followers of John (the view that they all went over to Jesus is over-simple),
and that the question of John and Jesus was a much more important ingredient in
debate about Jesus in the early church than is often recognized.

44. See R.J. Porter, 'That You May Know...: An Exegetical and Historical
Analysis of the Arguments Used by the Author of 1 John to Reassure his Readers of
the Authenticity of their Christian Faith and Experience' (MPhil thesis for Westminster College, Oxford, and the Open University, 1993).

New Testament. The story gave scope to those arguing for John's superiority to (or at least equality with) Jesus,[45] to people advocating an adoptionist Christology, and to the Corinthians with their over-realized eschatology and their special interest in baptism and charismatic experiences.[46] In response to such ideas we find all the Evangelists in their different ways being careful to put John the

45. It might have been argued that the baptism story shows John to have been one who baptized not just with water, but with the Holy Spirit! So was Jesus just a prophet like John, indeed a prophet taking his inspiration from John? The New Testament insistence on associating Spirit-baptism with Jesus could be to counter such a view (including in Acts 19.1-7).

46. It is not possible to prove that people like the Corinthians were familiar with the story of Jesus' baptism, but it is possible (1) to show that they knew many Jesus-traditions (see P. Richardson and P. Gooch, 'Logia of Jesus in 1 Corinthians', in D. Wenham [ed.], *The Jesus Tradition Outside the Gospels* [Gospel Perspectives, 5; Sheffield: JSOT Press, 1985], pp. 39-62; E.E. Ellis, 'Traditions in 1 Corinthians', *NTS* 32 [1986], pp. 481-502; and Wenham, *Paul*); (2) to argue for Paul's familiarity with the baptism story (see above); (3) to show the Corinthians' interest in baptism, for example 15.29 on the mysterious practice of baptism for the dead.

Various scholars have postulated links between Corinthian enthusiasm and Johannine Christianity (see n. 19 above), and indeed have connected both with the 'Q' tradition; we have already noted how Mt. 11.27/Lk. 10.22 has been linked to both 1 Corinthians and the Fourth Gospel. It has been argued that we have a 'gnostic' trajectory in early Christianity, going from Q to the Fourth Gospel to gnosticism via (among other places) Corinth. See J.M. Robinson and H. Koester's significant work, *Trajectories through early Christianity* (Philadelphia: Fortress Press, 1977). I suspect that there is a grain of truth in this view, but that the true picture is somewhat different. What we have is not a distinctive 'gnostic' Christianity within the early church (comparable to Jewish Christianity and Pauline Christianity). Rather we see the young church on a broad front wrestling with the traditions that they had received (including the baptism of Jesus) and trying to work out their significance. (On this sort of process in Corinth, see my 'Whatever Went Wrong in Corinth?', *ExpTim* 108 [1997], pp. 137-41). The traditions concerned and indeed some of the tendencies exhibited in Corinthian and Johannine Christianity could (and indeed would) lead some in gnostic directions. But in the early period it was less gnosticism and more the sacramental and charismatic nature of early Christianity that is the key to what was going on. And the sacramental and charismatic features of early Christianity are to be traced back not to Greek gnosis (at least not primarily), but rather back to the Palestinian roots of Christianity, to Jesus and the early church. There is no need to doubt that Acts is right to portray the earliest Christian church as a baptist, charismatic community, or that the Gospels are right to associate Jesus with baptism and charismatic power, and further back still to John the Baptist and indeed to the Essenes (with their emphasis on lustrations, the Spirit and revealed mysteries).

Baptist in his place and the Synoptic Evangelists not even mentioning Jesus' Judaean ministry alongside John. We find Paul in Corinthians, the author of 1 John and perhaps the author of Mark's Gospel all emphasizing the cross to counter a charismatic spirituality that emphasized baptism and the power of the Spirit.[47] As for the Fourth Gospel, the writer does not suppress the story of Jesus baptizing like John, but he has the Baptist speak emphatically about Jesus' superiority and uniqueness. Jesus in the Fourth Gospel is not 'a son' like any other Christian, but is 'the son', with Christians being 'children' of 'my father *and* your father' (1.12; 20.17).

If there is anything in these various suggestions and if such tensions were surfacing in the Johannine church when the Fourth Gospel was being written, then the author's energetic engagement with the question of Christology and his sustained affirmation of Jesus as the Christ and the Son of God make sense. He insists that the fleshly Jesus is divine, that he was from the beginning, and that in him (and nowhere else) is life.

There is an interesting parallel in Paul's epistle to the Colossians, where Paul (or the Pauline author) is countering those who 'would make a prey of you by philosophy and human deceit according to human tradition, according to the elemental spirits of the universe, and not according to Christ' (2.8-12). The nature of the heresy is disputed, but it seems that the heretics, as the author regards them, were putting Christ down. In response, the author emphasizes the supremacy of Christ, speaking of Christ as the image of the invisible God, the first-born of all creation, as the one in who all things were created, in whom the whole fullness of deity dwelt, and in whom there is fullness (i.e. of life). The language is strongly reminiscent of the Fourth Gospel (especially the prologue) and, moreover, both texts portray the cross as a victory (over the prince of this world in the

---

47. In Mark the only baptism mentioned after the start of Jesus' ministry is a baptism of suffering (10.38-39). It is one of the puzzles about the Synoptic Gospels that Jesus starts his ministry in a 'baptist' context, but then water baptism does not feature in the ministry of Jesus until we reach the resurrection and the age of the church (so Matthew and Luke). Was baptism not a feature of Jesus' ministry (despite the testimony of the Fourth Gospel to a baptizing ministry in Judea), but only of John the Baptist and the church? Or have the Synoptics deliberately played down the links between John and Jesus, because they were controversial? On this see Sefa-Dapaah, 'Investigation'.

Fourth Gospel, over the principalities and powers in Colossians). There is no need to argue for any very close connection between Colossians and the Fourth Gospel or between the heresies countered in the two books (though Colosse is near Ephesus, the city traditionally associated with the writing of the Fourth Gospel); but both suggest a situation in which some people are offering a relatively low Christology, and in which the canonical authors respond by affirming the supremacy and the pre-existence of Christ, his adequacy for salvation, and his victory.

It seems, then, that the Fourth Evangelist wrote his Gospel in a situation of christological controversy, a controversy that did not just involve Christians and Jews, but also Christians and those much closer to them—followers of John the Baptist, and even people who were or who had been part of the Christian community. Such a situation explains the Evangelist's almost obsessive interest in the question of Christology and his sustained attempt to exalt Jesus. It helps explain the strongly realized eschatology of the Fourth Gospel: the author wants to make it clear that life is to be found in Jesus, now, and that there is no other way (as some of his contemporaries were suggesting). It helps to explain his interest in the Spirit: if the heretics were people who made much of the Spirit and of their experience of the Spirit, then it became important to define the work of the Spirit and to insist that the Spirit is closely associated with Jesus (witnessing to Jesus, teaching about Jesus, continuing the work of Jesus).[48] It also helps explain the strong emphasis on 'loving one another': if the Fourth Gospel was written after a split had taken place in the church,[49] then it is understandable that the author of the Fourth Gospel has a big interest in Christian unity and love (Jn 17). Abiding in Jesus and in the vine which is the church is especially important at a time when some have gone out, not 'abiding' with us (cf. Jn 15; 1 Jn 2.19).

48. So too in 1 John, where going back 'to the beginning' (the beginning of the Christian story in Jesus) is emphasized (1.1-3)

49. Many scholars would argue that the Gospel was written before the epistles, but, even if they are right, it is quite likely that the split described in 1 John may have been anticipated, manifesting itself already.

5. *Conclusion*

This article has not resolved all the questions over the origins of the Fourth Gospel. But it has raised major questions about the Jamnian consensus and has offered the beginnings of an alternative, and I think preferable, explanation of the Fourth Gospel's distinctives. I have argued (1) that the distinctives arise out of a very early Christian tradition, not a rather late mutation in the evolution of Christian doctrine; and (2) that John's special emphases are better explained in terms of the sort of christological debates that I have described than more narrowly in terms of a church–synagogue split at the end of the first century.[50] This has important implications for a consideration of the historicity of the Fourth Gospel, and means that its claim to be based on the eyewitness testimony of 'the beloved disciple' deserves more respect than it is sometimes given. That is not to say that the Fourth Gospel is a verbatim account of Jesus' words and actions, and that the Johannine Evangelist has simply selected different material than the Synoptic Evangelists.[51] It is hard to deny that John has often put the traditions into his own words and presented them artistically and creatively. The extent of his creativity is difficult to assess, but it is less significant than most scholars have supposed, and may be more in presentation and less in substance than is often thought.

50. W. Sanday (*The Criticism of the Fourth Gospel* [Oxford: Clarendon Press, 1905], pp. 216-35) argues, rightly in my view, that the christological similarities between Paul, the Fourth Gospel and Synoptic sayings such as Mt. 11.27 are to be explained via 'a connection in the main underground' of early Christianity (not through Pauline influence on the Fourth Evangelist).

51. But that may well be one further factor explaining his differences. He may be clarifying what the previous Gospel traditions had left obscure, whether on Jesus and baptism, or on other matters. The story of Lazarus, for example, may have been deliberately ignored by the Synoptists, perhaps for the sake of Lazarus, but the Fourth Evangelist feels able to use the story, and to make his points through it.

THE WISDOM OF TOO MUCH ESCHATOLOGY

Alan Le Grys

Among the many perceptive observations in his magisterial study of the Fourth Gospel,[1] John Ashton draws attention to the preoccupation in a great deal of earlier scholarship with the link between apocalyptic and eschatology. As Ashton points out, this fixation on eschatology tended to generate a distorted view of first-century apocalyptic literature: to put it crudely, too many New Testament scholars regarded eschatology and apocalyptic as synonymous. They are not. As his Oxford colleague Chris Rowland has demonstrated, eschatology is at best only one element among many that *sometimes* appears in certain types of text. It does not define the genre of apocalyptic as a whole. That is a much broader category, and includes all forms of Jewish and Christian writing reflecting a belief that human agents are capable of perceiving divine reality. Some of those revelatory disclosures (almost coincidentally) reflect on matters concerning the end-times, but it simply does not follow that all apocalyptic is eschatological.[2]

Armed with this insight, Ashton goes on to reaffirm (albeit in modified form) John's apocalyptic credentials. Although John does not appear to maintain a lively interest in futurist eschatology,[3] there are clear features of the Gospel which betray a common heritage with Jewish apocalyptic: the link with the Wisdom tradition, the 'mystery of two ages', the two stages of enlightenment in which the Spirit-Paraclete plays a crucially important role as *angelus interpres*, the

---

1. J. Ashton, *Understanding the Fourth Gospel* (Oxford: Oxford University Press, 1991). This essay is offered as a small token of admiration for John's scholarship and gratitude for his friendship and support as a colleague in Oxford over the past five years.

2. Ashton, *Understanding*, pp. 383-87, citing C. Rowlands, *The Open Heaven* (London: SPCK, 1982).

3. This needs to be carefully qualified, of course: Jn 5.19-29 and 6.40 are but two examples of passages with strongly futurist elements.

mashal tradition, and the two level drama in which activity on earth is seen as a mirror image of events in heaven. Seen in this light, the startling innovation of the Gospel is that God's foreordained plan of redemption is no longer limited to auditions and visions conveyed through secondary agents, but has been brought into full effect through the definitive embodiment of Wisdom in the λόγος incarnate (Jn 1.14).[4] Divine truth is literally revealed in the flesh (cf. Jn 18.38).

This shift in perspective moves John away from an exclusively eschatological context and back in the direction of an underlying Wisdom tradition.[5] In the process, it perhaps helps to explain one of the more puzzling aspects of John's pneumatology: why, when the Evangelist tends to play down the futurist element in his eschatology, does John insist that the Holy Spirit was available to the disciples only as a future event, *after* the death and resurrection of Jesus (Jn 7.39)? In striking contrast to the Synoptic Gospels where Jesus already has access to the eschatological power of God (e.g. Mt. 12.28),[6] the Spirit in John is singularly absent during the teaching ministry. Jesus is neither a spirit-filled charismatic, nor an exorcist engaged in conflict with demonic spiritual powers.[7] Even after the crucifixion, the Spirit is not given the Pauline status of an eschatological ἀρραβών (2 Cor. 1.22; 5.5), the ἀπαρχή of a new creation (Rom 8.23): the παράκλητος is little more than an extension of the presence of Jesus (Jn 14.18, 25-26). Could it be that this change of perspective is simply symptomatic of John's underlying apocalyptic-Wisdom framework?

A brief review of some of the evidence may perhaps help to answer the question. The *TDNT* I article on πνεῦμα lists any number of different fields of meaning for Spirit. Putting aside for a moment the range of possibilities found in non-biblical literature, it appears that there are at least seven or eight different associations found in the Septuagint alone.[8] Of these, only one turns out to be directly concerned with eschatology. The rest include the Spirit as wind, breath of life, God-given ability to understand and to act properly, and the

---

4. Ashton, *Understanding*, pp. 405-406.

5. See also G. von Rad, *Wisdom in Israel* (Nashville: Abingdon Press, 1972), pp. 263-83.

6. C.K. Barrett, *The Holy Spirit and the Gospel Tradition* (London: SPCK, 1947), pp. 153-54.

7. E. Schweizer, *TDNT* I, p. 892.

8. W. Bieder, 'πνεῦμα', *TDNT* I, pp. 881-82.

power of blessing and discipline. Supremely, however, the biblical evidence suggests that the Spirit is linked with Wisdom (e.g. Wis. 9.17-18). The eschatological connection is a secondary development.[9]

Unlike Paul and the Synoptics, therefore, John buys into the primary Wisdom trajectory. For him, Jesus is either the embodiment of divine Wisdom herself,[10] or perhaps the λόγος child of Wisdom (Wis. 18.14-19).[11] So he does not need to be empowered by the Spirit—that goes with the package. In any case, as the 'firstborn of Creation' (Prov. 8.22), he already enjoys the closest possible intimacy with the Father (Jn 10.30). Further, as the Spirit is fully present in Jesus, there could obviously be no other divine presence apart from him—not at least until after the 'glorification' removed the limitations of the incarnation and enabled others to share his Spirit. This is actually acted out in narrative form in the post-Easter encounter in the Upper Room: the Spirit Jesus breathes onto the disciples is quite literally his own (Jn 20.22). This is received not so much as an eschatological pledge but as a kind of (lesser?) substitute, another παράκλητος in lieu of the embodiment of σοφία-λόγος (Jn 14.16; cf. Jn 19.30). This is the Spirit who will bring the disciples the apocalyptic insight they need to achieve a proper understanding of heavenly reality—he will literally guide them 'into all the truth' (Jn 16.13).

Yet this presents a paradox. For all that John tends to pull the Spirit away from eschatology towards the apocalyptic-Wisdom trajectory, Paul by contrast seems to be moving in exactly the opposite direction.

For example, almost by universal assent[12] 1 Corinthians is thought to address what is (from Paul's point of view) the problem of 'over-realised' eschatology. A group of πνευματικοί think they have σοφία and this has led them to behave in ways Paul finds morally unacceptable. Perhaps believing themselves to be already in a superior state (1 Cor. 4.8), he thinks they need to be reminded that the best is yet to

---

9. On the close connection between Wisdom and Spirit see also E. Schüssler Fiorenza, *Jesus: Miriam's Child, Sophia's Prophet* (London: SCM Press, 1994), pp. 135-50.

10. R.E. Brown (*The Gospel according to John I–XII* [AB; Garden City, NY: Doubleday, 1966], pp. 521-23) draws attention to the close connection between Wisdom and λόγος.

11. Schüssler Fiorenza (*Jesus*, p. 138) gives some evidence for seeing λόγος as the son of σοφία.

12. E.g. G. Fee, *The First Epistle to the Corinthians* (NICNT; Grand Rapids: Eerdmans, 1987), pp. 7-13.

come (1 Cor. 15.12-49). The eschatological resurrection remains only a future possibility, not a present reality. In the meantime, the Corinthians must learn to behave properly.

In an interesting study, Alexandra Brown examines how Paul works through a competing cluster of apocalyptic and eschatological ideas in the crucially important introduction to this letter (1 Cor. 1–4).[13] She argues that the key is the cross: Paul adopted a rhetorical strategy which sought to persuade the Corinthians to reorder their perceptions around the ethical logic of the death of Jesus. Thus, in 1 Cor. 1.18–2.16 the cross is the apocalyptic (revelatory) moment in which the 'mystery' (2.1) of 'God's plan secret and hidden' (2.7) is finally disclosed 'through the Spirit' (2.10). This secret plan undermines human values and reverses normal perceptions: 'God's foolishness is wiser than human wisdom, and God's weakness is stronger than human strength' (1 Cor. 1.25).[14] In short, the cross is a model of powerlessness and humility which provides the absolute paradigm for proper Christian living.

Brown goes on to suggest that Paul was an advocate of speech-act theory before its time. According to J.L. Austin, words can basically be placed in two distinct categories: constatives, which try to describe reality, and performatives, which attempt to change it. Performatives, however, can be broken down into two further sub-groups: perlocutionary, which attempt to effect change by virtue of their assumed authority ('I arrest you *in* the name of the law'), and illocutionary, which effect change by virtue of their own inherent power (e.g. the response 'I will' in the marriage service effects a change of status simply by expressing consent).

Applying this to 1 Corinthians, Brown argues that the 'word (λόγος) of the cross' (1 Cor. 1.18)[15] belongs to the latter sub-group of illocutionary words—statements capable of transforming perception through their inherent performative function. Echoing Luther, she suggests that the power of the 'message of the cross' is enough (Paul hopes) to shift attention away from the present achievements of believers (the 'wise') towards an unfulfilled future hope, and in the process bring about a long overdue change in inappropriate (un-Christlike) behaviour.

---

13. A.R. Brown, *The Cross and Human Transformation: Paul's Apocalyptic Word in 1 Corinthians* (Philadelphia: Fortress Press, 1995).

14. All biblical quotations are from the NRSV unless otherwise stated.

15. My translation.

Paul sets out to achieve this objective by adopting three familiar rhetorical strategies. First, he attempts 'dislocation' or the undermining of present social values (1 Cor. 1.18–2.6). Then, he appeals to an authoritative revelation (2.7-10) to establish the basis for his distinctive point of view. Finally, he moves the argument to closure by appealing to shared values—the assertion of an assumed common outlook (2.14-16).[16] Having argued to his own satisfaction that the revelatory power of the cross is sufficient to make the point, Paul moves on with remarkable ease to rebuke, challenge and correct the objectionable behaviour he associates with Wisdom theology (1 Cor. 3 onwards). The self-seeking assertive power and superior elitist behaviour of 'the wise' must be put to death on the cross which alone enables those who share the common mind to 'think [and therefore behave—1 Cor. 13?] like Jesus'.

The persuasive force of this argument turns on an apocalyptic disclosure about the significance of the cross: the Corinthians' perception of a present painless but superior status (the possession of Wisdom) must be exchanged for a future hope which leads to a final victory over the cosmic powers only after death and resurrection (1 Cor. 15). One of the spin-offs, however, is that the work of the Spirit is disengaged from the Wisdom context assumed by the Corinthians (1 Cor. 2.10-14) and replaced with the more characteristic Pauline emphasis on the already/not yet tension (1 Cor. 12–14). In other words, the Spirit is moving across the apocalyptic-revelatory spectrum back in the direction of eschatology.

It would appear, therefore, that although Paul and John work with similar ideas, they end up with mirror images of their shared apocalyptic-eschatological-Spirit heritage. Care is needed: a straightforward either/or pattern is obviously too simplistic. Nevertheless, it might perhaps be said in broad terms that Paul tends to move away from an emphasis on present Wisdom theology in favour of a futurist eschatology, whereas John prefers to play down futurist elements in favour of the present reality of λόγος-σοφία embodied in Jesus.

For all that, there is one point where they obviously agree: for both of them, the moment of revelatory disclosure is the cross. Paul says as much in 1 Cor. 1.18—the cross alone reveals the secret and hidden mystery of God which thwarts 'the rulers of this age' who 'crucified the Lord of glory' (1 Cor. 2.1, 7-8). According to Brown, this 'word

16. Brown, *The Cross*, pp. 150-67.

of the cross' has performative power, so for Paul the givenness of the crucifixion is enough to effect the necessary change in outlook. Jesus is no longer a 'stumbling block' (1 Cor. 1.23), but 'the crucified Lord of glory (δόξα)'.

John is less direct, of course, though curiously δόξα turns out to be part of his vocabulary for the cross (e.g. Jn 17.2-5). The ὥρα of the crucifixion not only brings about eschatological judgment but also glorifies Jesus (Jn 12.27-32) and releases the Spirit (Jn 19.30; 20.22). So, as Bultmann might have said, there is a certain *dass*-ness about the cross for both of these authors in which the δόξα or otherness of God cannot be disguised. Both Paul and John seem to agree that the sheer fact of the death of Jesus is enough to effect a radical change in perceptions.

But perhaps the parallel can be stretched (or is it over-stretched?) even further. For Paul, it is more precisely the *word* (λόγος) of the cross which brings about the required change in values. To use Brown's phrase, Paul is a 'speech-act'ivist.[17] Nowhere does John call the cross a 'word' as such, of course. And yet, it is precisely the λόγος of Jn 1.1-18 who is eventually crucified. Here perhaps is the archetypal 'speech-act'ivist if ever one were needed. Jesus' *words* (ῥήματα) are spirit (6.63), eternal life (6.68), words of God (8.47), divisive (10.19: λόγους) and judgmental (12.47-48), but always God-given (14.10). The word performs the task of disclosing the presence of God in Christ lifted up on the cross.

So why is it, given the huge overlap of language and beliefs, that Paul and John took a similar cluster of Wisdom, apocalyptic and eschatological ideas and pushed them in opposite directions? The clue, perhaps, is the very word δόξα both of them choose to use in connection with the crucified λόγος.

Since the pioneering work of Gerd Theissen,[18] it has become almost commonplace to interpret the interaction in 1 Corinthians against a background of social tension. Theissen argues that there are enough hints in the text to show that the Corinthian church was split between two major component groups: the relatively rich believers who provided the buildings for the house-church to meet and the wherewithal for the shared eucharistic meal, and the relatively poorer members of

17. Brown, *The Cross*, p. 19.
18. G. Theissen, *The Social Setting of Pauline Christianity* (Edinburgh: T. & T. Clark, 1982).

the lower classes who were socially and economically inferior. The honour-shame culture of the first-century Graeco-Roman world ensured that this produced an entirely predictable social structure within the community: it would have been taken for granted that the richer believers were the (superior) benefactors whilst the poorer members were relegated to an inferior dependent client status. It was, suggests Theissen, these richer patrons who were identified by Paul as the 'strong'—an elitist group of the 'wise' who knew how to behave in the present age of the Spirit. By contrast, the 'weak' represent those who were not convinced about this 'enlightened' behaviour and harboured continuing doubts and unease. They were swept along by their social superiors, however, either because they were afraid of making fools of themselves, or because they could not afford to cause offence. If this is correct, the function of 1 Corinthians is to undermine the superior status of the 'strong' and enhance the position of the 'weak' by rebuking the unacceptable behaviour of the so-called 'wise'.[19] Paul does not push the argument too far, of course—like everyone else he still needs benefactors! Instead, he cites his ministry as a practical example of how to modify superior status in the interests of the community as a whole (1 Cor. 9). The result is a compromise in the form of *love patriarchalism*, or how to live with the tension between Christian idealism (Gal. 3.27-29) and Graeco-Roman social reality.

Putting Theissen and Brown together, it could be said that Paul sets out in 1 Corinthians to rein in the corrupting influence of the 'strong'. He adopts a rhetorical strategy which will undermine the elitist Wisdom and over-realised eschatology package by directing attention towards the performative 'word of the cross'. The result, he hopes, will be a change in epistemological perception which allows the presence of God to be disclosed in the humble self-giving sacrifice of Jesus, the κύριος τῆς δόξης.

Enter Malina *et al.* δόξα, it appears, is more than just the כבד of the Hebrew Scriptures. It is also *reputation* or status within the honour-shame code.[20] By using a word straight out of the standard cultural vocabulary, Paul declares his intention of subverting received social values. Reputation or status within the community is now to be associated with the values of the cross—especially humility and self-giving.

19. Theissen, *Social Setting*, pp. 69-143.
20. B. Malina, *The New Testament World: Insights from Cultural Anthroplogy* (Atlanta: John Knox, 1981), p. 48.

Much the same could be said about the use of δόξα terminology in John: it might mean the weight of the divine presence, but to Hellenist ears it would be difficult to miss the overtones of reputation and status. As in Paul, normal social values are being subverted: reputation now depends on being lifted up, a pattern of behaviour which can be likened to the servant-like activity of washing people's feet (Jn 13.1-35). δόξα is routed from God through to the disciples via Jesus (Jn 17.22) and is available to all those who share the communal perception of the superior value of servant-like behaviour.

Unlike the Corinthian situation, however, the social signals in John suggest that the receiving community is not dominated by a powerful elite with an exaggerated sense of their own self-importance, but a tiny minority group living in a hostile environment and struggling to maintain a coherent sense of identity.[21] This community, therefore, does not need to be brought down a peg or two but needs strengthening through encouragement and support. The δόξα revealed on the cross is not a threat to their status—as with the Corinthian elite—but a promise of *enhancement* within an insecure and threatening social environment through a sharing of divine qualities. Unlike their Corinthian colleagues, the Johannine community need reassurance, not rebuke. It comes in the form of Wisdom incarnate: the presence of God's δόξα (reputation *and* glory) received through the death of Jesus ensures the coming of the Comforter (παράκλητος: Jn 16.12-15).

It is this contrast in the social situation facing the Corinthians and the Johannine community which perhaps helps to explain the curious divergence in otherwise similar language. Paul thinks the Corinthian elite have an over-realised enthusiasm and sees the remedy in terms of a firm reminder of the unfulfilled nature of Christian hope. John, on the other hand, thinks his community has too much reserve. His remedy is to enhance the value of their self-perception by describing them as a community blessed with the Spirit of divine Wisdom.

In short, Paul thinks his congregation have too much wisdom and not enough eschatology. John sees exactly the reverse: his community under threat already has far too much eschatological hassle. What they need is Wisdom.

21. R.E. Brown, *The Community of the Beloved Disciple* (New York: Paulist Press, 1979), pp. 93-144.

THE GOSPEL AND THE WRATH OF GOD IN ROMANS 1

Steve Finamore

This essay is an attempt to understand Paul's language about the ὀργὴ θεοῦ which is mentioned at 1.18 and described in chs. 1–3 of his letter to the Christians in Rome. It concentrates on 1.16-32 and in particular on vv. 17-18 and uses an understanding of the theories of René Girard to try to gain fresh insights into the text.

It is generally accepted that Rom. 1.1-15 forms an introductory section and that 1.16-17 states the theme of the letter: the gospel is the power of God for salvation to all who believe for God's δικαιοσύνη is revealed in it. The first major section is said to begin at 1.18 and is usually thought to end at 3.19-20 with the declarations that every mouth is silenced and the whole world (not just one group or another) accountable to God, for no flesh can be put right with God on the basis of the works of the Law. Having thus summed up the state of humanity, Paul can proceed to 3.21 and state how God's δικαιοσύνη has been revealed and the effect which this has on the human condition.

On this basis it is often argued that 1.18–3.20 states the problem and that 3.21 begins the account of God's solution. Within this structure, Rom. 1.18-32 is taken to be a description of the state of all or a part (i.e. the Gentiles) of humanity; it presents humanity under the wrath of God.

Broadly speaking, such a breakdown of the text is acceptable. However, a number of issues are raised, two of which will be addressed herein. First, the very idea of the wrath of God raises theological questions, while the description of its effects in 1.18-32 raises both theological and anthropological questions, not the least of which concerns the mechanisms or means by which the wrath operates. Secondly, there is the issue of the connection which exists between the revelation and operation of the wrath of God and the revelation and operation of the δικαιοσύνη of God in and through the gospel. The two issues are related and discussion of one inevitably raises the other. I shall begin with the second because it leads into a discussion of the text itself.

Before proceeding, a translation of δικαιοσύνη is required. The commentaries and translations offer righteousness, justice, faithfulness, covenant faithfulness and uprightness. And these are just the more popular options. I should be reluctant to enter the debate, especially since I have no space to defend my proposal. However, I offer the translation 'integrity' as a possible alternative. It carries the idea of uprightness and of faithfulness, particularly in the sense of commitment to promises given. Furthermore, it carries the sense of a commitment to truth and to acting in ways that are in keeping with one's own character.

Romans 1.17-18

While our Greek texts quite rightly offer us a new paragraph at 1.18, a number of commentators point out that v. 18 is closely related to the preceding verse. In v. 17 we read that δικαιοσύνη γὰρ θεοῦ ἐν αὐτῷ (that is, in the gospel) ἀποκαλύπτεται, while in v. 18 we find, ἀποκαλύπτεται γὰρ ὀργὴ θεοῦ ἀπ' οὐρανοῦ. It seems likely that the thoughts are intended to be in parallel with one another and if they are one must ask in what way the wrath of God is related to the gospel. The key words are ἀποκαλύπτεται and γάρ.

Bockmuehl has carried out a very helpful study of Paul's use of revelation language and explores its past, present and future dimensions.[1] An examination of Paul's use of the verb ἀποκαλύπτω shows that it nearly always has an eschatological context. Excluding Ephesians and the Pastorals from consideration, Paul uses the verb in the following places: Rom. 8.18, 'the coming glory to be revealed to us'; 1 Cor. 2.10, 'God has revealed to us that which he has prepared for those who love him'; 1 Cor. 3.13, 'the work of each will be manifest on that day because it will be revealed with fire'; 2 Thess. 2.3, 'the man of lawlessness is revealed'; 2.6, 'he may be revealed in his time; 2.8, 'and then the lawless one will be revealed'. There are also two uses of the verb in Galatians, at 1.16 and 3.23, 'But when...God was

1. M.N.A. Bockmuehl, *Revelation and Mystery in Ancient Judaism and Pauline Christianity* (WUNT, 2.36; Tübingen: Mohr [Paul Siebeck], 1990).

pleased to reveal his son in me' and 'we were kept under restraint until faith should be revealed'. These refer to past events yet, it might be argued, refer to the fulfilment of God's promises and purposes in Christ and so have an eschatological aspect to them. There are a couple of non-eschatological uses; these are Phil. 3.15, 'if any of you are otherwise-minded, God will reveal this to you', and 1 Cor. 14.30, 'but if anything be revealed to another'. Paul's use of cognates is extensive and these frequently have an eschatological dimension too. Therefore, it is likely that Paul's thought in Rom. 1.17-18 has an eschatological dimension. His use of ἀποκαλύπτω in 1.18 may contrast with his use of φανερόω in the following verse.

The verb ἀποκαλύπτεται has the same form in both verses; it is present and passive. In v. 17 we might translate 'The integrity of God is being revealed in the gospel'. Furthermore, since it is God who is responsible for this revelation, we should probably understand a divine passive, allowing us to paraphrase the words as 'In the gospel God is causing his own integrity to be revealed'.

Paul's gospel is a narrative which concerns the life, death and resurrection of Jesus (Rom. 1.4). Paul's conviction is that these events and the narrative that represents them generate a process of the revelation of God's integrity. This belief is eschatological: first because this revelation is the promised and anticipated divine vindication of God's own character; and secondly because, while the revelation is operating in history, it will culminate in the day of judgment. God's integrity has always been in existence but is now revealed in such a way that it generates a process which is worked out in history and which will culminate in the eschaton.

Since it is a parallel thought, the verb ἀποκαλύπτεται in v. 18 probably has a similar meaning. This implies that the wrath of God is a process that is connected in some way to the gospel. It is, after all, revealed ἀπ' οὐρανοῦ. In every other case, except one, where Paul uses the phrase 'from heaven', he is referring to Christ: 1 Cor. 15.47, 'The second man is from heaven'; 1 Thess. 1.10, 'To wait for his son from heaven'; 1 Thess. 4.16, 'The Lord himself will descend from heaven'; and 2 Thess. 1.7, 'When the Lord Jesus is revealed from heaven'. The exception is Gal. 1.8 which refers to the possibility of an angel from heaven preaching another gospel. In every case except for Galatians the reference is eschatological. This observation serves to support the contention that the wrath of God is, like the integrity of

God, an eschatological phenomenon. It is, in some sense at least, a new or newly revealed phenomenon and this implies that it is in some way related to the gospel.

As to the word γάρ, while it is conceivable that it could carry an adversative sense, it is, according to Bauer, usually used to express cause, inference or continuation, or to explain.[2] It is therefore normally translated by the word 'for' or the word 'because'. It seems that the revelation of God's wrath is, so far as the text is concerned, closely related to the revelation of God's δικαιοσύνη in the gospel.

Most commentators touch on these issues when discussing the words γάρ and ἀποκαλύπτεται and they arrive at a remarkable number of different conclusions. Many are uncomfortable with the idea of the wrath of God and are resistant to the idea that it is closely related to the gospel. It is worth examining some of the exegetical positions which have been adopted.

The Views of Some Exegetes

Bornkamm accepts that the gospel heralds both salvation and judgment.[3] The two are related in Paul's thought at 2 Cor. 2.15, 'For we are the aroma of Christ to God among those who are being saved and among those who are perishing.' He also cites 2 Cor. 4.3 and 1 Cor. 1.23. However, in his view, the wrath of God is not a part of the gospel as such.

He summarizes the available views on the connection between the wrath of God and the gospel as juxtaposition and succession. In the former, the ἀποκαλύπτεται is regarded as timeless; a description of the way of the world. The revelation of God's wrath is not related to the content or to the effects of the gospel. On this view, in its pure form, the wrath of God is not really related to the final judgment; the eschatological dimension is lost and Paul is thought to be speaking of a process which occurs entirely within history.

C.H. Dodd is associated with a position of this kind and his views about God's wrath have proved influential and are discussed by almost all the commentators. He writes that 'there is something impersonal about the "Wrath of God"' and that 'Wrath is the effect of human sin',

2. BAGD, pp. 151-52.
3. G. Bornkamm, 'The Revelation of God's Wrath: Romans 1–3', in *Early Christian Experience* (London: SCM Press, 1969), pp. 47-70.

the term being used 'not to describe the attitude of God to man, but the inevitable process of cause and effect in a moral universe'. For Dodd, this is something that is the case and has always been the case; there is nothing new that has happened in the gospel as far as the operation of God's wrath is concerned.[4]

Dodd is often accused of allowing his exegesis to be influenced by his theological concern to avoid ascribing the emotion of anger to God. Nevertheless, his reasons for this are understandable and his position has influenced the view taken in this essay. He is, for example, correct to point to human responsibility for, and involvement in, the phenomenon Paul calls the wrath of God, and he is right to be concerned that God should be understood to act in ways which are consistent with his own character as it is revealed in Jesus. However, Dodd's view is inadequate because it loses the eschatological dimensions of God's wrath; it also fails to acknowledge God's involvement in initiating the wrath or the connection between the wrath and the gospel. Finally, Dodd does not discuss the anthropology which would enable a process of the kind he envisages to operate. His may be an accurate observation about the effects of certain kinds of behaviour but it is hardly of great explanatory value.

Hanson takes Dodd's understanding of the wrath of God in Paul and develops it, applying it to the whole of the New Testament. In the process, it ceases to fit Bornkamm's category 'juxtaposition'; it is discussed here because of its relationship to Dodd's view. Hanson regards the wrath of God as something impersonal that has always been operating within history. However, he attempts to deal with one of the objections which have been raised to Dodd's view by linking God's wrath to the gospel. He does this by arguing that although it, like God's δικαιοσύνη, existed before the Christ event, its operation is fully revealed in Christ.[5]

He develops his argument with reference to the wrath of the Lamb in the book of Revelation. He believes that the author has a similar view to Paul's. The judgments recorded in Revelation 6, for example, are precipitated by the cross of Jesus and by the martyrdoms of his followers. These judgments take place in history and anticipate those

4.   C.H. Dodd, *The Epistle to the Romans* (MNTC; London: Hodder & Stoughton, 1932). See also, *The Meaning of Paul for Today* (Glasgow: Collins Fount Paperbacks, 1978 [1920]).

5.   A.T. Hanson, *The Wrath of the Lamb* (London: SPCK, 1957).

of the eschaton. Hanson argues that 'The wrath here is not purely eschatological; it is a process, stretching from the Cross to the Parousia', and that 'The crucifixion and its consequences in history are the means by which... wrath is manifested.'

There is a great deal to be said for this perspective. Hanson has brought out the connection between the wrath and the gospel and the link between the cross and the eschaton. However, it is unclear why the impersonal laws of the universe should function in such a way. Furthermore, it is not clear why the process should be ascribed to God or to the Lamb.

G.B. Caird has an approach similar to Dodd's although he tries to avoid overstating the impersonal nature of God's wrath; he regards God as being actively involved in the process described in Rom. 1.18-32. However, he seeks to qualify the link between vv. 17 and 18 by arguing that ἀποκαλύπτεται has different meanings in the two verses. In v. 17 the δικαιοσύνη is not a disclosure of God's character but a process which has broken in; to be revealed is to come into operation. Caird argues that it cannot have this meaning in v. 18 because the wrath of God came into operation at the fall. The wrath of God was invisibly operative before Christ but has now become visible to faith. The righteousness of God only becomes operative in the gospel.[6]

Certainly, those who advocate a 'juxtaposition' view have to find some way to break the link between vv. 17 and 18 and so to deny that they are in any way parallel. Dodd, whose commentary is based on the Moffatt translation of the Bible, found his job already done for him.[7] Moffatt translates the γάρ of v. 18 as 'but' and Dodd adopts this translation without question, regarding the word as an 'adversative conjunction' and thus allowing the two verses to stand in contrast to one another. He regards it as unthinkable that God's wrath and God's righteousness should be in any way identified. Fitzmyer's solution is to translate 'for' but to agree that the righteousness or 'uprightness' of God and the wrath of God stand in contrast to one another. The former saves humans from the latter.[8] As already indicated, if this

6.   G.B. Caird, *New Testament Theology* (L.D. Hurst [ed.]; Oxford: Clarendon Press, 1994).

7.   J. Moffatt, *A New Translation of the Bible Containing the Old and New Testaments* (London: Hodder & Stoughton, 1934).

8.   J.A. Fitzmyer, *Romans: A New Translation with Introduction and Commentary* (AB; London: Geoffrey Chapman, 1993).

were Paul's meaning, it would be an unusual use of the word γάρ. Such a rendering should only be adopted if no other option is available.

The view which Bornkamm calls 'succession' is based on a salvation-historical understanding of Paul's thought. According to this view, the wrath of God characterizes the epoch that has ended with the dawn of the age of the gospel. Until this point only God's wrath was being revealed. Now his righteousness is also being revealed or is being revealed instead. However, this view does not take sufficiently seriously the fact that the verbs in vv. 17 and 18 are exactly the same. Nor can it deal with the fact that the period prior to God's revelation in Christ is elsewhere described by Paul not as the time of God's wrath but as the time in which sins were passed over ἐν τῇ ἀνοχῇ τοῦ θεοῦ; the forbearance of God (Rom. 3.26).

Bornkamm's own understanding is that the existence of God's revelation in the world is the rightful basis for the revelation of God's wrath, God's judgment on humanity. The wrath process has occurred before and has been recognizable. What is new is the eschatological dimension. Only now, in the gospel, is the world put in the light of the event, that is the judgment of God, to which history is directing it. This could not be discerned on the basis of revelation in creation. Bornkamm writes, 'In the light of the previous revelation of God in creation and law, the world cannot announce that its time has come. The possibility for this is disclosed only through the "now" that has dawned over the world in the revelation of God's "righteousness" in Jesus Christ.'[9] This is the eschatological 'now' of salvation history that ushers in the new age. Hence the revelations of δικαιοσύνη and wrath belong together and the γάρ explicitly establishes the link.

There is a great deal to be said for interpretations of this kind. Käsemann speaks of the revelations of God's wrath and of God's righteousness as being two different aspects of one and the same act of revelation, vv. 17 and 18 being regarded as 'deliberate antithetical parallels'. The wrath of God was already present in the world but was unrecognized and only comes to light along with the gospel. He writes that

> the eschatological present implicitly illuminates the past which was previously concealed. This is not the result nor is it the true point of the gospel, but its reverse side. It is not merely something of which man now

9. Bornkamm, 'The Revelation of God's Wrath', pp. 47-70

becomes conscious from within but an event which encounters him from
without and which is therefore characterized as eschatological revelation.

Justification delivers some of us from the wrath to which the whole
world is subject. God hands others of us over to the wrath; God is at
work in this process in what Käsemann calls 'a hidden way'.[10]

Both Robinson and Dunn take similar positions.[11] They regard the
two revelations as two different sides of the same coin, as one revelation having two different kinds of effects. Robinson argues that God is
involved in both processes. The process called the wrath of God
appears impersonal but this is because of the depersonalizing effects of
sin. In fact everything exists by virtue of its relationship to God.

Cranfield argues that the wrath of God is, like the righteousness of
God, revealed in the ongoing proclamation of the gospel. The two
revelations are two aspects of the same process. Behind the revelation
of wrath in the proclamation of the gospel lies the revelation of the
wrath of God in the gospel events themselves, for the reality of the
wrath of God is revealed in Gethsemane and at Golgotha.[12]

Here Cranfield is close to the thought of Barth. The gospel is the
revelation of the divine verdict and one aspect of the verdict is God's
wrath. The death of Christ is at the heart of the gospel and is the revelation of wrath. The times of ignorance have been overlooked in the
forbearance of God, but now the gospel is being proclaimed and all
humanity is being brought to the point of decision. In his commentary
to the Romans Barth writes, 'The wrath of God is the righteousness of
God—apart from and without Christ'.[13]

This approach is on the right lines. Käsemann may be right to say
that the wrath of God is not one of the results of the gospel, but it is
one of its side-effects. The wrath of God may have been operative
before the gospel but its operation becomes recognizable and becomes
more accentuated and more thoroughgoing as a result of the gospel.
To ignore or to reject the gospel will leave humans caught up in the

10. E. Käsemann, *Commentary on Romans* (ET; London: SCM Press, 1980),
p. 35.

11. J.A.T. Robinson, *Wrestling with Romans* (London: SCM Press, 1979).
J.D.G. Dunn, *Romans 1–8* (WBC, 38a; Dallas, TX: Word Books, 1988).

12. C.E.B. Cranfield, *A Critical and Exegetical Commentary on the Epistle to the
Romans* (ICC; Edinburgh: T. & T. Clark, 1975).

13. K. Barth, *The Epistle to the Romans* (ET; London: Oxford University Press,
6th edn, 1933).

process which Paul calls the wrath of God. Those who accept the gospel and conform their lives to it will be saved from that process or kept safe through it. Bockmuehl arrives at a similar conclusion and states that both God's righteousness and God's wrath are being revealed in the gospel events and in the gospel proclamation. He writes,

> No doubt God has from time to time manifested his wrath in the past: but now in particular with the historical inauguration of the gospel, and apparently with its subsequent proclamation, the heavenly wrath of God has begun to come to its eschatological realization.[14]

Thus, the best interpretation of Paul's thought at this point takes seriously the parallel between vv. 17 and 18 and therefore accepts that the revelations of God's wrath and δικαιοσύνη are closely related to one another and that both are eschatological processes which have roots in the gospel events and in the oral proclamation of those events by the church. The events have a once and for all nature but their re-presentation in the proclamation of the church allow them to have a continuing effect. This effect either brings humans to salvation or produces the effects described by Paul in Rom. 1.18-32. These processes anticipate and culminate in the last judgment; they are a fore-taste of the future. Any adequate account of the processes which are involved must allow God's actions to reflect his character and still take seriously the genitive θεοῦ; the wrath process is in some way God's.

Reference will now be made to the theories of René Girard to attempt to demonstrate why all this should be so and to offer some account of the social and cultural mechanisms which underlie the operations of these processes in history. Girard's ideas not only cover literature, culture and revelation in Christ, they also have an eschato-logical dimension which makes them particularly appropriate for an analysis of the present kind. He offers an interpretative framework for understanding human society, culture and history and, I suggest, offers us a meaningful way to appropriate the eschatological language of the New Testament. My intention is to show that his views fit the historical processes which Paul describes in Rom. 1.18-32.

---

14. Bockmuehl, *Revelation and Mystery*, p. 141.

The Theories of René Girard

According to Girard, whose views are derived from his engagement with Durkheim, Freud and the structural anthropology of Lévi-Strauss, the cultural differentiation which is the basis of every human society is founded on murder; acts of violent exclusion. These violent founding acts are represented in the myths which form the ideologies which legitimate cultures. In every case this involves a fundamental misrepresentation for the myths justify the founding violence. The victim is arbitrary yet the myth which represents the victim's story asserts his or her guilt. The myth will also tend to sacralize the murdered victim.[15]

Girard's key anthropological idea is mimesis. This has two related meanings. The first, which we might call representational mimesis, is derived from literary criticism where the term has come to be used for the means by which a representation of reality in a myth, a ritual, a text or a drama becomes a perception of that reality in the mind of a performer, reader or hearer. This is important because mimesis can play us false; that is to say, it can, and it normally does, produce a false perception of reality. Mimesis in this sense is also important, of course, because both the telling of myths and the telling of the gospel rely on it: to tell a founding story is to allow that story to shape the perceptions of the hearers; to proclaim a myth or the gospel is to re-present a past event so that it has efficacy in the present. Thus, when myths about cultural origins are told the effect is to re-present the foundation of society, to reinforce the founding lie and thus to reinforce the ideology and hence strengthen cultural differentiation. The same is true of the performance of rituals. These often involve sacrifice or exclusion and this is a representation of the original murder.

15. Of Girard's major works, the most relevant are *Violence and the Sacred* (Baltimore and London: The Johns Hopkins University Press, 1979), translated from *La violence et le sacré* (Paris: Grasset, 1972); *The Scapegoat* (London: Athlone Press, 1986), translated from *Le bouc emissaire* (Paris: Grasset, 1982); *Things Hidden Since the Foundation of the World* (with J.-M. Oughoulian and G. Lefort; London: Athlone Press, 1987), translated from *Des choses cachées depuis la fondation du monde* (Paris: Grasset, 1978); *Job: The Victim of his People* (Stanford, CA: Stanford University Press, 1987), translated from *La route antique des hommes pervers: essais sur Job* (Paris: Grasset, 1985); *'To Double Business Bound': Essays on Literature, Mimesis, and Anthropology* (London: Athlone Press, 1988).

The second kind of mimesis might be called imitative mimesis. This is regarded as the fundamental human drive. We learn language and culture by imitating models. It is this drive which enables infants to learn to behave and to speak languages. It is this drive which makes us respond to advertising; that makes us want the Mars Bar that somebody else is eating. Mimesis in this sense tends to make people the same; it makes us want the same things and behave in the same ways.

Mimesis is therefore not compatible with cultural differentiation and slowly but surely undermines human culture. When people desire and seek to acquire the same things, rivalry develops and violence can result. Cultures therefore have all kinds of prohibitions which prevent people imitating one another's desires and from attempting to acquire one another's sexual partners and chattels. Thus, prohibitions, especially in the realms of sexual behaviour (that is, rules about incest, marital fidelity, heterosexuality and so on) and in the form of rules about property rights, have the effect of preventing this kind of mimetic violence. Together, prohibitions, myths and rituals act as the pillars of culture.

However, when imitative mimesis proves stronger than the prohibitions and the reinforcing effects of representational mimesis mediated through myth and ritual, cultural differentiation is undermined; desires, acquisition, rivalry and violence, in the form of vengeance, become imitated and the human society concerned lapses into a state of undifferentiation which is experienced as disorientation and chaos. This is resolved only by an act of unanimous violence which establishes a new cultural order. Human culture therefore has a cyclical nature. Order is slowly undermined by imitative mimesis. This creates a crisis, experienced as chaos, which is resolved by an act of unanimous violence, the misrepresentation of which founds and legitimates and provides the ideological framework for a new cultural order.

So, all human cultural order rests on violence. And it rests on a misrepresentation of that violence, a violence which is justified by the false ascription of guilt to the victim. This helps to explain why all human cultures react to crises in the same ways: they look for scapegoats to persecute. They seek their own sense of identity and they seek to shore up their own network of cultural differences by the violent exclusion of others. This is how cultures were founded and this is how they are sustained.

The gospel, however, changes this situation. It repeats the story found in mythology and enacted in rituals from all over the world. It describes the death of a scapegoat. However, the gospel acknowledges, even declares, the innocence of Jesus. The culture—the crowd, the Romans—unanimously regarded its victim as being guilty of the offences for which he is punished. From this perspective and indeed from that of his disciples, Jesus' death demonstrates that his claims are unfounded. Yet the canonical Gospels, the documents that tell of his death, break with all human culture and declare this scapegoat to be innocent of the charges against him and vindicate his claims. In doing this the Gospels reveal the founding lie, the misrepresentation of the violence at the root of all culture. They reveal our scapegoating and our exclusivist behaviour for what it is. The gospel is revelation in that it confronts us with the truth about ourselves and our victims.

Many understandings of atonement see it as a kind of covering; it covers over the cracks which have appeared in culture; it is a means of restoring or renewing the cultural order. The acts which people have done which transgressed prohibitions and undermined the cultural order are covered over and disregarded. This is true of pagan understandings of sacrificial rituals and of some Christian understandings of the work of Christ. It is also true of some Old Testament understandings of atonement; the Hebrew word כפר can mean both 'cover over' and 'propitiate by sacrifice'. These understandings seem to rest on the idea that a deity requires the death of a victim to appease his or her anger at breaches of prohibitions. Girard's view is that breaches of prohibitions and mimetic rivalry generate violence which finds an outlet in sacrificial rites. Religious explanations which ascribe the violence to a god are a rationalization of the phenomenon.

Girard's understanding of the effect of Jesus' death is very different. He sees it not as a covering but as an uncovering; an uncovering of the roots of culture, the unveiling of the lies about the justness of the existing cultural order and about the guilt of its victims. Once this revelation is perceived, the order of the culture concerned cannot endure. So, the cross is seen not as a sacrifice but as a deconstruction of sacrifice and as an unveiling of the sacrificial structures on which human societies are founded. It confronts us with the truth about ourselves and so offers the prospect of change.

Sacrificial language is quite rare in Paul but there are a number of texts where he uses sacrificial imagery. This is not fatal to Girard's case or to the use made of his thought in this paper. There are two possible approaches. One is to accept the traditional readings of these passages and argue that Paul was unable to be consistent in pursuing his own best insights and therefore occasionally lapsed into sacrificial thinking. The other is to re-examine the texts to see if we have not misunderstood them. Hamerton-Kelly has attempted to read Paul in the light of Girard and offers an example of the second approach.[16]

One of the most significant of Pauline texts which uses sacrificial imagery is a part of the presentation of the gospel to which Rom. 1.18-32 is leading: 3.25. Jesus is put forward by God as an ἱλαστήριον in his blood through faith in order to demonstrate God's δικαιοσύνη. Hamerton-Kelly tries to demonstrate that Paul's language here subverts traditional understandings of sacrifice. In sacrifice, humans offer something to God in order to affect God's disposition. The thing sacrificed is taken into the realm of the sacred to be offered. Here, however, it is God that does the offering. The natural conclusion is that this is done, not for God's own benefit but for the benefit of humans in that it has the potential to affect their disposition. Furthermore, God's son passes from the sacred into the non-sacred to be offered. If this is a sacrifice, concludes Hamerton-Kelly, it is a most unusual example. He goes on to argue that we should not understand Paul as arguing that humans deserved to suffer the wrath of God and that God substituted a propitiatory offering to himself to bear that wrath in our place. Rather, we should understand the wrath of God as the process of human vengeance and violence of which Christ was the target and victim. In bearing that wrath, Jesus does not take our place and so hide our violence from us. Instead he represents it to us, enabling us to take responsibility for it and so have the possibility to change our way of being human. It is in this sense that Christ stands for and represents the many. The cross of Christ affects sin not by changing God but by revealing sin and thus changing sinners. In this understanding, Hamerton-Kelly is close to some existing understandings of atonement which keep the term 'sacrifice' but which reinterpret it; Frances Young and Paul Fiddes are examples.[17]

16. R.G. Hamerton-Kelly, *Sacred Violence: Paul's Hermeneutic of the Cross* (Minneapolis: Fortress Press, 1992).

17. P. Fiddes, *Past Event and Present Salvation: The Christian Idea of Atonement* (London: Darton, Longman & Todd, 1989). F.M. Young, *Sacrifice and the Death of Christ* (London: SCM Press, 1975); *Can These Dry Bones Live?* (London: SCM Press, 1982).

In any event, whichever approach to Paul's sacrificial language we choose to adopt, to those who believe, to those who realize the violent and arbitrary nature of human culture and their own part in that, the gospel offers an alternative: a non-acquisitive mimesis not based on violence but based on the behaviour of Jesus; the mimesis of the kingdom of God.

The gospel revelation about the innocence of the victims, of the lie and the violence which is the basis of our cultures, changes the situation drastically. Since we are aware, even as we carry out scapegoatings and persecutions, that our victims are, or may be, innocent, the cultural order of the societies which have been influenced by the gospel can never be re-established. They cannot use representational mimesis of their founding myths to reinforce their cultural differentiation. So, the cultural order of such societies will be slowly undermined as mimesis breaks down the vestiges of cultural differentiation and they will enter a violent crisis of differentiation. This is the eschatological dimension of Girard's thought. No renewal of the normative human cultural order is now possible; we will enter a cultural crisis and destroy ourselves before the scapegoating mechanism, which has previously resolved such crises, can operate. This process, the undermining of order by mimesis, has always been apparent in human history but, because of the gospel, it has entered a new and final stage.

On the other hand, the gospel revelation also offers humanity an alternative; the possibility of life in Christ. Those who behave like Jesus will, by welcoming the victims and the outcasts—in Paul's case, embracing the Gentiles—challenge the cultural order of which they are a part. They will also cause it to respond violently to such activity as it seeks to reinforce itself. This response will never be wholly successful because the idea that the victims are in fact innocent, and that the distinction between 'good', legal, legitimate violence and 'bad' violence is in truth arbitrary, is too widely acknowledged. Furthermore, the silent testimony to the truth of the Christian martyrs reveals the lie at the basis of society just as the death of Jesus did. In other words, Christian testimony, the proclamation of the gospel, both promotes the alternative to the existing way of being human and contributes to the process by which the existing cultural order is subverted.

Girard's Ideas as an Interpretative Grid for Romans 1.1-18

Let me make it clear that this argument is not an attempt to demonstrate that the apostle had a Girardian view of society. Rather it suggests that Paul understands that the proclamation of the Christ event is an eschatological phenomenon because it must herald the close of the existing world order. It has two parallel effects: one which has the potential to transform the world, to produce a new world with a new way of being human, and the other which will see humanity launched on a cycle of violence which ends in self-destruction. The gospel offers to the whole of humanity its final choice between these two effects.

Paul calls one of these effects the revelation of God's integrity. God has revealed what is right and true of himself and has shown humans what they are like. Those who grasp these truths and live accordingly will, Paul believes, be saved. The other effect, the one with which this article is primarily concerned, Paul calls the revelation of the wrath of God. This is the process of cultural disintegration which the revelation of the gospel generates or accelerates. This a process which has always been present in the world. However, this time there can be no resolution of the kind there has been in the past; this time it is final: the gospel heralds the eschatological wrath of God. It is because the process is one which has always been present in culture that Paul's description has parallels with descriptions of human decline found elsewhere. The difference is that this time, when human culture descends into chaos, we shall be unable to emerge.

Certainly, the effects described by Paul are those that a Girardian understanding would lead us to expect. Furthermore, as Hooker (followed by Dunn) has pointed out (although her findings have been challenged by Fitzmyer), Romans 1 reflects the events described in the opening chapters of Genesis.[18] This could be because Paul had Genesis in mind or it could be that both are attempts to describe the same cultural phenomenon.

In v. 18 Paul demonstrates his intuitive understanding of the human dilemma: humans have lived in accordance with a lie and suppress the truth. This is the root of the problem. The fact of a transcendent creator can be known but is in practice suppressed in favour of the gods

18. M.D. Hooker, 'Adam in Romans 1', *NTS* 6 (1959–60), pp. 297-306.

who are served in the violent rituals of paganism; the gods of the realm called 'the sacred'; the gods of violence. These are the idolatrous religions of which Paul speaks in v. 21, with which the revealed truth of the gospel is to be contrasted. These are 'the god of this world [who] has blinded the minds of the unbelievers' (2 Cor. 4.4). The unbelievers are those whose minds have been darkened and who, like Adam, have exchanged and will again exchange the glory of the immortal God for images (Rom. 1.21-23). Paul elsewhere urges us to exchange the old, Adamic way of being human for Christ's new way. Girard offers us an understanding of the lie which Paul claims lies at the heart of our cultures, our ways of being human.

In addition, Girard argues, and it certainly would have been true in Paul's context, that all idolatry is linked to sacrifice and thus to the gods of violence. It is certainly the case that sacrifice is a very common social phenomenon and is linked to nearly every pagan religion of which we have knowledge. Its practice was widespread in the Roman Empire and it was, of course, vital in the form of Judaism known to Paul. It is usually said that Paul regards idolatry as the root of human problems. This is very close to being true; it is a primary consequence of cultural acceptance of the primal lie. Paul is aware of the misrepresentation that lies behind idolatry and of which all humans are vaguely aware but which most choose to suppress, probably because to collude in the lie makes social life easier (or even possible or conceivable). Idolatry is linked to mimesis. The invisible God is (mis)represented in the form of a creature. Humans choose to render worship to the representation and accept the false religious rationale for worship that goes with it. The god is thought to demand victims and the effects of mimesis ensure that a violent god will have violent worshippers. Humans are trapped in idolatry and thus in sacrificial thinking and hence in violence.

Human cultural order founded on violence is unstable. Mimesis induces people to break prohibitions and the system of differentiation which is the basis of culture is undermined. Furthermore, since God has acted in the gospel to reveal the founding lie of culture, it may be said that God gives humans up (1.26) to the next stage of the cycle, for the awareness of the truth about cultural victims, a truth for whose revelation God is responsible, undermines the effectiveness of a culture's attempts to renew itself.

As cultural differentiation breaks down, the cultural prohibitions against incest, adultery and so on become perceived to be purely cultural, and hence arbitrary, phenomena. There is no divine sanction to enforce them and no apparent likelihood of retribution. Therefore, people do not fear the consequences of breaching them; they feel able to act on desires which were previously kept in check. These prohibitions are vital to the survival of the culture and once they are breached, mimetic rivalry and hence violence must become more and more common. This is the next stage to which humans are given up (1.28) as the society of which they are a part disintegrates and murder, strife and ruthless behaviour become common. There remain no cultural values by which behaviour can be assessed and so the cultural crisis gets worse and worse. This process has happened in the past and will be repeated in the future. The future process will, because of the gospel, be worse and will be impossible to resolve in the normal way, because people will no longer be able to convince themselves of the guilt of their victims.

Paul's account of the downward spiral of humanity caught up in the wrath of God is a good description of a crisis of differentiation. There is reason to believe that Paul and Girard have similar phenomena in mind. Or perhaps it would be better to say that Girard offers us a helpful, contemporary, interpretative grid for understanding Paul. In either case, there is reason to believe that the proclamation of the gospel would contribute to such a process. Since the process could not be resolved it would be eschatological. Thus the revelation of the gospel is linked to the eschaton.

There are, apart from the gospel, two possible responses to this process. One is to be involved in the process as described in Romans 1. The other position is found in Romans 2. This is the self-righteous position to which so many of us are prone. It is an attempt to exclude and to scapegoat the sinners; this amounts to an attempt to revert to the founding lie. The gospel offers a third alternative; it is revealed by God and stands over against the alternatives offered by human culture. Paul refers to the gospel at 1.16-17 and discusses it in more detail in 3.21–15.21.

Conclusions

The wrath of God is God's in that it is initiated by the revelation of the gospel which breaks into human culture and exposes the violence on which it is based. The violence is not God's but humanity's; the responsibility for the effects of the process lie with humans rather than with God. However, it is God's process in that it is God who has acted in a way which generates the process and prevents its resolution. God has acted so that humans are liberated from their endless cycles of cultures founded on violence and lies. God's own action is non-violent and exposes violence and untruth in human society. However, the result of this is that human violence has the potential to be greater than ever and to be resolved only by complete self-destruction.

The process can be escaped only insofar as humans recognize the lie which has deceived them in the past and embrace the truth manifested in the death of Jesus and re-presented in the gospel. Mimesis cannot be escaped in either of its forms. In the first, literary-critical sense of the word, the mimetic representation of the founding lie must be replaced by mimetic representation of the gospel. In the second, imitative sense, the mimesis of the desires and acquisitions of others must be replaced by a mimesis of Jesus. In such a way the wrath of God will be averted and the expected new world will dawn. As Girard says, 'The time has come for us to forgive one another. If we wait any longer there will not be time enough.'[19]

The contention of this article is that the best interpretation of Rom. 1.17-18 understands the gospel to be an agent for the revelation of God's wrath and of God's integrity; the two are related for both are processes set in train by the Christ-event and its representation in the gospel. This twin process is eschatological because it presents humanity with a final crisis in which the choices are the gospel or destruction. Rom. 1.18-32 describes the cultural effects of the eschatological wrath of God. Such an interpretation raises certain questions about the cultural mechanisms which might underlie such a process. This article suggests that Girard's theories offers a plausible and appropriate contemporary explanation of this process and shed light on the phenomena which Paul describes.

---

19. Girard, *The Scapegoat*, p. 212.

Peter Oakes

This article is based on part of my thesis, 'Philippians: From People to Letter',[1] the first half of which is a study of the church at Philippi. One chapter models the development of the Roman colony of Philippi. The next considers the social structure of a church likely to arise in that context. A further chapter discusses evidence in the letter of suffering in the church. It then considers what this was likely to involve. I conclude that the most likely form of long-term suffering in Philippi would be economic suffering caused by breakdown of some relationships with non-Christians. The breakdowns would largely be caused by non-Christians seeing that converts have stopped honouring the gods.[2] Such suffering would tend to be more acute among the poorer, more dependent, Christians.

In the second half of the thesis, I imagine how certain aspects of the letter were likely to sound to Philippian Christians. I consider Christ's accession to Lordship in the light of the Philippians' experience of imperial ideology. I also consider the relationship between the themes of suffering and unity, as they would be heard by Philippians listening to 1.27–2.11. Before either of these investigations, I try sharpening my perception of the material on suffering in the letter by listening to the letter from the viewpoints of two imaginary hearers. One of them has suffered a great deal, the other has suffered very little. The imaginary hearers are reconstructed from my social data about types of people likely to be in the church. They are essentially vehicles for helping me to use the social data in engaging my imagination in the study of the text.

1. Oxford DPhil thesis, 1995, supervised by Dr N.T. Wright.
2. See M. Goodman, *Mission and Conversion: Proselytizing in the Religious History of the Roman Empire* (Oxford: Clarendon Press, 1994), p. 105; R.L. Fox, *Pagans and Christians* (Harmondsworth: Viking, 1986), pp. 38, 95, 98.

Jason is a Greek of Macedonian descent. He is married to Chloe, who is also a Greek Christian. They have four young children. Jason's forebears farmed near Philippi but his own profession has been as a goldsmith, working for his cousin. He was spared any agonizing over whether to continue doing work for temples because, as soon as his cousin found out that Jason had become a Christian, he sacked him. For the last eighteen months, Chloe and Jason have faced a desperate financial struggle, keeping their family alive through Jason doing casual farm-labouring, mainly for other Christians, and Chloe doing some very poorly paid work as a waitress in her second-cousin's tavern. Six months ago, Jason was involved in a fight after a discussion with some former friends. He ended up with a night in jail and, since then, has found casual labour harder to find—even from Christians. Jason thinks of himself as something of a hero. To their great regret, he and Chloe did not manage to send any money to Paul.

Penelope, along with her husband Isidoros, was one of the most generous contributors to Paul's gift. She and Isidoros moved to Philippi from Asia and run a business importing fine Italian pottery—made in one of the areas from which many of the colonists' grandparents came. When a number of their customers found out that Penelope and Isidoros had become Christians, sales dropped by twenty per cent and, on one morning, thirty-nine pots were smashed. However, much of the business is from farmers in the countryside, and people have tended to forget, or have decided that they do not mind too much. Neither Penelope nor Isidoros gets involved in any high-profile (or even rather low-profile) attempts to persuade others to become Christians, and Isidoros, who rents some land near the town, has become rather less ready to employ certain people in the congregation. However, the couple are regular attenders of church meetings and were, as noted above, among the most generous contributors to Paul's gift. Penelope is a little unsure of how good a Christian she is, in the light of the heroics of people such as Jason (and Paul).

Jason was pleased that there was no direct reference to the gift in 1.1-11: he had been very disappointed that they had not managed to contribute to it. Instead, Paul, knowing the difficulties at Philippi, had focused on their fellowship with him in their continuing faithfulness to the gospel (v. 5), faithfulness even to the extent of sharing Paul's chains (v. 7)—which was generous of Paul since none of them was facing a trial for his or her life. Paul encouraged them by promising that God would sustain them through their difficulties right through to Christ's return (v. 6). He also acknowledged the value of their ministry of evangelism in Philippi (v. 7)—although Jason was slightly galled by the insistent πάντας (vv. 4, 7 [twice], 8), especially at this point (end of v. 7). Did Paul not realize that one of the main problems at Philippi was that people like Isidoros were not pulling their weight? Jason was also caused to reflect a little by the prayer for increased love (v. 9), but decided that Paul was *probably* thinking about the wealthier Christians failing properly to help people like him and Chloe. Jason was encouraged by v. 10, feeling that he had weighed the importance of various things and had gone for the things that really counted. (In this, he was slightly fooling himself, since the differences between what had happened to him and to Penelope arose principally from the difference in their prior social circumstances, rather than from some difference in how they acted when they became Christians.)

Penelope was pleased by Paul's warm expression of gratitude for the gift in 1.1-11. He clearly continued to value highly his relationship with the Philippian community. He recalled their friendship with him and financial support of his mission (v. 5) and expressed his confidence that God would enable them to continue their support (v. 6). He saw them as being thus involved in everything that he did or suffered for the gospel (v. 7). As the word πάντας came up at the end of v. 7, a momentary uncharitable thought went through Penelope's mind, about those who had not contributed to the gift. But she realized that neither she nor Paul would dream of regarding those less well off in the church as not having participated fully, in some sense, in the gift to him. She wondered whether the prayer for ἀγάπη (v. 9) was directed towards Euodia and Syntyche: she knew that Paul knew about them. Penelope was a little disturbed by v. 10. In the light of the more zealous activities of people like Jason, were she and Isidoros really making the most important things their priority?

Jason had been waiting to hear a letter from his suffering hero. In 1.1-11, he heard Paul expressing warmth towards the Philippians as they shared with him by going through the same suffering. Penelope had been waiting to hear from the missionary she supported. In 1.1-11, she heard Paul expressing appreciation for their financial support. Each hearer 'filled in' relatively open terms in the text from their own perspective.

If my two hearings are plausible, this has implications for four contexts: Philippi; reception in the modern context; Paul's writing of the letter; the general study of the text.

What would happen in Philippi? This might depend on how closely Penelope and Jason were in communication. If they were in different house-churches, the divergence in the hearings might go unnoticed, especially if each person was in a house-church whose members shared their kind of perspective. If Penelope and Jason communicated and realized the divergence, there might be an authoritative figure who would express the community's standard interpretation. This might or might not correspond with Paul's intention. It would be more likely to do so if the authoritative figure was Epaphroditus or someone else close to Paul. An alternative scenario would involve Jason and Penelope agreeing that Paul intended both hearings: that he had left the text deliberately open. Such a decision would reflect the hearers' expectations about Paul—as would many features of their hearings anyway. Jason and Penelope could also simply disagree about Paul's intention.

It is interesting to note that thoughts about Paul's intentions seem likely to be more important in a process of arbitration than in the original hearing. Although the hearers' expectations about Paul are always important as they hear, the hearers' own perspectives are a very strong factor too. In a process of arbitration, the hearers' perspectives must, conventionally, be subordinated. A factor agreed by both parties must dominate. The most obvious role remaining for the hearers' own perspectives would be in motivating them to defend their original hearing.

Leaving aside the issue of arbitration, there is the question of the function of the passage as it is heard. Jason and Penelope each hear the passage in their way and the passage seems to function well for each of them. It functions to bind each of them closer to Paul as he identifies with each at an appropriate point. It also functions to encourage each in their particular Christian walk: Jason as he stands firm under suffering; Penelope as she applies her money to the relief of need.

If, after arbitration, Penelope decides that the passage should be heard in Jason's way, the passage stops functioning effectively for her in the way that it did. It will start functioning in a different way— probably by making her think that she ought to be behaving more like Jason does, which she would expect to result in suffering. If Jason, who has not contributed to Paul's gift, decides that the passage should be heard in Penelope's way, it would probably become dysfunctional. Jason would hear Paul thanking people other than him in the church for their gift. At best, Jason is likely to be only a spectator of the passage. At worst, the passage might distance Jason from Paul somewhat. This would be the opposite of the function which Paul clearly intends for all the Philippian hearers.

Considering reception in the Philippian context sheds light on the issues involved in reception in the modern context. All the same issues seem to be present, although various factors differ in degree. This difference is most pronounced in the factor of communication between people or groups who hear the text in different ways. In the modern context (and in any context since the letter was first heard widely), lack of communication is endemic. This is, first, because the hearers of the text will belong to groups far more separated from each other— physically, culturally, and in terms of experiences—than two house- churches in Philippi. Another factor hampering communication is dis- trust and dismissal. Some groups will think that hearings by some other groups are not worth listening to.

There are also two specific areas of change between Philippi and now. First, there is now no Epaphroditus who may have discussed the letter with Paul as he wrote it. Also, none of us knows Paul person- ally, as many Philippians did. This places a limit on the point we can reach in appeal to Paul's intention as arbiter. This limitation is coun- teracted to an extent by our possession of the wider corpus of Paul's letters. Another resource that we have is centuries of traditions of hearing of the passage by others. A second area of change is in the balance between modes of receiving the passage. I would imagine that most people still hear the passage read out, rather than reading it themselves. However, when it is read out it would tend then to be expounded by a preacher. Even if some explanation of the letter was given in Philippi, it is unlikely to have been such a decisive shaping of the hearing as is produced by preaching. Also, many do read the pas- sage. This differs from Jason and Penelope's hearing primarily in its inherent individualism. This difference, however, should not be exag- gerated. People read against a background of group norms on how such passages—or this specific passage—should be read. Conversely, Jason and Penelope do each hear as individuals, as well as as part of a group. In particular, each Philippian hearer has his or her own combination of life-experiences which will shape his or her perspective.

Reception in the Philippian context sheds light on the modern context. It also sheds light on Paul's writing of the letter. It does this by raising a number of fresh issues about what Paul may be doing.

A particularly striking conclusion about Jason and Penelope's hearings is that the text performs the same functions for each of them precisely by their hearing it in different ways. The functions it performs are of drawing the hearer closer to Paul and of encouraging the hearer in his or her own kind of Christian walk. This works for Jason via references to suffering, and for Penelope via references to financial giving. This raises the question of whether Paul might have meant this to happen. He could have chosen, say, 'fellowship in the gospel from the first day until now' (v. 5) as a deliberately open expression which could function successfully for various hearers, who might have differing ideas of what 'fellowship in the gospel' consisted of.

Alternative possibilities are raised by considering the overall flow of Paul's rhetoric (informally or formally understood) through the letter and then placing 1.1-11 within that flow. One such possibility begins from the observation that, if there are both sufferers and non-sufferers in the church, Paul has, by 1.27-30, decisively placed himself on the side of the sufferers. I would argue that the central issue of the letter is involved with this (notice the pervasive theme of suffering: 1.12-26, 27-30; 2.6-8, 17-18, 25-30; 3.9-11; 4.11-13; these are only the explicit passages). If the central issue does involve some sort of taking sides on Paul's part, and if he only wants to present the issue directly from 1.27 onwards—having prepared the ground first—then Paul may well want to leave his language very open in 1.1-11 so as to draw both parties with him into the heart of the letter.

Finally, all this has implications for the general study of the text. If we are going to describe the attributes of a particular text, we need to observe its various features. Jason and Penelope provide two angles from which to observe the text. As with a three-dimensional object, different features become visible when the object is viewed from different angles. Each fresh type of hearer can potentially make us aware of previously unobserved features of the text. This is true for various types of modern hearer as well as for various reconstructed types of ancient hearer. Of course, as with viewing objects, some angles may reveal less than others and some objects look similar from several viewpoints.

Which features of the text count as interesting will depend on the objectives of the reader. Features observed via Jason and Penelope ought to be of interest to most readers. They raise important questions for our understanding of the life of people in early churches undergoing suffering. They raise important questions about who Paul expected as his hearers and how he addressed their situation. They make us ask questions about the concrete ways in which the New Testament texts were first (and are now) heard—questions which we would otherwise leave too blurred.

APPENDIX

An Assessment of Scholars' Views on Philippians 1.7

A cogent objection to the above reading would arise if Phil. 1.7 could be shown to fit unambiguously either a 'Jason'- or a 'Penelope'-type hearing. Scholars have argued vigorously for each option, with the recent majority favouring the 'financial support' model over the 'suffering' one. Of the two I would see the 'suffering' model as the more likely to reflect Paul's intention. However, the points on which the decision turns seem sufficiently unclear to allow the likelihood of the passage being heard in different ways by different Philippians.

καθώς ἐστιν δίκαιον ἐμοὶ τοῦτο φρονεῖν ὑπὲρ πάντων ὑμῶν, διὰ τὸ ἔχειν με ἐν τῇ καρδίᾳ ὑμᾶς, ἔν τε τοῖς δεσμοῖς μου καὶ ἐν τῇ ἀπολογίᾳ καὶ βεβαιώσει τοῦ εὐαγγελίου συγκοινωνούς μου τῆς χάριτος πάντας ὑμᾶς ὄντας.

Lohmeyer makes this verse a key text in his commentary. He argues that the only thing which can give an objective basis to συγκοινωνούς is if the Philippians, like Paul, are suffering. The warmth of the friendly language in the letter arises precisely because the Philippians are sharing with Paul in this way.[3] J.B. Lightfoot links v. 7 with vv. 29 and 30 and explains the συγκοινωνούς as 'if I have suffered, so have you; if I have laboured actively for the gospel, so have you'. He takes τῆς χάριτος in the sense of v. 29: God granting, as privileges, both preaching and suffering.[4]

A wide range of scholars disagree with these two great exegetes, arguing that, instead of v. 7 referring to the Philippians' suffering, it refers to the Philippians' financial and other support of Paul. Beare writes, 'The words are simply a grateful recognition that they are with him by their sympathy and by their prayers, and sustained themselves by his cheerful steadfastness.'[5] Caird's view is that, 'By their help

3. E. Lohmeyer, *Der Brief an die Philipper* (Göttingen: Vandenhoeck & Ruprecht, 1928), p. 26.

4. J.B. Lightfoot, *St Paul's Epistle to the Philippians* (London: Macmillan, 1885), p. 85.

5. F.W. Beare, *A Commentary on the Epistle to the Philippians* (New York: Harper, 1959), p. 53.

and sympathy they have taken partnership shares in his commission'.[6] Gnilka's perspective could be somewhat wider. He sees here an active element in their participation in the gospel—but he does also think that the verse refers to their sending money.[7] O'Brien ties the grace directly to the giving: '[I]t must mean that God in his grace had prompted the Philippians to alleviate Paul in his imprisonment'.[8] This demonstration of God's grace at work in the Philippians gives Paul grounds for confidence in the Philippians' position (vv. 3-6).[9]

The vocabulary and syntax of 1.7 seem to leave open the options of seeing a reference either to the Philippians' suffering or to their giving. For help in deciding on Paul's intention here, we need to go further afield, to vv. 29-30 and to Paul's general theology and self-understanding.

Following Lightfoot's lead, vv. 29-30 offer a possible explanation of v. 7. The Philippians share in χάρις because their suffering ἐχαρίσθη. In this they are sharers with Paul because they are τὸν αὐτὸν ἀγῶνα ἔχοντες. A reasonable explanation of the language of 1.7 which is available in the same letter must generally be preferred over one which has to be constructed from supposition.

One might respond that the συγκοινωνούς is equally explained in Philippians under the 'financial support' reading of v. 7. One could cite 4.14, συγκοινωνήσαντές μου τῇ θλίψει.[10] However, there is a crucial difference in syntax between 1.7 and 4.14. 4.14 follows Rom. 12.13, ταῖς χρείαις τῶν ἁγίων κοινωνοῦντες.[11] In both verses, κοινωνέω is about providing for someone rather than about receiving along with someone or from someone. 1.7, on the other hand, is like Rom 15.27, εἰ... τοῖς πνευματικοῖς αὐτῶν ἐκοινώνησαν τὰ ἔθνη, in which the nations do receive a share in the spiritual things.[12] In 1.7, the Philippians definitely receive a share in the grace. Any attempt to make the συγκοινωνούς of 1.7 perform both functions, meaning 'shared' in the sense of 'provided' (which is the meaning in 4.14) and 'shared' in the sense of 'receiving', looks like exegetical sleight of hand. 1.7 seems unequivocally to mean 'received, alongside me, a share of grace'. Even if Paul is thinking about financial support rather than suffering, we cannot draw in 4.14 as an explanation of his language.[13]

As well as explaining Paul's language in 1.7, vv. 29-30 may explain his overall

6.   G.B. Caird, *Paul's Letters from Prison (Ephesians, Philippians, Colossians, Philemon)* (New Clarendon Bible; Oxford: Oxford University Press, 1976), p. 108.

7.   J. Gnilka, *Der Philipperbrief* (HTKNT, 10.3; Freiburg: Herder, 1968), p. 49.

8.   P.T. O'Brien, *Commentary on Philippians* (NIGTC; Grand Rapids: Eerdmans, 1991), p. 70.

9.   Note the flow of O'Brien's argument up to the 'it must mean' sentence.

10.   J.L. Houlden, *Paul's Letters from Prison* (PNTC; Harmondsworth: Penguin, 1970), pp. 53-54 loosely suggest this.

11.   Lightfoot (*Philippians*, p. 174) sees the usage of κοινωνεῖν as indicating that of συγκοινωνεῖν.

12.   Cf J.D.G. Dunn, *Romans 9–16* (Dallas: Word Books, 1988), p. 743; J.B. Lightfoot, *Saint Paul's Epistle to the Galatians* (London: MacMillan, 1880), p. 218 (on Gal. 6.6).

13.   In contrast, a good parallel to 1.7 would be a verse which is remarkably similar to 4.14, Rev. 1.9, Ἰωάννης... συγκοινωνὸς ἐν τῇ θλίψει.

argument in vv. 3-7. Verse 29 provides a reason for something in v. 28: either for the Philippians receiving salvation or for their stand acting as ἔνδειξις of destruction and salvation. Taking the former option, the fact that the Philippians had been granted to suffer for Christ would be the reason for Paul's confidence in their salvation. The relevance of this to vv. 3-7 is fairly direct. Verse 7 begins, καθώς ἐστιν δίκαιον ἐμοὶ τοῦτο φρονεῖν. The referent of τοῦτο must be v. 6 or, probably, vv. 3-6 as a whole[14]—Paul's joy and confidence in the Philippians and their future. There seems to be a pattern of argument which is included in both vv. 3-7 and vv. 28-30: the Philippians have χάρις, which is in common with Paul, and which is grounds for confidence in their salvation. Especially when we note that in each case the χάρις is connected with suffering, the parallel with the argument in vv. 28-30 looks very strong.

The parallel with vv. 28-30 also makes vv. 3-6 seem a very Pauline argument. The 'financial support' model of v. 7 struggles to do this. The argument using the 'financial support' model is something like, 'You have supported me (and the work of the gospel) financially, therefore you share with me in grace, therefore I am confident of your salvation'. One feels rather sorry for the Corinthians who were so forcefully denied this road to assurance! Using the 'suffering' model of v. 7, we have, 'You have suffered, therefore you share with me in grace, therefore I am confident of your salvation'. Rom. 8.17 comes to mind, as do other parts of Philippians, especially 3.9-10. The picture is of a faithful Pauline church being seen by Paul as following his own road of suffering for the gospel. This gives Paul joy and confidence in their salvation. The 'financial support' model would seem less likely to flow from the pen of Paul.

Hawthorne's view of v. 7 is, from a general Pauline perspective, particularly problematic. He sees 'grace' as referring to 'Paul's apostolic commission to preach the gospel handed him by God... and in which the Philippians have shared by making it financially possible for him to carry out this work of evangelism... Paul sees himself as an extension of the Philippian Christians...'[15] Clearly, if we were to replace 'Philippian' with 'Corinthian', the sentence would appear very dubious. It is, however, far from certain that putting 'Philippian' back into the sentence really clears the problem. In fact, it may be that an objective behind 4.11-13 is for Paul to refute Hawthorne's conclusion.[16] Paul says to the Philippians: I value my close relationship with you, but I am not an extension of you. It is noticeable, both in Acts and in his letters, how little Paul seems to operate as the field-worker of any church, notably the church at Antioch. In marked contrast to modern missionary practice, Paul the Apostle is not responsible to a sending church. The Jerusalem leaders have some sort of an originating and authoritative role in his thinking, but Paul certainly does not act as though he is a field-worker answerable to them. It seems unlikely that Paul saw himself as 'an extension' of any group.

---

14. J.-F. Collange, *The Epistle of Saint Paul to the Philippians* (trans. A.W. Heathcote; London: Epworth, 1979), p. 47; O'Brien, *Philippians*, p. 66.

15. G.F. Hawthorne, *Philippians* (Waco, TX: Word Books, 1983), p. 23.

16. See Hawthorne, *Philippians*, p. 195.

Finally, O'Brien raises the objection that the addition of μου to τοῖς δεσμοῖς excludes the possibility of the Philippians' suffering in v. 7.[17] This does not seem forceful. If Paul wanted to say that the Philippians' sufferings should be categorized with his, then the μου seems quite natural.

O'Brien's verdict on Lohmeyer's reading of v. 7, 'this view has rightly been rejected by New Testament exegetes',[18] while reasonable given the extremeness of Lohmeyer's martyrological reading of the letter, needs revision when discussing the more general 'suffering' model of v. 7 as presented by Lightfoot. From the point of view of Paul's intention, my exegetical sympathies are, therefore, more with Jason's reading than Penelope's. However, if the scholars are reasonable in being divided on the interpretation of 1.7, i.e., if 1.7 may, with only a slight interpretative push (such as whether the first μου makes a difference), be understood in two differing ways, then the strong possibility is raised that the differences in life-experiences of the various first hearers will have led them to interpret the verse differently.

17.   O'Brien, *Philippians*, p. 70.
18.   O'Brien, *Philippians*, p. 70.

WRESTLING WITH HEBREWS:
A NOTE ON τετραχηλισμένα AT HEBREWS 4.13

John Muddiman

Dr John Ashton chaired the New Testament research seminar in Oxford when this short paper was delivered. He did so with the characteristic fairness and wit, sharp insight and rare learning that we shall so miss as he retires. Although the Epistle to the Hebrews is more of a sermon than a letter and to that degree, in broad outline, not too difficult to understand, timeless and self-contained, it does have many points of exegetical and textual obscurity in detail, one of which is the subject of this paper.

The problem of τετραχηλισμένα at Heb. 4.13 can be quite simply put: the context demands 'exposed' or 'laid bare', which the translations invariably offer, but this word cannot have that meaning.

The passage on the word of God (Heb. 4.12-13) poses several other questions, which have a bearing, to a greater or lesser degree, on our problem and I will briefly refer to six of them, before we return to address it directly.

1. It is unclear whether 4.12 begins a new paragraph or continues the one which began at 4.1.[1] If it continues with a clinching argument, as the γάρ might suggest, then that would favour the view that the word of God is Scripture, since Psalm 95, the text being expounded, finishes with a sharp warning: 'I swore in my wrath they will by no means enter my rest'.[2] However, the majority of paragraphs in Hebrews begin with γάρ or οὖν—such is the sermonic style ('It all

---

1.   J. Moffatt (*Hebrews* [ICC; Edinburgh: T. & T. Clark, 1924], p. 54) begins a new paragraph at v. 11.

2.   As for example W.L. Lane (*Hebrews 1–8* [WBC; Waco, TX: Word Books, 1991], p. 102), who writes 'those who remain sensitive to the voice of God in scripture may discover that God's word is also a lethal weapon'. But Scripture is not so unequivocal for our author: see 1.1, πολυμερῶς καὶ πολυτρόπως.

follows, my friends!'). A new paragraph here would lend weight to a more christological interpretation of the word and this passage might then form an inclusio with 1.1-4 (see especially 1.2, 'God spoke in a son'; and cf. 1.3 with Wis. 7.25-26 and 18.15).[3] In between these two views—the minimising scriptural and the maximising christological interpretations—are those that take the word of God to be preaching and the author's own cutting exhortations that periodically slice through the exposition,[4] and this view is preferable, particularly when taken in conjunction with the next observation.

2. There is, even for this author, a surprisingly high incidence of hapax legomena in these two verses: τομώτερος, διϊκνέομαι, μερισμός (in the sense of division; contra 2.6 where it means distribution), ἁρμός, μυελός, κριτικός, ἀφανής and of course τραχηλίζω. This may mean that some traditional, perhaps hymnic, formulae are being used . But more likely it simply means that, freed momentarily from the vocabulary of the LXX text on which he is commenting, the author expresses himself here in his own, more distinctive and more fluently hellenistic style. Thus, 4.12-13 is a relatively free-standing exhortation, similar to passages like 5.11-14 and 12.12-17, which interestingly also use athletic metaphors.

3. Verse 12, taking up the image of a double-edged sword, speaks of division between two or three pairs of terms:[5] soul and spirit, joints and marrow and probably also thoughts and intentions of the heart. Are subtle distinctions being made between these terms or are they taken to be close synonyms? If the former, the emphasis would be on the depth of the word's penetrating discrimination; if the latter this is a mere rhetorical flourish, i.e. the word is so sharp as to separate the conceptually inseparable. To take each pair in turn: apart from the possibility of a more neutral use of ψυχή in one quotation (10.38) the author uses it in a positive sense elsewhere, of the spiritual dimension

3.   As argued by H. Clavier, 'Ο ΛΟΓΟΣ ΤΟΥ ΘΕΟΥ dans l'épitre aux Hébreux', in *New Testament Essays* (Festschrift T.W. Manson; A.J.B. Higgins [ed.]; Manchester: University of Manchester Press, 1959), pp. 81-93 and J. Swetnam, 'Jesus as Λογος in Heb 4:12-13', *Bib* 62.2 (1981), pp. 214-24. But compare the counter-arguments of G. Trompf, 'Conception of God in Hebrews 4:12-13', *SJT* 25.2 (1971), pp. 123-32.

4.   For this sense of the word of God, compare 4.2 and 13.7.

5.   Unless the division is between the first spiritual pair, and the second physical pair, as P.E. Hughes argues: *A Commentary on the Epistle to the Hebrews* (Grand Rapids: Eerdmans, 1977), p. 165, and see also n. 7.

of the human person (6.19; 12.3; 13.7). πνεῦμα, however, has a wide range of meanings in Hebrews, including angelological and in the strict sense theological usages; but we also find an anthropological use at 12.23, 'the spirits of the just', where the author could equally well have written 'the souls of the just'. That points in the direction of synonymity. The second pair, however, points the opposite way. There is a clear difference between joints and marrow, literally speaking: one is bone, the other is soft and mushy stuff. Indeed, one might have expected bones, ὀστέα, and marrow as the more obvious pairing.[6] The second pair is odd in another way: if the physical terms are 'merely metaphorical equivalents'[7] for soul and spirit, then one might expect them to come first; putting them afterwards implies that they make an additional point.[8] So, perhaps there is some other reason for preferring to speak of joints here, even though it disrupts the pattern; I shall suggest one below. The third pair are without doubt synonymous. If one were to insist on finding a distinction, ἐνθύμησις might have the added notion of an imaginative or mental construct, while ἔννοια is more reflection on given data. Philo's λόγος τομεύς, dissecting analytical reason, would have been capable of such a fine distinction; but the λόγος of Hebrews 4.12 is moral incisiveness, which gets to the bottom of human guilt, and that is a rather less pedantic and hair-splitting exercise.[9]

6.   It is, I suppose, just conceivable that this is the point, that while it is easier to get the marrow out of straight bones, at the joints it is more twisted up, so to speak, and difficult to get at!

7.   Moffatt, *Hebrews*, p. 56.

8.   That sin can reside in the members is not a strange thought for a New Testament writer (Rom. 7.23; Jas 4.11; 1 Pet. 2.11), nor for a Greek philosopher; Plato for example identified the extrusion of marrow through porous bone as the cause of sexual desire (see *Timaeus* 86D).

9.   Swetnam ('Jesus as Λογος in Heb 4:12-13', see n. 3) proposes a highly unusual interpretation; he suggests that the controlling idea in this passage is that of spiritual circumcision of the heart, basing his view on implicit typological parallelism between Jesus and Joshua (p. 217; see already Origen, *Homilies on Joshua* 36.2). He therefore prefers to draw the the dividing line between soul and spirit on the one hand, and joints and marrow, by metonymy for physical nature, on the other. The variant reading in some late minuscules of σώματος for πνεύματος might reflect the same interpretation (if it is not simply lapse into cliché). But Swetnam's view is fraught with difficulty. There is nothing to indicate an allusion to circumcision here (or anywhere else) in Hebrews; joints and marrow are not involved in that operation; and more importantly, this interpretation requires taking v. 12 as a positive idea—the

4. The sequence of thought between vv. 12 and 13 also raises a problem. The imagery of v. 12 is that of sharpness and penetration while that of v. 13 is of exposure to scrutiny. In this connection it is worth just mentioning the singular variant of Codex Vaticanus which has ἐναργής for ἐνεργής—the word is not 'living and active', but 'living and clear'. This at least has the merit of making a connection with the exposure idea in v. 13, though at the expense of the correlation with living, ζῶν, in v. 12, and it may be just a slip. There is some correlation of course between the two ideas; it is not unnatural to speak in English of a penetrating gaze and I do not want to overstate the problem. I refer to it only because some commentators[10] have wanted to exploit the sequence of v. 12 and v. 13 for their interpretation of τετραχηλισμένα, to which we will be ready to turn after two more difficulties have been mentioned.

5. There is a marked contrast between the images of this short passage, the sharp penetrating sword that exposes the inner self and leaves one open to the gaze of God, and the images with which the author continues in vv. 14-16 of a high priest able to sympathise, sharing our temptations and giving us access to the throne of grace with all its attendant benefits. This could be a deliberate balancing of the themes of judgment and mercy but again some have attempted to see more of a sequential progression of thought, from the wielding of the sacrificial knife to the rather more gentle priestly tasks of representation and intercession.

6. And finally, the meaning of the final phrase in v. 13 πρὸς ὄν ἡμῖν ὁ λόγος. We have several choices here ranging from the banal to the sublime. Comparing the similar phrase just a little further on, at 5.11, περὶ οὗ ἡμῖν ὁ λόγος, we might translate 'the eyes of him about whom we are speaking'. 'Impossibly flat' according to Moffatt. While it is clear that the main subject of the sermon is the high priest, so that 5.11 is understandable emphasis in context, it is not so clear why the author would want to underline that 4.12-13 is his subject, because he does not revert to the sword imagery again. Secondly, taking ὁ λόγος

---

cauterising of the flesh—while v. 13 changes to a negative idea of judgment, on which see the next section.

10. So H. Attridge, 'The Epistle to the Hebrews: A Commentary on the Epistle to the Hebrews', in *Hebrews* (Hermeneia; Philadelphia: Fortress Press, 1989), *ad loc.* Swetnam, however, is forced by his interpretation to take the καί at the beginning of v. 13 in an adversative sense.

as a minor semitism 'business' or 'affair', we might translate: 'with whom we have to deal'. But it can be questioned whether the semitic idiom would be so clear to the reader, especially in a paragraph where the language is more normally hellenistic than Septuagintal. Alternatively, calling on the technical Greek sense of λόγος as a bank account, we might translate 'with whom we have to reckon', and that would have the advantage of spelling out the consequences of the all-seeing eye of God in terms of judgment day and reckoning. This is perhaps the most common view, but there is a problem with it. When elsewhere λόγος clearly means an account or reckoning, as at 13.7 or at Lk. 16.2 or 1 Pet. 4.5, it always appears with ἀποδίδωμι, which makes the financial metaphor clear. Finally, picking up the echo with λόγος in v. 12, the translation has even been suggested: 'the eyes of him with whom the Logos is present for us'.[11] This is a hugely christological climax rather than a lame conclusion. But there are grave problems; we would have to take αὐτοῦ as God rather than Christ, and more importantly, would the author just throw in a dramatic piece of Johannine Christology as an undeveloped aside? We shall offer later a slightly different rendering of the final phrase of v. 13, consistent with the interpretation proposed for the whole verse.

7. And so, at last, to our main problem, the sense of τετραχηλισμένα at Heb. 4.13. The verb does not occur in the LXX, though the noun τράχηλος is common enough (85 times). The same word is used for both neck and throat (both the back and the front). There are a couple of peculiar Hebrew idioms that are worth mentioning because they explain this rather high incidence: 'to fall on the neck' is to embrace, especially between men at moments of tearful emotion; 'stiff-necked' of course meaning obdurate and disobedient, and puting 'a yoke round the neck' as a symbol of slavery. But there is not a single reference anywhere in the LXX to cutting the neck or the throat of a sacrificial victim. To return to the verb, its uniform sense in classical Greek is to grab hold of someone by the neck in a wrestling match, to twist the neck and to weaken one's opponent by cutting off his windpipe.[12] It has a metaphorical use of being oppressed by circumstances which probably also derives from the technical usage in Greek wrestling

11. See Clavier, 'Ο ΛΟΓΟΣ ΤΟΥ ΘΕΟΥ'; Swetnam, 'Jesus as Λόγος in Heb 4:12-13'.
12. E.g. Plutarch, *Anton* 33.4 and *Moralia* 521b.

rather than, say, carrying heavy burdens attached to a yoke round the neck.[13]

The problem then becomes only too clear. Hebrews says 'no creature is hidden before him, but everthing is naked and...'—we would expect some synonym for 'naked exposed', such as 'laid bare', but what we get is 'naked and throttled to the eyes of him' etc. How can 'throttled' mean 'exposed'? Commentators have agonised over this issue. Héring notes the fact that 'hold by the neck' and 'overpower' are the only meanings attested for the Greek verb and adds wryly: 'Exegetes determined to find in τετραχηλισμένα a synonym for γυμνά have performed acrobatic feats to justify the meaning.'[14] The gymnastics of the commentators are indeed entertaining; they speculate that the neck might hang forwards and down in shame, or on the contrary be pulled back forcibly in public humiliation. Alternatively, gathering up loose threads from some of the problems I mentioned earlier, Attridge suggests that the sword of the word is thought of as a sacrificial knife and that τετραχηλισμένα 'derives from the sacrificial sphere, where it refers to bending back the victim's neck prior to slaughter'.[15] The difficulty with this attractive solution is that, as we have seen, there is no lexicographical precedent for it in classical Greek nor anything in the LXX which would justify it.

The only support to which Attridge is forced to appeal is Theophrastus's *Characters* 27. This is about the ὀψιμαθής, 'the late developer', who makes a fool of himself horsing about like an adolescent. Sheer incompetence and ineptitude is the essence of this character. He picks up the latest slang, but garbles it in the pub (v. 2); he does not know his left from his right foot in elementary military drill (v. 3); at the ancient equivalent of the football match ('heroes' festivals'!) he runs through the streets with the hooligans (v. 4). Then

13. Particularly frequent in Philo: *Omn. Prob. Lib.* 159; *Mut. Nom.* 81; cf also *Rer. Div. Her.* 274; *Vit. Mos.* 1.297; *Cher.* 78.

14. J. Héring, *L'Epître aux Hébreux* (Paris: Delachaux & Niestlé, 1954), p. 47. He continues in the same vein: 'Cette manière de torturer les textes par des explications tirée par les cheveux ('Schulmeistererklarungen') ne peut que discréditer l'exégèse'.

15. Attridge, 'The Epistle to the Hebrews', p. 136; cf. also Swetnam, 'Jesus as Λογος in Heb 4:12-13', p. 222, 'exposed as a victim ready for sacrifice; all God has to do is deliver the blow'; and see P. Proulx and L. Alsonso Schökel, 'Heb 4:12-13, componentes y estructura', *Bib* 54 (1973), pp. 331-39.

follows the relevant incident for our purposes (v. 5): ἀμέλει δὲ κἄν του κληθῇ εἰς Ἡράκλειον, ῥίψας τὸ ἱμάτιον τὸν βοῦν αἴρισθαι, ἵνα τραξηλίσῃ. Here he is invited to a party at a shrine of Hercules, presumably in a private house rather than a public temple, and rips off his cloak to choose the bull in order to throttle it. The slight oddity that more than one bull might appear to be available to choose from led one erudite German editor to prefer the variant reading of the Vatican ms. V, αἱρέσθαι 'to raise or pull up' instead of αἱρεῖσθαι 'to choose'.[16] He then explained that 'to raise up' was used technically to hoist a sacrificial victim into position and went on to reinterpret τραξηλίσῃ as meaning 'expose the throat to the sacrificial knife'. This fancy continues to haunt the translations of Theophrastus, even those which prefer the other reading.[17] But surely it is clear that the bull is not going to take any serious harm from these sexagenarian antics; the whole point of the character of 'the aging hippy' is that he makes a mess of everything he attempts. In the following verse, continuing the wrestling motif, he goes off straightaway to the palaestra to work out with the lads. The remainder of this hilarious piece develops the point: he sits through several performances of a musical to learn the numbers by heart (v. 7); he turns his initiation into eastern mysteries into a beauty contest (v. 8); at the sauna he wriggles his bottom vigorously to show that he is well brought up (v. 14) and when the women start their dance he insists on joining in and humming the tune (v. 15). To suppose that he slaughters a bull in the midst of such buffoonery is simply to miss the joke.

In Heb. 4.13 τετραχηλισμένα is not a sacrificial but a wrestling metaphor; and in wrestling matches no sharp instruments are allowed! The metaphor is suggested by the preceding word γυμνά which is the equivalent of οὐκ ἀφανής in the preceding clause, and that is a perfectly natural association: one is, after all, 'gymnos' in a 'gymnasium'.[18] Throttled then refers to a decisive neck hold and the perfect

16. Meier; see R.G. Ussher, *The Characters of Theophrastus* (London: Macmillan, 1960), *ad loc*, who rightly resists it. The host gives the late developer a choice of opponent, and he takes the hard option, emulating the feats of Hercules, by choosing to wrestle the bull!

17. E.g. P. Vellacott, *Theophrastus, the Characters* (Harmondsworth: Penguin, 1973), p. 57: 'he chooses the bull, so that he can bend back its neck for slaughter'.

18. The author uses the verb γυμνάζω twice elsewhere, 5.14 and 12.11 (see also 1 Tim. 4.7 and 2 Pet. 2.14) in the technical sense of 'to exercise naked, to train'.

tense refers to the result of such a hold, namely to be floored and winded; hence the connotation of exposure. I would translate 'naked and spreadeagled to the eyes of him who keeps our score'.[19] Sudden switches of metaphor like this, from sharp sword to victory in wrestling, are not without parallel in our author when left to his own fertile imaginative devices. One might compare the 'firm and fast anchor of the soul' at 6.19 which suddenly introduces a breath of sea air into the Jerusalem Temple.

If one wanted to plumb the depths of the author's imagination even more deeply and fathom his subconscious—a dangerous proceeding admittedly—and ask why a wrestling match should have occurred to him here, I would make just one final tentative suggestion. He has spoken of joints and marrow in v. 12 and naked and throttled at v. 13 and in a similar exhortatory passage later other parts of the anatomy appear: 12.12, 'Lift your drooping hands and strengthen your weak knees and make straight paths for your feet'. Notice the joints! He goes on 'so that what is lame may not be put out of joint' (ἐκτραπῇ, technical word, again, for dislocation—a perennial hazard of the sport of wrestling).[20] In the same context, at 12.16, the author refers to the story of Esau and Jacob, as he has earlier at 11.20. It is not perhaps irrelevant to recall that Jacob stole his brother's blessing by putting goat skins on the naked parts of his neck (Gen. 27.16, where the two words 'naked' and 'neck' occur together in the Hebrew Bible); even more relevantly, Jacob wrestled with a supernatural opponent in Genesis 32 and won a greater blessing at the price of a dislocated joint, and yet he called the place Peniel because he had seen God face to face and survived. I am not suggesting that this scene would have been consciously in mind already at Heb. 4.13. What I am suggesting is that there is no need to struggle against the plain evidence of the Greek lexicon that τραχηλίζω means to bring a wrestling opponent down by

19. In the context, the notion of an account or tally (see above) might reasonably be rendered thus.

20. Metaphors from hellenistic athletics are remarkably frequent in Hebrews. Apart from 4.12-13 and 12.12-13, see the references at n. 18, and some at least of the following: the high protein diet, 5.14; the front runner, 6.20; training, 10.32; running the race without encumbrances, 12.1; the team captain, 12.2; fatigue, 12.3; the competitors, 12.4; physical education, 12.6. Athletic metaphors are not uncommon in Paul: boxing, 1 Cor. 9.26; track, Gal. 2.2, 1 Cor. 9.24, Phil. 3.13-14; training, 1 Cor. 9.25; and the winner's crown, 1 Cor. 9.25.

a decisive hold on the neck. One might hope to limp away from such an encounter—with a sore neck certainly, but not a slit throat. Hebrews never suggests that the eternal High Priest selects *us* as his sacrificial victim; on the contrary he volunteers himself for that role.

AUTHORSHIP AND CANONICITY: SOME PATRISTIC EVIDENCE

Mark Edwards

Up to the present century, it appears to have been the common view
of Christians that if we accept a writing as canonical we identify its
author as a saint. Luther stripped the New Testament of those books
which he did not believe to be written by Apostles or their compan-
ions; and the sanctity of the Old was compromised by Spinoza's argument that Moses could not have prophesied his death in Deuteronomy.
During the first three centuries the Bible of every Christian was the
Septuagint; but by the end of the fourth it was unusual to accord the
full authority of the canon to those portions which existed only in
Greek. It should not be thought, however, that adherence to the Septuagint, either then or at an earlier time, was based on an erroneous
belief in the antiquity of its contents. With regard to certain texts,
both Greek and Hebrew, that the Jews described as 'Writings', it was
possible for the most distinguished exegetes to ignore the date suggested by tradition, or even by the title of the work itself, without
apparent prejudice to the writer's orthodoxy or their own.

I

From Jerome's time to Pusey's it was thought a test of Christian
orthodoxy to maintain the exilic dating of the book of Daniel.[1] Christian exegetes were glad to show, and may have been the first to notice,[2]
that most of the events described in the prophecies are historical, and
culminate in the attempt of King Antiochus Epiphanes to destroy the
independence of the Jews. To modern eyes, the obvious conclusion is

1. The triumph of the critical school is announced by W.M. Sanday, *Inspiration*
(London, 1893), pp. 215-20.
2. See P.M. Casey, 'Porphyry and the Origin of the Book of Daniel', *JTS* 27
(1976), pp. 15-33.

that of the pagan critic Porphyry (232/4–c. 305), that these events were not foretold by Daniel in the time of Nebuchadnezzar, but recorded as they happened by a second-century writer who concealed his name under one of more authority, and gave credit to his unfulfilled predictions by ascribing to the seer a premonition of the facts already witnessed by the present generation. But Porphyry, as Jerome did not fail to note, was an infidel, an apologist for persecution; and even though the Jews excluded Daniel from the canon of the prophets,[3] they do not appear to have thought that its late appearance must betoken a later time of composition.

Christians before Jerome were obliged to believe still more, for the book of Daniel is longer in the Septuagint version, and the accretions cannot be translated back from Greek to Hebrew. This was already evident to Julius Africanus in the third century AD, but Origen (185–c. 254) misused his erudition to deny it,[4] and the comments of his contemporary Hippolytus on the story of Susannah presuppose that it is true in fact and canonical enough to justify an allegory.[5] Hippolytus (d. 235?) saw the Bible as a perfect and sufficient revelation, the only antidote to heresy, and his *Commentary on Daniel*, perhaps the first by a Christian, goes on to apply its prophecies to Antiochus as examples of fulfilled vaticination; yet when he comes to explain those which have not yet been accomplished, he implies that such events as have been verified took place within the lifetime of the seer:

> Having therefore narrated what had already occurred and been fulfilled in his own times, he announces to us another mystery, making a revelation of the last days (*Commentary on Daniel* 4.48).

Hippolytus does not deny the author his gift of prophecy, but presumes that, like Isaiah or Jeremiah, he spoke mainly to his time while leaving certain enigmatic utterances to be deciphered at the end of history. Since he believes that Daniel is a figure of the Babylonian exile, it would seem that he does not think him the author of every portion of the book that bears his name. Nor, on the other hand, does he express the fear that his words will offend the pious or diminish

---

3. As noted e.g. by Sanday, *Inspiration*, pp. 100-102, and by J. Barton, *Oracles of God* (London: Longmans, Green & Co., 1986).

4. See Eusebius, *Hist. Eccl.* 6.31.

5. Though it may be doubted whether the author of the *Commentary on Daniel* wrote the *Refutatio Omnium Haeresium*, the former is almost always agreed to be the 'real' Hippolytus and is known to have been a scourge of heresy.

their belief in the inspiration of the prophecies. And since he makes no objection to the title of the book at any point, it would appear that he is willing to subscribe to an erroneous attribution where the text itself is sacred to the church.

II

The same may be true of Origen, who though he is reported to have doubted the Pauline authorship of Hebrews, does not hesitate to cite it in his writings as the work of 'the Apostle'.[6] To him its chief use is that it asserts the coeternity, and perhaps also the consubstantiality, of the first and second persons in the godhead;[7] the verse in which it does this has a parallel, as he notices, in the Septuagint writing called the Wisdom of Solomon.[8] Among the early fathers, it is Origen who cites this work most frequently, regarding it (unlike the first book of Enoch) as sufficient in itself to prove a doctrine,[9] and nowhere does he state that it should not be ascribed to Solomon.

Nevertheless the preface to his commentary on the Song of Songs assumes the Hebrew canon, which admits no more than three works by that author:[10]

> First, let us examine why it is, that since the churches of God acknowledge three books written by Solomon, that of them the book of Proverbs is put first, the one called Ecclesiastes second and the book Song of Songs has third place. The following ideas have been able to come our way about the subject. There are three general disciplines by which one attains knowledge about the universe. The Greeks call them ethics,

6. See Eusebius, *Hist. Eccl.* 6.25.11 for Origen's doubts, which even as quoted do not amount to rejection of Pauline authorship. In the same chapter Eusebius records Origen's catalogue of the Hebrew writings of the Old Testament; he does not, of course, include Wisdom of Solomon, though he does not expressly exclude it, as he excludes the Maccabean histories.

7. On this intricate question see G.C. Stead, *Divine Substance* (Oxford: Clarendon Press, 1977), pp. 211-12.

8. Cf. Heb. 1.3 and Wis. 7.25, both cited at *De Principiis* 1.3.5 and in the answer to the first charge against Origen in Pamphilus's *Apology*.

9. Thus Enoch is cited with Ps. 138 at *De Principiis* 4.4.8. Wis. 7.16 is cited alone in the Greek text of *De Principiis* 3.1.14 (following Koetschau).

10. Prologue to *Commentary on the Song of Songs* in *Origen: On Prayer etc.* (trans. R. Greer; Classics of Western Spirituality series; London: SPCK, 1979), pp. 231-32.

physics and enoptics; and we can give them the terms moral, natural and contemplative... Solomon, since he wished to distinguish from one another and to separate what we have called earlier the three general disciplines, that is, moral, natural and contemplative, set them forth in three books, each it its own logical order.

It is not a question simply of what is extant in the Hebrew; the church is said to recognise no other book by Solomon, and he himself is alleged to have conceived a single project, which he completed in three books. Origen remarks that some Greeks posited a fourth discipline, called logic, which is either a further stage or else a method that informs the other three; he never suggests that Solomon would have felt the need of any such addition. Origen's scheme is grounded in the Trinity, anticipating both the Augustinian theory of signs and the threefold way which mysticism was to espouse in its ascent to God;[11] for him as for the churches, there was no need of a fourth.

III

Jerome, Athanasius and Cyril of Jerusalem exclude the Wisdom of Solomon from the Old Testament, while the author of the Muratorian Fragment seems to think it a better candidate for the New.[12] Nevertheless, an African Code of 419, endorsing the whole of the Septuagint as Scripture, ascribes no fewer than five untitled books to Solomon.[13] Elimination shows that the fifth is Sirach, and the omission of this book from other lists is said by Munier to show that Augustine's doubts as to the authorship of the volume had prevailed.[14] But why should there be any thought of Solomon, when the author names himself and was acknowledged by his admirers among the rabbis to have written after the era of prophetic inspiration? It may

11. See my 'Being, Life and Mind: A Brief Inquiry', forthcoming in *Syllecta Classica* (1998).

12. See Athanasius, *Festal Letter* 39; Cyril, *Catechetical Homily* 4.35. Both differ slightly from our Old Testament canon. On the Muratorian Fragment see G. Hahnemann, *The Muratorian Fragment and the Development of the Canon* (Oxford: Clarendon Press, 1992); see also n. 16.

13. Most conveniently consulted in H.R. Percival, *The Seven Ecumenical Councils of the Undivided Church* (repr.; Grand Rapids, 1991 [1899]), p. 454.

14. See C. Munier, 'La tradition manuscrite de l'Abrège d'Hippone et le canon des écritures des églises Africaines', *Sacris Erudiri* 21 (1972–73), pp. 43-44, esp. p. 52.

have been only in Africa that Sirach ranked among the books of Solomon, and so it will have been only there that anyone was disposed to ascribe it to him. We cannot suppose, however, that Augustine meant to contradict the council, for he repeatedly acknowledges that the canon is created by conciliar definition;[15] nor, on the other hand, can we believe that one who swayed the council of Carthage so decisively in 417 would have been so lightly contradicted by an African assembly in 419. The use of Solomon's name implies no more than a decision to accept the canonicity of the volume, and the council thus upholds Augustine's view that the whole Greek Bible is to be received as Scripture. He himself merely clarifies the view of his fellow-bishops by ensuring that the honorific title which they gave the book did not give rise to a false belief about its authorship:

> For those two volumes, one of which is entitled Wisdom, the other Ecclesiasticus, are called Solomon's on account of a certain likeness; for Jesus Sirach is most commonly said to have been their author. Since, however, they have deserved to be received as authoritative, they are numbered among the prophets (*De Doctrina Christiana* 2.13).

Augustine is not contradicting anyone, since it is clear enough that he never expected any learned person to imagine that these writings came from the pen of Solomon. The author of the Muratorian Fragment is another who includes Wisdom in his canon while ascribing it to other hands, and seemingly without any apprehension that he might be either eccentric or offensive.[16] This, we may note in passing, is no proof that he was writing in the fourth century,[17] for Origen's case reveals that the ubiquitous ascription of the book to Solomon in the earlier period was conventional, and does not imply that he was ever thought to have been its author. Defenders of the Septuagint could not but be aware of the distinction drawn by Jerome and Rufinus between those works which might be read in church and those that were, in the stricter sense, canonical; they could not dispute the scholarship which

---

15. See *Epistle* 64.3; Munier, 'La tradition', p. 55 n. 37.

16. See Hahnemann, *The Muratorian Fragment*, pp. 9-14, 200-205. The fragment states that the book was written *ab amicis Salomonis in honorem ipsius*; if this is a mistranslation of a Greek original which (like Jerome) attributed it to Philo, the author must have added the last three words.

17. As Hahnemann (*Muratorian Fragment*) argues throughout. His account of patristic testimonies on pp. 200-205 does not take acccount of the Prologue to Origen's *Commentary on the Song of Songs*.

underlies the Vulgate, and in any case the acceptance of the Maccabean histories by Augustine and the council of 419 can hardly rest on any misapprehension of their date.[18] When the Africans, therefore, included Sirach among the books of Solomon, they were merely saying, like Augustine, that it showed the inspiration of a prophet. The premises of modern criticism may exclude from an author's canon any writings which do not attain his 'constant level of value';[19] our evidence here implies a different principle, which can even extend one author's name to the writings of another where a common level of value was discerned.

18. See Augustine, *De Doctrina Christiana* 2.13, and the African Code, as cited (n. 13).

19. Quoting M. Foucault, 'What is an Author?', in P. Rabinow (ed.), *The Foucault Reader* (Harmondsworth: Penguin Books, 1984), p. 111.

WHAT'S IN A WORD?
AN INTRIGUING CHOICE IN THE SYRIAC *DIATESSARON*

Sebastian Brock

The recovery of a large proportion of the Syriac original of Ephrem's *Commentary on the Diatessaron*[1] confirmed that a number of distinctive readings in quotations from the Gospels by Syriac writers did indeed, as scholars had often suspected, have their origin in the Syriac *Diatessaron* (whether or not these go back to Tatian is a question to which we shall return later). Several of these distinctive readings display an interest in associating the Gospel text with passages in the Old Testament, evidently in order to incorporate certain features of the gospel message within the wider framework of biblical salvation history as a whole.

Although Ephrem does not offer any comment on John the Baptist's diet (Mt. 3.4; Mk 1.6) in his *Commentary on the Diatessaron*, a number of later witnesses indicate that the Syriac *Diatessaron* replaced the 'locusts and honey' by 'milk and honey',[2] the intention evidently being, not just to provide John with a vegetarian diet, but to introduce a typological dimension: John, the baptizer of Jesus, whose baptism constitutes the fountainhead of Christian baptism, already feeds on the 'milk and honey' of the promised land which the newly baptized were from an early date described as entering.[3] In a similar vein the *Gospel according to the Ebionites*, by neatly altering ἀκρίδες, 'locusts', to ἐγκρίδες, 'cakes', introduces a reference to manna, whose taste,

---

1. L. Leloir, *Saint Ephrem: Commentaire de l'évangile concordant (MS Chester Beatty 709)* (Dublin: Hodges Figgis, 1963), and *Saint Ephrem: Commentaire de l'évangile concordant (MS Chester Beatty 709). Folios additionels* (Leuven: Peeters, 1990).
2. See my 'The Baptist's Diet in Syriac Sources', *OrChr* 54 (1970), pp. 113-24.
3. Later, more literally minded Syriac commentators wondered how John could have found milk in the wilderness, and so specified that it came from gazelles.

according to the Septuagint, was like ἐγκρὶς ἐν μέλιτι (Exod. 16.31). Here the typological reference is historically more logical, in that John's upbringing is made to correspond to the desert wanderings, prior to the crossing of the Jordan into the promised land.

Another example is provided by the alteration, in Mt. 16.18, of 'doors of Hades' into 'bars of Sheol', employing the Greek word μοχλός.[4] The purpose of this small change was, as Robert Murray perceptively saw,[5] to provide a phraseological link with Ps. 107 (106).16 (cf. Isa. 45.2) where God 'has broken the gates of brass and cut the bars in sunder' (both LXX and Peshitta have μοχλοί). Since this passage was frequently taken by early Christian writers to refer to the descent of Christ into Sheol, the phraseological link introduced into the Syriac *Diatessaron* was evidently intended to serve as an invitation to the reader to interpret these words of Jesus (whose precise meaning has puzzled many commentators over the centuries) as having reference to his coming descent to Sheol and resurrection. To judge by the fact that later Syriac commentators fairly regularly understood the passage as referring to the descent and resurrection, the alteration had very much the desired effect.[6]

It is to another distinctive reading of the Syriac *Diatessaron* that I should like to turn in this *opusculum donaticum* in honour of John Ashton. At both Lk. 1.35 and Jn 1.14 the Syriac *Diatessaron* introduces the single verb *'aggen* to render the two different Greek verbs, ἐπισκιάσει and ἐσκήνωσεν. Since it is by no means obvious how best to translate *'aggen* (the causative of *gnn*, a root from which *gnona*, 'bridal chamber', derives), it is preferable for the present purposes to leave it untranslated here; what is important to realize is that it is not an obvious choice for either of the two Greek verbs, the former of which could much more readily have been rendered by *'attel*, 'overshadow' (causative of *tll*; cp. *tellala*, 'shadow'), and the

---

4. Ephrem, *Commentary on the Diatessaron* 14.1.

5. R. Murray, 'The Rock and the House on the Rock', *Orientalia Christiana Periodica* 30 (1964), pp. 356-62, and his *Symbols of Church and Kingdom* (Cambridge: Cambridge University Press, 1975), pp. 324-28; see also my 'Some Aspects of Greek Words in Syriac', in A. Dietrich (ed.), *Synkretismus im syrisch-persischen Kulturgebiet* (Göttingen: Vandenhoeck & Ruprecht, 1971), pp. 95-98.

6. As R. Murray points out, the later Syriac exegetical tradition sees Christ as breaking out of Sheol, and so the 'bars of Sheol' are not able to restrain him, or the departed.

latter by *shken*, 'reside, dwell, tabernacle'. What, then, led to the surprising choice of *'aggen* to cover both Greek verbs? An examination
of the use of this verb in the Peshitta Old Testament and in the Tar-
gumim (in neither of which is it at all common) is instructive. In both
the verb *'aggen* is restricted to a rather specialized usage, for in the
great majority of cases God is the subject and the verb is intransitive:
'God *'aggen* over...'

As far as the limited number of occurrences in the Peshitta Old
Testament is concerned, it is worth noting that *'aggen* renders the
Hebrew root שׂכך, 'cover, screen', in Exod. 33.22 and Job 1.10; 3.23.[7]
In the first two of these passages the verb unusually has an object: God
causes his hand to cover over (so Hebrew) someone. In all these cases
the idea of 'covering over' in the underlying Hebrew is essentially
associated with protection, and this likewise applies to those passages
where *'aggen* is not surprisingly used to translate the Hebrew cognate
גנן, usually rendered 'protect, defend'.[8] Interestingly enough, the
Peshitta always avoids using the root גנן where the Hebrew has מגן,
'shield', whether or not this is used as a epithet for God. The verb
'aggen further occurs in the Peshitta Old Testament only in Ps.
138(137).8 (rendering Hebrew גמר, 'perfect'), and Jer. 17.17, where
מַחְסִי אַתָּה, 'you [God] are my shelter', is rendered "*aggen* [imperative]
over me'. It is in fact only in these two passages and in Job 3.23 that
we have an exact parallel to the construction *'aggen 'al* ('over') which
occurs in Lk. 1.35, and nowhere do we have a parallel to *'aggen* + *b-*
'in', of Jn 1.14. Furthermore, none of the Peshitta Old Testament
occurrences of the verb *'aggen* provides a context which might offer
any clue why this verb should have been singled out for use in Lk.
1.35 and Jn 1.14.

Turning to the Targum tradition, it is at the outset striking to discover that the verb (always with God as subject) is almost entirely
confined to the Palestinian Targum tradition. As far as constructions
are concerned, אגן + על (of persons)[9] occurs at Gen. 7.16 (*Neofiti*

---

7.   The same root probably underlies the Peshitta at Job 29.4.

8.   2 Kgs 19.34; 20.6; Isa. 31.5; 37.35; 38.6; Zech. 9.15; 12.8. The verb also
occurs a few times in the Syriac translations of Ben Sira, Wisdom, 4 *Ezra* and the
Apocalypse of Baruch.

9.   For details of this and other constructions, see my 'From Annunciation to
Pentecost: The Travels of a Technical Term', in E. Carr, *et al.* (eds.), *Eulogema:*

margin), 15.1 (*Neofiti* margin), Deut. 33.12 (*Neofiti* and *Pseudo-Jonathan*), and a single time in *Targum Jonathan* (Isa. 4.5). Although אנן + -בְּ does indeed also occur in the Palestinian Targum a number of times, the preposition there has the sense 'with' (usually 'with my Memra'), not 'in', and it is always accompanied by *'al*, 'upon, over' of the recipients of the divine action. One of these passages in fact deserves particular notice. At Exod. 12.13 *Neofiti* renders the Hebrew וּפָסַחְתִּי (traditionally translated 'and I will pass over') by ואפסח ואגן במימרי עליכון, 'I will "pass over" and I will *'aggen* over you with my Memra' (margin: ...ויחוס ויגן מימרי, 'my Memra will protect and *'aggen*...). In this passage (and likewise at 12.23, 27, where the verb פסח again occurs) we have in *Neofiti* witness to two out of the (at least) six different interpretations of this puzzling root that were current in antiquity.[10] The linking of פסח with *'aggen* was certainly inspired by Isa. 31.5, where the two Hebrew roots, פסח and גנן, are used in parallel: 'As birds flying, so will the Lord Sabaoth protect (יָגֵן) Jerusalem; he will protect (וְגָנוֹן) and deliver it, he will pass over (פָּסוֹחַ) and preserve it'. Both in Exodus and in Isaiah, the immediate consequence of this action (evidently protective) by God is deliverance.

The Passover narrative of Exodus 12 is certainly the most weighty—from the point of view of salvation history—of the passages where *'aggen* occurs in the Palestinian Targum, and accordingly one is strongly inclined to suggest that a knowledge of the Palestinian tradition of rendering פסח by *'aggen* could be the factor underlying the choice of *'aggen* in Lk. 1.35 and Jn 1.14 in the Syriac *Diatessaron*, the intention being to introduce into the Gospel texts there the typological link between Christ 'the Lamb of God' (Jn 1.36) and the paschal lamb. Although this suggestion must inevitably remain speculative, the thinking behind it is entirely in harmony with the typological links that subsequent Syriac writers saw between the conception of Christ and the Passover narrative of Exodus 12. This can be seen most

Studies in Honor of Robert Taft S.J. (Studia Anselmiana, 110; Rome: S. Anselmo, 1993), p. 90.

10. Further details can be found in my 'An Early Interpretation of Pasah: *'aggen* in the Palestinian Targum', in J.A. Emerton and S.C. Reif (eds.), *Interpreting the Hebrew Bible: Essays in Honour of E.I.J. Rosenthal* (Cambridge: Cambridge University Press, 1982), pp. 27-34. This interpretation of *pasah* is also known from the Mekilta (ed. Lauterbach, I, p. 185).

notably from certain passages in Ephrem (d. 373) and Jacob of Serugh (d. 521).

Ephrem and other early Syriac writers were able to calculate the date of the annunciation (and hence conception of Christ) as the 10th Nisan;[11] this was neatly arrived at by assuming that Zacharias's entry into the sanctuary (Lk. 1.9) took place on the Day of Atonement (10th Tishri), and then adding the six months of Lk. 1.26, 36. The assumption is of course unhistorical, but it goes back well before Ephrem's time to the second century and the *Protogospel of James*—which makes the tradition more or less contemporary with Tatian, and so certainly not subsequent to the date of the Syriac *Diatessaron*. The typological significance of this date is brought out by Ephrem in his *Commentary on Exodus* 12.2-3:

> The (paschal) lamb is a symbol of our Lord who came to the womb on the tenth of Nisan. For from the tenth of the seventh month [i.e.Tishri], when Zacharias was told about the birth of John, up to the tenth of the first month [i.e. Nisan], when the announcement was made to Mary by the angel, constitute six months. That was why the angel said to her 'This is the sixth month for her who had been called barren' [Lk. 1.36]. On the tenth, therefore, when the (paschal) lamb was confined [Exod. 12.3], our Lord was conceived, and on the fourteenth, when it was slaughtered [Exod. 12.6], he whom the lamb symbolized was crucified.

In Exodus 12 it is, as we have seen, only the Palestinian Targum tradition, represented by Neofiti's margin, which employs *'aggen* to render פסח, whereas the Peshitta has the causative from the same root as the Hebrew, *'apṣaḥ*.[12] What sense the Peshitta translator intended there is unclear, but from the fourth century onwards Syriac writers regularly link both the verb and the noun *Peṣḥa* with 'joy', which is the normal sense of the Syriac root *pṣḥ*. Although no variant reading is found to *'apṣaḥ* in the Peshitta text of Exodus 12, it is striking that the poet Jacob of Serugh actually introduces the verb *'aggen* into this

---

11. For this date for the annunciation, see my 'Passover, Annunciation and Epiclesis', *NovT* 24 (1982) [Festschrift for J.D.M. Derrett], pp. 222-33; J.F. Coakley, 'Typology and the Birthday of Christ on 6 January', in R. Lavenant (ed.), *V Symposium Syriacum* (Orientalia Christiana Analecta, 236; Rome: Pontificum Istitutum Studiorum Orientalium, 1990), pp. 247-56; and A. de Halleux, 'Le comput ephrémien du cycle de la nativité', in F. van Segbroeck *et al.* (eds.), *The Four Gospels 1992: Festschrift Frans Neirynck* (Leuven: Peeters, 1992), pp. 2369-82.

12. The *ṣadhe* in the Syriac root is due to the proximity of *pe*.

context in his Homily *On the Passover in the Law*, where he says[13] 'Who, apart from His [sc. the Word's] power, *'aggen* over your doors [Exod. 12.23]?', and a few lines later, 'The Hidden Symbol [i.e. Christ, the True Lamb] *"aggen*, saved, delivered and rescued...' (the wording of Isa. 31.5 will also have been in Jacob's mind). Jacob knows indirectly of a number of Jewish traditions, and so it is perfectly conceivable that his choice of *'aggen* here might have been due to an awareness of the use of that term in Exodus 12 in the Palestinian Targum tradition, although one should not rule out the possibility that he has simply transferred back to Exodus 12 what had already by his day become something of a technical term in Syriac in the context of divine action. It is to this aspect that we next turn briefly.

The Syriac *Diatessaron*'s choice of *'aggen* at Lk. 1.35 and Jn 1.14 was never 'corrected' by means of some more literal translation in any of the various subsequent revisions of the Syriac Gospels, the Old Syriac, the Peshitta, and the Harklean, all of which were content to take it over even though renderings closer to the two underlying Greek verbs were readily at hand.[14] This in itself is an indication that the verb quickly acquired in Syriac certain rather specialized sacral connotations. That *'aggen* had become early on something of a technical term designating immanent divine activity among humanity can be readily seen from its reappearance in the Peshitta New Testament translating a variety of different Greek verbs.[15] Furthermore, it was not long before the verb became associated with liturgical invocations to the Holy Spirit, and something of its chronological progress from one liturgical context to another can actually be charted.[16] Thus the *Hymns on Epiphany* (attributed to Ephrem, but probably slightly later) use *'aggen* in the context of Christian baptism, while in fifth-century writers such as Narsai and Jacob of Serugh, it appears in

13. P. Bedjan (ed.), *Homiliae Selectae Mar-Jacobi Sarugensis* (Paris/Leipzig: Harrassowitz, 1910), V, p. 633.

14. There is in fact some evidence that *'aggen* may have replaced an earlier Syriac verb used in the context of the incarnation, *shra* 'dwell, reside (in)', which also has a Targumic background: see my 'The Lost Old Syriac at Luke 1.35 and the Earliest Syriac terms for the incarnation', in W.L. Petersen (ed.), *Gospel Traditions in the Second Century* (Notre Dame: University of Notre Dame Press, 1989), pp. 117-31.

15. E.g. Acts 10.44; 11.15, where the Greek has ἐπέπεσεν, '(The Holy Spirit) fell upon...'

16. For these developments details can be found in 'From Annunciation to Pentecost', pp. 71-91.

descriptions of the eucharistic epiclesis, where indeed it also features in the Syriac translation of the influential anaphora of St James, translating ἐπιφοιτάω. Moving into the sixth century, *'aggen* begins to be used in connection with the Pentecost narrative, and indeed it even replaces the Peshitta's '(tongues of fire) sat upon (the apostles)' at Acts 2.3 in some subsequent quotations of the entire passage.[17]

The choice by the author of the Syriac *Diatessaron* of *'aggen* at Lk. 1.35 and Jn 1.14 was thus one of great consequence for later Syriac tradition, whether or not one accepts the suggestion that he made that choice in the light of the Palestinian Aramaic tradition concerning פסח in Exodus 12. But who was this author, and how is the Syriac *Diatessaron* in these passages related to the Western diatessaron tradition? Recent scholarship has veered once again in the direction of seeing Syriac as the original language of Tatian's *Diatessaron*,[18] and if this is correct, then the choice of *'aggen* can with a fair degree of certainty be attributed to Tatian himself. If, however, Greek was the original language of Tatian's harmony, then of course the Syriac translation could date from several decades—or more—after Tatian's return to the East in the early 170s. This is not the place to go into the intricacies of the diatessaron problem,[19] and it must suffice here simply to note that no trace of the Syriac *Diatessaron*'s reading in these two passages can be found in any of the Western diatessaron witnesses; the same, moreover, applies to the even more distinctive readings concerning the Baptist's diet and the 'bars' of Sheol. This in itself suggests that the Syriac *Diatessaron* tradition had something of an independent development (though this does not in itself necessarily rule out Tatian as its author). Whatever may be the reality of the matter, it is at least fairly clear from a number of different passages that the author of the Syriac *Diatessaron*, beside having certain encratite concerns, also had

17. Notably in John of Dara (ninth century): see 'The Lost Old Syriac at Luke 1.35', pp. 127-30.

18. Thus especially W.L. Petersen, 'New Evidence for the Question of the Original Language of the Diatessaron', in W. Schrage (ed.), *Studien zur Text und Ethik des Neuen Testament* (Festschrift H. Greeven; Berlin: de Gruyter, 1986), pp. 325-43.

19. A helpful guide here is W.L. Petersen, *Tatian's Diatessaron: Its Creation, Dissemination, Significance and History in Scholarship* (Vigiliae Christianae Suppl., 25; Leiden: Brill, 1994). Further possible complications have been introduced by M.-E. Boismard's *Le Diatessaron de Tatien à Justin* (EBib NS, 15; Paris: Gabalda, 1992), whose views seem to me highly speculative.

a specific interest in introducing, by means of his specific choice of wording, new associations and links with passages in the Old Testament.[20]

20. In this context it is significant that the Syriac *Diatessaron* (like the Old Syriac after it) seems to have adapted at least some Old Testament quotations in the Gospels to the form of text found in the Peshitta Old Testament: see J. Joosten, 'The Old Testament Quotations in the Old Syriac and Peshitta Gospels: A Contribution to the Study of the Diatessaron', *Textus* 15 (1990), pp. 55-76.

WILLIAM TYNDALE—A MARTYR FOR THE BIBLE?

Henry Wansbrough

It is a pleasure to offer to John Ashton on his retirement a few reflections on a particular biblical translation. Long ago, as students of Classical Honour Moderations together, we learned together some of the art of translation. The piece also serves as a glance at the application of classical learning to scriptural scholarship in a former age.

Bible translations can be indicative of the spirit of their age. In an age of devotion St Bede's translations were directed primarily to prayer. In an age of revolt Wycliffe's translation was a symbol of protest against oppression. In an age of reconstruction the clutch of English translations after the Second World War was perhaps a symbol of a new recourse to religion as hope for a shamed world. So William Tyndale's first edition of the New Testament in English has been claimed as the cornerstone of English Protestantism, spread round the world with British colonialism. For this reason in his *Thomas More*[1] Richard Marius even asserts that 'From a cultural perspective, the year 1525 has a much better claim to mark the end of the Middle Ages than the traditional date of 1485'. Yet, less than ten years after the publication of his New Testament, Tyndale had been kidnapped by the Catholic authorities in the Netherlands, condemned as a heretic and degraded from his priesthood, and had died an excruciating death by garrotting, his body burned at the stake. Nevertheless he made an indelible mark on the English language, and nowadays any Christian would applaud his powerful desire to translate and bring the text of the Bible to the people.

It is challenging to form a picture of Tyndale and his fundamental motives. As it is, he is a figure on the margins of the European Reformation. Was it inevitable that he should be? Born on the borders of Wales, he was educated first at Oxford (BA 1512, MA 1515) and

1. London: Dent, 1984, p. 312.

then at Cambridge, at a moment when the new learning was beginning to spread at those universities. As early as 1488 William Grocyn had begun teaching Greek at Oxford, though John Colet's famous lectures on Romans in 1496–99 were still based on the Latin text.

Cambridge seems to have been the more eager for Greek learning. It is even claimed that some Greek graffiti on the wall of a monastic cell at Magdalene College may date from before 1500. Erasmus was in Cambridge (where he was thoroughly bored) between 1511 and 1514. In 1518 Richard Croke was appointed first Reader in Greek at Cambridge, whereas in the same year Thomas More found it necessary to write to Oxford encouraging the university to emulate its sister at Cambridge. This may seem unfair in view of the fact that two years previously Richard Foxe had founded Corpus Christi College, Oxford. The following year Erasmus was writing to the President of Corpus (with typical flattery) that Corpus was *inter praecipua decora Britanniae* on account of its *bibliotheca trilinguis*.[2]

At all events, Tyndale went to Cambridge between 1517 and 1521 and may well have participated in the hotbed of Lutheran discussion there. After his time at university Tyndale secured a post as tutor to the children of a Gloucestershire squire, Sir John Walsh, twice High Sheriff of Gloucestershire, and a man of substance. It is amusing to note that Tyndale there already showed his contentious tongue. Sir John kept a good table, so that 'there resorted to him many times sundry abbots, deans, archdeacons with divers other doctors and beneficed men'.[3] Master Tyndale 'spared not to show unto them simply and plainly his judgement in matters, and lay plainly before them the open and manifest places of the Scriptures, to confute their errors and confirm his sayings' to such good effect that 'at length they waxed weary, and bare a secret grudge in their hearts against him'. The influence of Erasmus may well have played a part in this. Tyndale seems to have translated Erasmus's *Enchiridion Militis Christiani*, which he presented to his master and lady.[4] 'After they had read well

2. Letter 990, in *Collected Works of Erasmus*, VI (Toronto: University of Toronto Press, 1982).

3. Foxe's *Book of Martyrs*, V (1838 edn).

4. There were 50 Latin editions of this work during Erasmus's lifetime. It was translated into German in 1520, Dutch 1523, Spanish 1527, French 1529, but the first English edition was not published until 1533. There seems to be no telling whether this was Tyndale's or not.

and perused the same, the doctorly prelates were no more so often called to the house, neither had they the cheer and countenance when they came as before they had.' The *Enchiridion*, originally published by Erasmus in 1503, was one of the most formative books of the age. In spirit it might be described as pre-Reformation, for Erasmus is critical of the church from within. Erasmus detested ceremonies, relics and pilgrimages. Two barbed remarks suffice to show the temper of the book:

> Would you like to win the favour of Peter and Paul? Imitate the faith of the one and the charity of the other, and you will accomplish more than if you were to dash off to Rome ten times.
>
> With great veneration you revere the ashes of Paul. If you venerate mute and dead ashes and ignore his living image, still speaking and breathing, as it were, in his writings, is not your religion utterly absurd? You worship the bones of Paul preserved in a relic casket but do not worship the mind of Paul hidden in his writings.[5]

At this stage such a spirit of criticism accords well with what we know of the fiery young Tyndale.

Foxe recounts another story which has plenty to say about both Tyndale's temper and his theology at this time.

> Master Tyndale happened to be in the company of a certain divine, recounted for a learned man, and in communing and disputing with him he drave him to that issue, that the said great doctor burst out into these blasphemous words, and said, 'We were better to be without God's laws than the pope's.' Master Tyndale, hearing this, full of godly zeal and not bearing that blasphemous saying, replied again and said, 'I defy the pope and all his laws', and further added that, if God spared him life, ere many years he would cause the boy that driveth the plough to know more of scripture than he did.

The last rejoinder shows that the discussion which led to the learned cleric's outburst would have been about the Scripture, Tyndale opposing the scriptural text to received ecclesiastical interpretation. Tyndale's final remark is strongly reminiscent of Erasmus's famous dictum in his preface to the first printed edition of the Greek New Testament in 1516. There Erasmus wrote, 'I could wish even all women to read the gospel and the epistles of Paul, and that the farmer may sing parts of them at his work, and the weaver may chant them

---

5. *Enchiridion*, in *Collected Works of Erasmus* (Toronto: University of Toronto Press, 1988), LXVI, pp. 71, 72.

when engaged at his shuttle, and the traveller with their stories beguile the weariness of the journey.'

The desire to bring the Bible to the people was in the air, and this inevitably involved translation. The language of religion was Latin. The Bible was in Latin, the Mass was in Latin, Church law, inscriptions and prayers were in Latin. Before Shakespeare and Marlowe, English was considered too rough and barbarous for any sacred use. Then Tyndale made the startling claim that English was actually more suitable for the Bible than Latin: it rendered more naturally 'the grace and sweetness' of the biblical text than did Latin.

But Englishing the Bible was suspect of heresy. The first attempt to translate the Bible was associated with Wycliffe and the Lollards a century before, and Wycliffe had been burnt at the stake for his efforts. The primitive character of Wycliffe's translation throws Tyndale's into the brightest possible relief, and makes only too clear why English was not considered suitable for a translation of the Bible. Two well-known biblical passages suffice to give a taste of Wycliffe's version:

> Gen. 1.1-2 In the first made God of nought heaven and earth. The earth forsooth was vain within and void, and darknesses were upon the face of the sea, and the spirit of God was born upon the water.

> Jn 1.5-7... and darkness comprehendiden not it. A man was sent from God to whom the name was John. This man came in to witnessing.

Furthermore, Wycliffe had translated from the Latin, which was then considered simply the Bible, and was the only version then available, but the new learning made a further revolution possible. Now it was possible to push back to the original Hebrew and Greek texts themselves. By 1500 Greek was beginning to be taught at the universities, and in 1506 Reuchlin's Hebrew grammar, *De Rudimentis Hebraicis*, was published (in the 1537 catalogue of Corpus Christi College library, this is still the only Hebrew book). However, this revolution was tainted too, for Luther was translating the Bible from Hebrew into German. This was perhaps why, when in 1522 Tyndale offered his services as a translator to the Bishop of London, he was turned away. It is interesting that as a sample of his work Tyndale presented Tunstall with a translation of the classical Greek orator Isocrates. Was it from Greek rhetoric that Tyndale derived his literary skill? In any case, the refusal must have been a serious disappointment, for Bishop

Cuthbert Tunstall was a friend of Tyndale's hero Erasmus, and an advocate of reform. It may well have been this rejection by ecclesiastical authority which finally drove Tyndale into the arms of Luther.

It is striking that, for all his objections to Tyndale's actual translation (see below), Thomas More grants that the clergy must bear the blame for the lack of a translation—in England alone of all Christian countries:

> surely the thing that maketh in this matter the clergy most suspect, and wherein it would be full hard to excuse them, is this, that they not only damn Tyndale's translation, but over that do damn all other, and as though a layman were no Christian man will suffer no layman to have any at all. But when they find any in his keeping they lay heresy to him therefore. And thereupon they burn up the book and sometime the good man withall... In all other countries of Christendom the people have the scripture translated into their own tongue and the clergy findeth no such fault therein.[6]

So William Tyndale emigrated to Flanders, and there set about his work of translating. After a mere two years, in 1526 his New Testament, translated from the Greek, arrived in England. As it reached the docks it was seized by the Bishop of London and burnt.

Tyndale and St Thomas More

Enough copies got through to make further action necessary, and in 1528 Tunstall commissioned the learned Thomas More, himself a humanist and friend of Erasmus, to counterattack. This More did in his *Dialogue Concerning Heresies*, which appeared in June 1529. There was no love lost between the two. More characterized Tyndale variously as 'a hell-hound in the kennel of the devil' and 'a drowsy drudge drinking deep in the devil's dregs'.[7] Consonant with More's famous penchant for mockery, some parts of the *Dialogue* are light-hearted and replete with a broad and bawdy humour which would hardly be considered edifying from the pen of a saint in a later age. In particular, the account of the goings-on at the shrine of St Valery

6. *Complete Works of Sir Thomas More* (New Haven: Yale University Press, 1961), VI, pp. 293-94.

7. Quoted by D. Daniell, *William Tyndale* (New Haven: Yale University Press, 1994), p. 277.

makes bracing reading. (In his reply Tyndale passes this section over with one sentence, as beneath contempt). When More comes to Tyndale's translation, however, little quarter is given.

More's chief objection is that Tyndale has been so influenced by Luther that his New Testament should be called 'Tyndale's Testament' or 'Luther's Testament' rather than 'New Testament'. Typical of More's detailed objections is his fight against Tyndale's use of three words, 'senior' instead of 'priest', 'congregation' instead of 'church', and 'love' instead of 'charity'.[8] Each of these translations is defensible in itself, and yet historically tainted by Tyndale's association with Luther. There can be no doubt that it was Tyndale's marginal theological comments which excited More's ire in the matter:

> It is to be considered that at the time of this translation [Tyndale] was with Luther in Wittenberg and set certain glosses in the margin, framed for the setting forth of the ungracious sect... Touching the confederacy between Luther and him is a thing well known and plainly confessed by such as have been taken and convicted here of heresy coming from thence.[9]

Indeed it is true that Tyndale was deeply affected by Luther; fourteen of the fifteen pages of his Prologue to the letter to the Romans are a straight translation from Luther. Nevertheless, Tyndale's impetus was different from, though related to, that of Luther. Apart from his marginal glosses, in his translation Tyndale's impetus was linguistic reform, an attempt to break away from the tired ecclesiastical terms overlaid with Latinity, in order to achieve an English which would speak to his 'boy that driveth the plough'. This claim deserves examination in detail, in particular with regard to the three words to which More objected.

(1) More complains that 'this word *senyor* signifieth nothing at all, but is a French word used in English more than half in mockery, when one will call another "My Lord" in scorn'. Clearly More capitalizes on the uncertain spelling of the day to assimilate the word to the French 'Seigneur'; it must have been a joke to call someone 'Mon Seigneur' in mock honour. Tyndale, however, was making a valid theological point. He uses 'priest' of the Hebrew priests of the Temple and of Christ the high priest. In the New Testament, however, the Greek word for priest is used only of Christ and the company of

8. *Complete Works*, VI, pp. 285-88.
9. *Complete Works*, VI, p. 288.

saints in heaven (in the letter to the Hebrews and the book of Revelation respectively); here Tyndale duly uses 'priest'. The Greek word
which Tyndale translated offendingly is *presbyteros*, literally 'an
older person'. In his reply to More, Tyndale admits that 'senior' is a
rare word, used mostly in the universities, but by the time More
objected Tyndale had himself emended the translation to 'elder'. It is
hard to find fault with Tyndale's choice of this word. There is no suggestion in the New Testament that these officials have any office as
sacrificing priests. They have much the same office—despite More's
explicit objection—as 'the aldermen of the cities', a council of elders
in the nascent Christian communities.

(2) To Tyndale's option for the word 'congregation' instead of the
more traditional 'church' More objects that not every congregation is
a church, but only a congregation of Christian people, 'which congregation of Christian people hath been in England always called and
known by the name of the church'. Tyndale in his reply[10] ripostes that
the word 'church' has too many senses. It is commonly used both for a
building and for the clergy, as well as 'another signification, little
known among the common people nowadays, a multitude or a company gathered together in one, of all degrees of people'. He energeti-
cally cites examples from Paul where the word signifies the multitude
of Christians gathered in a particular locality. He omits, surely deliberately, to mention the less palatable instances in the later Pauline letters where the same word means the church universal, the multitude
of Christians gathered throughout the world: his translation clearly
fits less well in Col. 1.18, 'And he is the head of the body, that is to
wit of the congregation' (or Eph. 1.22). Yet even here it is arguable
that Tyndale's 'congregation' reflects well the Old Testament concept
on which the New Testament concept of the People of God is founded,
the people gathered together by God to be his own possession.

Although the arguments put forward by Tyndale for his translations
of the two preceding words are perfectly legitimate, it is hard to avoid
the feeling that he is being disingenuous. It is a classic case of the situation where the context makes all the difference. The word 'congregation' had been used by Wycliffe in his translation, and it is hard
to avoid the suspicion that Tyndale's preference for the word was also

10. *An Answer to Sir Thomas More* (ed. H. Walter; Cambridge: Cambridge University Press, 1850), pp. 12-16.

influenced by Luther's similar use of *Gemeinde*. At the very least his motives must have been to avoid the overtones of traditional ecclesiastical teaching. Both 'priest' and 'church' have strong Catholic overtones, which have persisted to this day. More in fact explicitly accuses Tyndale of following Luther's 'damnable heresies' in his choice of words. 'Priest' is accordingly to be avoided because 'Luther and his adherents hold this heresy, that all holy order is nothing'. 'Church' is to be avoided 'because that Luther utterly denieth the very catholic church on earth and saith that the church of Christ is but an unknown congregation of some folk, here two and there three, no man wot where, having the right faith'.[11]

(3) The third example, 'love', is different, and there Tyndale seems merely to be preferring the simple and direct English word, consonant with his usual preference for straightforward English words above Latinate words such as More's preferred traditional word, 'charity', reflecting the Latin *caritas*. More relates this change to the Lutheran doctrine of salvation by faith alone: 'and therefore he changeth that name of holy virtuous affection into the bare name of love common to the virtuous love that man beareth to God and to the lewd love that is between fleck and his make'. To this Tyndale's reply is that 'charity' means nothing in good, plain English: 'Verily, charity is no known English in that sense which *agape* requireth';[12] it is used chiefly of almsgiving and mercifulness. These senses are too exclusively Christian for the word to have the general meaning which Tyndale demands. If a word is to 'bite' in translation, it must have a real meaning of its own. Anyone who has marvelled at Tyndale's version of Paul's hymn to love in 1 Corinthians 13 (repeated virtually unchanged in the familiar King James Version) can hardly object to the result, 'Love suffereth long and is courteous. Love envieth not', and so on.

The argument between More and Tyndale continues into such words as 'favour', which Tyndale substitutes for the more familiar 'grace', 'knowledge' substituted for 'confession' and 'repentance' preferred to 'penance'. In each case Tyndale prefers the word which is used in daily life to the word which had long acquired ecclesiastical overtones, and which in the heat of controversy Tyndale bitterly calls

11. *Complete Works*, VI, p. 289.
12. *Answer*, p. 21.

'juggled and feigned terms'.[13] In each case the word he rejects is basically a Latin word, reflecting the Latin heritage of the church.

Tyndale's Legacy

Nothing daunted, Tyndale set about the Old Testament too, and in 1530 the first five books were completed. He revised his New Testament and continued his work on the Old. He must have been about halfway through when he was kidnapped and imprisoned.

Even in his dank cell, where he suffered terribly from the ague, he thirsted to continue his work. In a letter to the prison governor shortly before his execution he wrote pathetically,

> I suffer greatly from cold in the head and am afflicted with perpetual catarrh. I ask to have a lamp in the evening; it is indeed wearisome sitting alone in the dark. Most of all I beg and beseech Your Clemency to urge the Commissary that he will kindly permit me to have the Hebrew Bible, Hebrew grammar and Hebrew dictionary, that I may pass the time in that study.

A few years later 'Matthew's Bible' was published by Tyndale's friend John Roger. Containing Tyndale's translations but without his name, it was licensed by Henry VIII. Nearly a century later the King James Version, the authorized version of the Bible, and the basis for virtually all modern English versions, was issued—an event which has been described as the coming of age of the Church of England. It relies heavily on Tyndale—up to 80 per cent in those parts which he had translated. The nobility, rhythm, freshness and even wit of this translation are his: 'Then said the serpent unto the woman, "Tush, ye shall not die"'. Where the King James Version does change Tyndale, it often shies away from his imaginative, daring version; the serpent's enticement fades to 'Ye shall not surely die'. Similarly the lively 'the woman saw it was a good tree to eat of and lusty unto the eyes' is softened to the pedestrian 'the woman saw that the tree was good for food and a tree to be desired'.

The debt of the English language to Tyndale is immense. There were biblical expressions for which no English equivalent existed. He invented such words as 'scapegoat' and 'passover'. Any number of expressions which have become proverbial were his: 'the powers that

13. *Answer*, p. 24.

be', 'the fat of the land', 'eat, drink and be merry'. His rhythms still haunt the language: 'Not unto us, O Lord, not unto us'. Some were too bold (more is the pity) and were 'corrected' by the King James editors, so that we lost such a wonderful blessing as 'every one of you swimmeth in love' (2 Thess. 1.2).

'FOR PAUL' OR 'FOR CEPHAS'?
THE BOOK OF REVELATION AND EARLY ASIAN CHRISTIANITY

Ian Boxall

Relocating the Black Sheep

The book of Revelation has become somewhat difficult to locate on the map of first-century Christianity. Traditionally classified together with the Fourth Gospel and the Epistles of John, it has more recently become the black sheep of the Johannine flock, at the very least relegated to the fringes of the Johannine tradition,[1] if not attributed to 'those who are not of this fold'. Alternative suggestions continue to be made: Adele Yarbro Collins defines the author as a Jewish Christian, probably Palestinian, itinerant prophet;[2] J. Massyngberde Ford has proposed that the work emanates from the circles of John the Baptist, with only minor editing clearly attributable to Jewish Christians;[3] more recently, within his impressive revision of the Tübingen hypothesis, Michael Goulder has placed both Revelation and the other Johannine writings within the Pauline stream.[4] Though on occasion he does admit, however implicitly, a more complex situation,[5] Goulder is generally clear about the main sentiments of John the seer of Patmos:

---

1. Some scholars prefer to speak more loosely of a Johannine 'school' or 'circle': e.g. O. Cullmann, *The Johannine Circle* (ET; London: SCM Press, 1976).

2. A. Yarbro Collins, *Crisis and Catharsis* (Philadelphia: Westminster Press, 1984), pp. 25-53.

3. J. Massyngberde Ford, *Revelation* (AB, 38; Garden City, NY: Doubleday, 1975).

4. For a popular statement of this, see M. Goulder, *A Tale of Two Missions* (London: SCM Press, 1994).

5. Goulder can speak of Revelation as written by 'a seer with sympathies for both the missions' (*Tale*, p. 66), a 'bridge' writing (p. 183), possessing 'Petrine strands' (p. 107).

he is 'another Pauline',[6] one of a number writing 'against Petrines in Asia Minor',[7] the area where, in his view, the Petrine–Pauline battle was fought the hardest.

Goulder's reconstruction rightly suggests that the identification of the Christian 'opponents' of John of Patmos may shed some light upon the place of the latter in the spectrum of early Christian thought. But are these most appropriately described as 'Petrines'? Alternative suggestions abound as to the identity of the Nicolaitans, the followers of 'Balaam' and the prophetess 'Jezebel': besides 'Petrine Christians' or 'Judaizers', we find, as in the original Tübingen school, their mirror image, Pauline Christians or 'pseudo-Paulinists',[8] as well as the less precise 'antinomians'[9] and 'gnostics',[10] the latter sometimes influenced by the later patristic traditions about the Nicolaitans.

In this essay I shall assess the hypothesis that the author of Revelation is a Pauline battling against the Petrines, arguing that, on the contrary, the book represents a non-Pauline reaction to certain trends within the Pauline tradition in Asia. In so doing, I shall focus upon one issue in particular, which is dealt with by both John of Patmos and, in somewhat greater detail, Paul of Tarsus: the problem of food sacrificed to idols. In the case of John, this issue is central to his critique of at least two groups of his opponents, namely, those who 'hold the teaching of Balaam' at Pergamum (Rev. 2.13-17) and the followers of 'Jezebel' at Thyatira (Rev. 2.18-29). But I shall also propose a more complex Christian situation for first-century Asia than that offered by the simple Tübingen hypothesis, appealing both to our general knowledge of Asian Christianity in the New Testament period and to information supplied by the book of Revelation itself with respect to these 'opponents'. In other words, if John is not a 'Pauline', this does not mean that he is automatically a 'Petrine'.[11]

6. *Tale*, p. 89.

7. *Tale*, p. 186.

8. E.g. H.B. Swete, *The Apocalypse of St John* (London: Macmillan, 1906), p. lxviii and pp. 36-37. Recognizing 'an element of truth' in the Pauline identity of the Nicolaitans, he prefers 'the spiritual descendants of the libertines who perverted the Pauline doctrine and against whom St Paul strongly protests' (p. 37).

9. E.g. R.H. Mounce, *The Book of Revelation* (NICNT; Grand Rapids: Eerdmans, 1977), pp. 98, 103-105.

10. E.g. G.R. Beasley-Murray, *Revelation* (NCB; Grand Rapids: Eerdmans, 1978), p. 86.

11. See now also C.K. Barrett, 'What Minorities?', in D. Hellholm, H. Moxnes

It is a pleasure to dedicate this paper to John Ashton, a wise teacher, and one who has made an enormous contribution to our understanding of the undisputed Johannine writings; I trust he will forgive this sortie into what some might call the 'Johannine hinterland'.

Christian Life in Asia

Why might one wish to challenge the identification of John of Patmos as a Pauline, albeit one with the occasional Petrine sympathy? First, such a clear-cut division of Christians into 'Petrines' and 'Paulines' fails to do justice to the evidence for Christianity within the Roman province of Asia in the New Testament period. Asia was one of the most fertile soils in which earliest Christianity took root, and one which has yielded a rich literary crop. But this only underlines the complexity of the Christian situation. Besides Revelation's perspective on seven Asian churches, history has bequeathed to us the letter to the Colossians (with its close association with Laodicea and Hierapolis: see Col. 4.13),[12] Ephesians, the Pastoral Epistles, and the letters of Ignatius of Antioch. There is also a wealth of evidence, particularly about Ephesus, in the Acts of the Apostles; ecclesiastical tradition has located the Johannine Writings in this city, and the Petrine stream has also laid some claim to influence in the province (1 Pet. 1.1). Thus we witness not only the potential interplay of Pauline, deutero-Pauline (of various kinds), Petrine and Johannine traditions, but also influences from the disciples of the Baptist (Acts 19.1-7)[13] and Hellenistic Jewish preachers like Apollos (Acts 18.24-28), set against a diverse tapestry of Jewish diaspora communities.[14] Against such a climate, one might

and T.K. Seim (eds.), *Mighty Minorities? Minorities in Early Christianity— Positions and Strategies* (Oslo: Scandinavian University Press, 1995), pp. 9-10.

12. The scholarly debate about the so-called 'Colossians heresy' has convinced many that the Pauline mission in the Lycus valley was threatened by a rival, non-Pauline, understanding of the gospel, 'insisting on self-abasement and worship of angels, dwelling on visions' (Col. 2.18).

13. A number of Johannine scholars have argued for the influence of followers of John the Baptist on the Fourth Gospel (regardless of its traditional association with Ephesus) and within the Johannine community: see e.g. R.E. Brown, *The Community of the Beloved Disciple* (London: Geoffrey Chapman, 1979). Ford (*Revelation*) has argued that the Apocalypse of John itself derives from Baptist circles.

14. E.g. P.R. Trebilco, *Jewish Communities in Asia Minor* (Cambridge: Cambridge University Press, 1991).

expect to find diverse influences upon New Testament texts from Asia, even in those texts clearly attributable to a particular Christian strand. It is not surprising, for example, that scholars have often claimed Pauline influences upon 1 Peter, a text claiming to be in the Petrine tradition. To divide all Asian Christians into either 'Petrines' or 'Paulines', therefore, would appear to underestimate both the range of Christian traditions in that area and the criss-crossing of and interplay between those traditions.

Certainly John of Patmos can be expected to have some exposure to Pauline Christianity: he writes to, and his letters suggest intimate knowledge of, churches having some explicit connection with the Pauline mission (Ephesus, Laodicea, Thyatira). Indeed, Elisabeth Schüssler Fiorenza has argued for some affinity between Revelation and the Pauline tradition.[15] But John's knowledge of Pauline traditions does not necessarily make him a Pauline. As Schüssler Fiorenza herself states, with reference to verses in Revelation which echo both the Fourth Gospel and Paul: 'Rev. 21.6-7 would thus indicate that the author could have been familiar with the Johannine as well as the Pauline school tradition without belonging to one of them'.[16] In the event, she concludes that the Apocalypse contains more affinities in language, tradition and form with the Pauline than with the Johannine tradition, although she designates John of Patmos as a member of an early Christian prophetic-apocalyptic school.

But this should warn us against speaking simply of 'Pauline' and 'Petrine' churches in this area, or even of a simple battle between these two. Rather, the evidence suggests that individual churches were divided within themselves, and not simply into two camps (e.g. Rev. 2.2, 6, 14-15, 20-23). This would appear to hold true not simply for the seven churches of the Apocalypse. We know, for example, that Paul faced opposition in Ephesus (1 Cor. 16.9; cf. 15.32), and this may well have come from fellow Christian missionaries.[17] The author of the Pastorals arguably faced opposition from fellow Paulines who

15. E. Schüssler Fiorenza, 'The Quest for the Johannine School', in *The Book of Revelation: Justice and Judgment* (Philadelphia: Fortress Press, 1985), pp. 85-113.

16. Schüssler Fiorenza, 'The Quest', p. 101.

17. E.g. C.K. Barrett, *The First Epistle to the Corinthians* (BNTC; London: A. & C. Black, 2nd edn, 1971), p. 389: 'possibly non-Christians, possibly Jewish Christians'. 2 Tim. 1.15 also has Paul declare that 'all who are in Asia have turned away from me'.

differed in their interpretation of that tradition, particularly in the realm of eschatology.[18] Further, the author of Colossians seems to warn against a rival Christian movement or philosophy, perhaps influenced by Jewish mystical traditions, among the churches of the Lycus valley (e.g. Col. 2.16-19). Indeed, over thirty years ago Austin Farrer already pointed to the similarities between the thought of Revelation and the 'Asianized Judaism' attacked in Colossians: strict adherence to Jewish food laws; interest in angelology, the heavenly bodies and the elements of the world; insistence on visionary experience.[19] He concluded then that, if there were any connections, John of Patmos would represent a Christianized representative of that Judaism who had 'fully digested St. Paul's lessons', that is he would be closer to Paul than the 'Colossian teacher' attacked in the Pauline epistle. It may be, however, that the opposition in Colossae was more 'Christian' than the polemic of 'not holding fast to the Head' (Col. 2.19) might suggest, that the cryptic phrase θρησκεία τῶν ἀγγέλων (Col. 2.18) refers to worshipping along with the heavenly host (cf. e.g. Rev. 4-5; 4Q400-407) rather than angelolatry, and that there might be even closer links between the 'Colossian heresy' and the thought of Revelation than Farrer allowed. But whatever our conclusions, the letter to the Colossians does suggest some kind of rivalry to the Pauline mission in the Province of Asia.

Likewise, across the Aegean in Corinth, other influences beyond those of Paul were at work within a church he himself had founded (not simply the two very different shadows of the Palestinian Cephas and the Alexandrian Apollos but, more damagingly, the 'superlative apostles' of 2 Cor. 10–13). For this reason, is it strictly true to speak of even the Corinthian church as 'Pauline'? Still less, then, should we expect a church like Ephesus to be solidly 'Pauline', or 'Pauline' with 'Petrine' fringes. The literary deposit from Christians in that city suggests a more complex picture. At the time that Revelation was written, it is likely that this particular church was split at least three ways: between those who shared John's point of view, 'those who call themselves apostles', and a group known as the Nicolaitans (Rev. 2.1-8).

18. Hymenaeus and Philetus, who hold that 'the resurrection has already taken place' (2 Tim. 2.18), have been plausibly identified as Paulines of the kind who wrote Colossians/Ephesians.

19. A. Farrer, *The Revelation of St John the Divine* (Oxford: Oxford University Press, 1964), pp. 37-38.

In short, the obvious fact that John knows communities with Pauline members does not mean that he himself is happy with the Pauline tradition, at least as it is practised in his (post-Pauline) situation. Nor is knowledge of Pauline thought and language the same as sharing a Pauline stance. But there is evidence that, on certain issues, the seer of Patmos advocates a distinctly un-Pauline stance.

Opponents in Revelation

In the second place, the Letters to the Seven Churches, addressed as they are to specific Christian communities in Asia,[20] suggest that John is faced not with one set of 'opponents' throughout the province, but with different problems in the various congregations. The church in Ephesus is praised for its rejection of 'those who claim to be apostles but are not' (Rev. 2.2), as well as for hating 'the works of the Nico-laitans' (2.6). The teaching of these Nicolaitans has apparently made headway in Pergamum (2.15); it is somewhat unclear whether their teaching is identical to the 'teaching of Balaam' (2.14), namely 'that they [the people of Israel] would eat food sacrificed to idols (εἰδωλόθυτα) and practice fornication (πορνεῦσαι)'.[21] A similar charge of teaching Christians 'to practice fornication and to eat food sacrificed to idols' is laid against a prophetess in Thyatira, who is given the name of the pagan queen, Jezebel (2.20). Finally, two churches, Smyrna and Philadelphia, are praised for their endurance and fidelity, in the face of apparent hostility from 'those who say that they are Jews and are not, but are a synagogue of Satan' (2.9; 3.9); in the case of Smyrna, the latter's 'slander' (βλασφημία) may have con-tributed to the temporary imprisonment of some Christians (2.9-11). The 'synagogue of Satan' language suggests intra-Jewish polemic of the kind we find, for example, in the Qumran scrolls: the polemic of a community which still considers itself Jewish and seeks to deny that title to other Jews, rather than (as in the Fourth Gospel's use of οἱ Ἰουδαῖοι) one which has reached the point of no return vis-à-vis the

20. See C.J. Hemer, *The Letters to the Seven Churches of Asia in their Local Setting* (JSNTSup, 11; Sheffield: JSOT Press, 1986). This is true irrespective of whether the letters predate the visions (e.g. R.H. Charles, *Revelation* [ICC; Edinburgh: T. & T. Clark, 1920], I, p. 37), or are an integral part of Revelation.
21. Biblical citations are taken from the NRSV, except where noted.

synagogue community.[22] The 'so-called Jews', moreover, are cast in the role of persecutors and slanderers, not of false teachers, unlike those who receive the divine rebuke at Ephesus, Pergamum and Thyatira. These 'opponents' in Smyrna and Philadelphia, then, are almost certainly non-Christian Jews, perhaps instigators of local hostility towards their Christian brethren (2.9-10), pressurizing them to 'deny' the name of Jesus (3.8).[23]

Occam's Razor notwithstanding, one should avoid the tendency to harmonize all these into a composite group of 'opponents': it is probable that recent descriptions of the opponents as 'Judaizers' or 'Jewish gnostics' are the direct result of such a tendency.[24] Yet, at the very least, the evidence suggests opposition on two fronts (connected with non-Christian Jews on the one hand and fellow Christians on the other), but more likely points to several different 'demonized' groups within or related to the seven churches of the Apocalypse.[25]

All this calls for a more complex solution than one which reads Revelation as a Pauline criticism of the Petrines in Asia. Indeed, of the seven Asian churches named, only three have any explicit connection with the Pauline mission: Ephesus, Laodicea (cf. Col. 4.13), and, through Lydia (Acts 16.14), possibly Thyatira. Interestingly, neither Smyrna nor Philadelphia, the two churches which receive unconditional praise from the seer of Patmos (and which, therefore, can be expected to share John's Christian stance), are known to be congregations in the Pauline tradition, whereas Pauline Laodicea is unique among the seven in receiving only rebuke (3.14-22).

On the basis of the Christian literary deposit of first-century Asia, and of the evidence from Revelation itself, there are good reasons for

22. But the sentiments are not too far from those of Jn 8.44: 'You are from your father the devil.'

23. A plausible connection between Jewish hostility and Domitian's 'fiscus iudaicus' policy depends upon the traditional dating of Revelation to the 90s, one which is now no longer universally held.

24. E.g. H. Koester, *Introduction to the New Testament. II. History and Literature of Early Christianity* (ET; Philadelphia: Fortress Press, 1982), p. 253: 'perhaps Jewish-Christian gnostics.'

25. Yarbro Collins (*Crisis*, pp. 134-38) has suggested that at least some of John's rivals, and John himself, may well have been itinerant Christian prophets. This would account for John's intimate knowledge of the seven churches and his (disputed) claim to authority over all of them.

questioning a simple Petrine/Pauline dichotomy: the evidence rather suggests tensions on a number of fronts, from non-Christian Jews in Smyrna and Philadelphia, from rival apostles in Ephesus,[26] from Nicolaitans in Ephesus and Pergamum, who may be identical to the advocates of the teaching of 'Balaam' in the latter church,[27] and therefore promoting a similar Christian stance to 'Jezebel' in Thyatira. But even if we link the Nicolaitans-Balaam-Jezebel as the main Christian alternative to John of Patmos, there are good reasons for doubting their 'Petrine' allegiance. For there are some indications that on some issues the author of Revelation is the conservative 'Jewish Christian', advocating a non-Pauline, even an anti-Pauline response, while his prophetic rivals, 'Jezebel' and the followers of 'Balaam', are the Paulines in his midst.

Balaam, Jezebel and Food Sacrificed to Idols

Both Paul (in 1 Cor. 8–10) and the author of Revelation (in the letters to Pergamum and Thyatira: Rev. 2.12-29) discuss the appropriate Christian attitude to τὰ εἰδωλόθυτα, an issue which also exercises the 'Apostolic Council' of Jerusalem, according to traditions in Acts 15. In assessing the relationship between these first two writers on this particular issue, a number of questions need to be asked. What precisely was the issue of 'food sacrificed to idols', and the related 'immorality/fornication' in Revelation? How similar are the responses of Paul and John of Patmos, and to what extent are these determined by the 'Apostolic Letter' preserved in Acts 15? Finally, in the case of Revelation, what might John's designation of his opponents as 'Nicolaitans', 'Balaam' and 'Jezebel' tell us about his place in the spectrum of first-century Asian Christianity?

The Issue

In both 1 Corinthians 8–10 and the Letters to Pergamum and Thyatira (Rev. 2.12-29), the issue of εἰδωλόθυτα is far more than a narrow concern over diet: it concerns the legitimate level of Christian participation in surrounding pagan society. Leaving aside the issue of

26. The logic of the letter to Ephesus (2.1-7) would suggest that the 'so-called apostles' and the Nicolaitans are different groups.

27. See Charles, *Revelation*, I, pp. 52-53 for an ingenious attempt to link the two etymologically.

participation in religious cults, contact with idol meat was a distinct possibility for those Christians who shopped in the local market, took seriously social intercourse with pagan neighbours, or strove to promote business interests through membership of voluntary associations or trade guilds. In Corinth, this was particularly pressing for prominent church members such as Erastus, the οἰκονόμος τῆς πόλεως (Rom. 16.23),[28] Gaius (1 Cor. 1.14; Rom. 16.23) and Crispus the ἀρχισυνάγωγος (1 Cor. 1.14; Acts 18.8). But it appears to have been no less an issue for Christians living in the Province of Asia.[29] Thyatira, for example, was well known for its large number of trade guilds, and its most famous convert, Lydia, may well have been a businesswoman of some means, 'a dealer in purple cloth' (πορφυρόπωλις, Acts 16.14).[30] The issue of idol meat was essentially an issue about the appropriate Christian relationship to surrounding pagan society.

Evidence from elsewhere in Revelation supports the idea that the author is concerned with the relationship between church and empire. The vision of the two beasts in ch. 13 makes clear that worship of the first beast is not simply a matter of cult but of economics: '...no one can buy or sell who does not have the mark, that is, the name of the beast or the number of its name' (13.17). Participation in the life— political, religious and economic—of Roman Asia implicates human beings in the worship of the beast, and this is no less a danger for unwitting Christians, like 'Balaam' and 'Jezebel'. Similarly, the vision of the great harlot in ch. 17, and the ensuing lament over her, highlight both the economic dominance of this immoral city (notably in the laments of the 'merchants of the earth', 18.11-17)[31] and the seductive hold she may have even over members of the church ('Come

28. Particularly if this is the same Erastus who became aedile of the city, and who paid for the building of a pavement there. See J. Murphy-O'Connor, *St Paul's Corinth* (Wilmington, DE: Michael Glazier, 1983), p. 37; W. Meeks, *The First Urban Christians* (New Haven: Yale University Press, 1983), pp. 58-59.

29. This applies whether one dates Revelation to the 90s, in line with its traditional setting under Domitian and the development of the emperor cult, or, as some now prefer, in the 60s.

30. For a rather different assessment of the social status of Lydia, see I.R. Reimer, *Women in the Acts of the Apostles* (ET; Minneapolis: Fortress Press, 1995), ch. 3.

31. For a detailed discussion of this economic dimension, see R. Bauckham, 'The Economic Critique of Rome in Revelation 18', in *The Climax of Prophecy* (Edinburgh: T. & T. Clark, 1993), pp. 338-83.

out of her, my people, so that you do not take part in her sins, and so that you do not share in her plagues', 18.4).[32]

But what of the second issue which concerns the author of Revelation in both the 'teaching of Balaam' and the deception of 'Jezebel', that of 'practicing fornication/immorality' (πορνεῦσαι)? 'Jezebel' is described as having a 'bed' (κλίνη), as one with whom some Christians 'commit adultery', and as the mother of 'children' (2.22-23). Scholarship is divided between a literal and metaphorical interpretation. In favour of a literal interpretation is the evidence of 1 Corinthians, where Paul is concerned not only with idol meat but also with concrete cases of sexual immorality (1 Cor. 5; 6.12-20), as well as the presence of both εἰδωλόθυτα and πορνεία in the Apostolic Decree of Acts 15. However, there are reasons to prefer a more metaphorical reading in the case of 'Jezebel'. First, in general terms, one should bear in mind the nature of polemical language, which should not be taken at face value.[33] Stock phrases of abuse, particularly biblical ones, are the staple diet of religious polemic in the Judaeo-Christian tradition. Secondly, to take the language literally in this case would mean to postulate a situation in Thyatira far worse than anything Paul found in Corinth (multiple adultery or fornication), despite the fact that John can praise the Thyatirans for their 'love, faith, service, and patient endurance' (2.19). Thirdly, the noun πορνεία and the verb πορνεύω are used elsewhere in Revelation in a metaphorical sense: in relation to the unjust and idolatrous activity of the Great City, Babylon (Rev. 17.2; 18.3, 9).

But it is the identification of this prophetess with the Old Testament Queen Jezebel which finally tips the scales in favour of a metaphorical interpretation: πορνεία as religious 'harlotry', a synonym for idolatry (e.g. Hos. 4.12 LXX: πνεύματι πορνείας ἐπλανήθησαν καὶ ἐξεπόρνευσαν ἀπὸ τοῦ θεοῦ αὐτῶν). Jezebel is remembered in Jewish

---

32. There are a number of significant parallels between the biblical figure of Jezebel and Revelation's portrayal of the Great Harlot, Babylon (e.g. compare 2 Kgs 9.22, where Jezebel is remembered for her 'many whoredoms and sorceries', and Rev. 17.1-2; 18.23). Thyatira's 'Jezebel' is a shocking example of the inroads which the 'immoral city' has made even into the church, through Christian accommodation to what John perceives to be an idolatrous Roman imperial system. She (2.21), no less than Babylon (17.2), is guilty of πορνεία.

33. See L.T. Johnson, 'The New Testament's Anti-Jewish Slander and the Conventions of Ancient Polemic', *JBL* 108 (1989), pp. 419-41.

Understanding, Studying and Reading

tradition, not for sexual immorality, but for her introduction into Israel of the worship of Baal and her violent opposition to Yahwism and its classic defender, the prophet Elijah (e.g. 1 Kgs 16–19), and as a symbol of bloodshed and injustice (1 Kgs 21; 2 Kgs 9). Likewise, Balaam is remembered negatively for the apostasy of Peor (Num. 31.16), the P interpretation of an event also described in Num. 25.1ff., when the people of Israel played the harlot (LXX ἐκπορ-νεῦσαι) with the daughters of Moab, sacrificing to their gods. In both cases, πορνεία is adequately interpreted as idolatry.

The problem, then, was primarily one of avoidance of 'idolatry', the extent to which Christians might participate in pagan society, including the kinds of religious, economic and social intercourse implied by the eating of idol meat (though, of course, in the temples of Ephesus, Thyatira and Corinth, shades of sexual activity could not be ruled out completely). But how might we expect the division lines to be drawn within the early Christian communities? Allowing for the inadequacy of the simplistic Jewish Christian/Gentile Christian division, the avoidance of meat that had been sacrificed to idols, and indeed of idolatry in all its forms, was a particular concern for Jews, and the issue could be expected to divide those Christians (whatever their ethnic origin) who advocated a certain 'Jewish separatism' and at least the terms of the 'Apostolic Decree' on Gentiles, from those taking a more accommodating view of contemporary pagan society.[34] This general background stands, even granted Theissen's illuminating socio-economic account of the weak/strong division in Corinth.[35] Let us now turn to the various responses of the New Testament writers.

Responses
Among scholars who have recognized parallels between the situations in Pergamum and Thyatira and the situation in Corinth, there has often been a tendency to interpret the responses of Paul and the author of Revelation as essentially the same on this issue.[36] A wedge is drawn

34. The Jews in Sardis, for example, had provision made for 'suitable food' to be sold in the market, to avoid the danger of idol meat: see Trebilco, *Jewish Communities*, p. 18; Josephus, *Ant.* 14.261.
35. G. Theissen, *The Social Setting of Pauline Christianity* (ET; Edinburgh: T. & T. Clark, 1982), ch. 3.
36. E.g. Beasley-Murray, *Revelation*, p. 86: 'In that case John responded to the Nicolaitans in a similar manner to Paul in his dealing with the Corinthian liberals'.

between Paul and the Corinthian 'strong' to equal that between John and Balaam/Jezebel. But does an analysis of their respective responses really support such a conclusion, or is Paul's pastoral response more accommodating to his Corinthian brethren than John's message to his prophetic rivals?

The compromise position of the so-called 'Apostolic Decree', as recorded in the book of Acts, takes into account the Jewish Christian sensibilities of those associated with Jerusalem over a number of issues, including that of idol meat, and may well represent an early form of the so-called 'Noahic Commandments'.[37] Though dispensing with the requirement of Gentile circumcision in the New Age, the decree nevertheless places certain constraints upon Gentile converts:

> For it has seemed good to the Holy Spirit and to us to impose on you no further burden (μηδὲν πλέον ἐπιτίθεσθαι ὑμῖν βάρος) than these essentials: that you abstain from what has been sacrificed to idols (εἰδωλοθύτων) and from blood and from what is strangled and from fornication (πορνείας) (Acts 15.28-29).

The extent to which Luke has carefully preserved historical tradition about the decree, and in particular whether this is traditional wording or his own, continues to be hotly debated, as do a whole host of issues relating to the so-called 'Jerusalem Council' of Acts 15. Particularly pertinent in this discussion are the respective responses of Paul and the author of Revelation to the idol-meat issue: for Paul, writing to the Corinthians, seems either unaware of this letter or content to disregard it, while John appears not only to require a strict enforcement of it but even to echo its wording.

Paul's position on the eating of idol meat (1 Cor. 8–10) would surely have been regarded as a 'sell-out' by conservative Jewish Christians, his appeal to the principle of love notwithstanding, and is puzzling for its lack of reference to the 'Apostolic Decree'.[38] His carefully worded and complex answer, covering three chapters of his letter, reveals that he is treading a careful path through a difficult

---

37. See A.F. Segal, *Paul the Convert* (New Haven: Yale University Press, 1990), ch. 6; cf. *Jub.* 7.20-21; *Tosephta 'Abodah Zarah* 8.4, for alternative lists.

38. Is this because Paul is unaware of such a decree, or is he aware of it but rejects it or regards it as inappropriate for a church surch as Corinth? Or should we prefer the more complex thesis of J.C. Hurd, *The Origin of 1 Corinthians* (Macon, GA: Mercer University Press, new edn, 1983): that he has previously tried to enforce it in Corinth (in his 'previous letter'), but now attempts a compromise?

issue. Despite his sympathies for the 'weak', Paul nevertheless numbers himself among the 'strong', seeing eating itself as a matter of indifference (1 Cor. 8.8; 10.25-26), unless it should offend the weaker brethren. For Paul, where and why one eats is more important than what. He is clear that it is permissible for a Christian to eat meat from the local market, or at a dinner hosted by a pagan neighbour, unless it offends against conscience (1 Cor. 10.23-30). He seems to recognize the detrimental effect not only upon wealthy Corinthian patrons but, by extension, on the whole community, of a strict avoidance of idol meat. On the other hand, he is equally clear that participation in pagan sacrificial rites is to be condemned (1 Cor. 10.14-22), even if such are associated with demons rather than real 'gods' (cf. 1 Cor. 8.4-6). It is less clear, however, whether this would rule out participation in banquets in the precincts of a pagan temple, perhaps arranged by trade-guilds or voluntary associations; given 1 Cor. 8.7-13, it is likely that this is permitted, consciences allowing (v. 9, 'But take care that this liberty of yours does not somehow become a stumbling block to the weak'). This would fit with Paul's stance elsewhere: idol meat, like circumcision (Gal. 5.6) and special days (Rom. 14.5), is essentially a matter of indifference.

The author of Revelation, on the contrary, advocates an uncompromising stance with regard to this issue. In no way does he distinguish, as Paul seems to, between participating in a sacrificial meal in a pagan temple and eating idol meat in a non-cultic context, whether at home, in a temple dining-room or at a neighbour's house.[39] He condemns certain members of two churches, Pergamum and Thyatira, for eating food sacrificed to idols (εἰδωλόθυτα) and practicing 'immorality/harlotry' (πορνεῦσαι), two of the four practices expressly forbidden Gentile converts in the 'Apostolic Decree' of Acts 15.[40] In the letter to Pergamum, he describes this as 'the teaching of Balaam'; in that to Thyatira, it is attributed to a prophetess in the community

---

39. There is no obvious support from the text for the suggestion of Mounce (*Revelation*, p. 98) that εἰδωλόθυτα 'probably refers to meat which was eaten at pagan feasts rather than that sold in the open market after having been offered to idols'.

40. A number of scholars have pointed to echoes of the 'Apostolic Decree' in Rev. 2; besides the condemnation of 'idol meat' and 'immorality', the letter to Thyatira declares to the faithful that 'I do not lay upon you any other burden (βάρος)' (2.24), echoing the language of Acts 15.28.

whom he calls 'Jezebel'. If the 'teaching of Balaam' is to be identified with the 'teaching of the Nicolaitans' (2.15), then this 'liberal' Christian stance has also infiltrated the church in Ephesus, though without making much headway ('Yet this is to your credit: you hate the works of the Nicolaitans, which I also hate', 2.6). It is hard to see how this essentially pragmatic position of 'Balaam' and 'Jezebel' differs from the approach that Pauline Christians might take, particularly the 'strong' in cities like Corinth (apparently with the apostle's own blessing), or, we might presume, Ephesus and Thyatira. In the face of such teaching, John advocates a harsh rejection of idol meat which would lead to Christian non-participation in Roman society.[41]

Balaam and Jezebel

Do the names attached to John's opponents in the churches, notably 'Balaam' and 'Jezebel', help to shed further light upon their position in the spectrum of early Christian opinion, and indeed that of John? It is unlikely that the name 'Jezebel' was claimed for herself by the prophetess of Thyatira, given the overwhelming negative connotations of Queen Jezebel in Jewish tradition, but was probably given her derogatorily by John himself. She clearly sees herself as a Christian 'prophetess', one who speaks the true words of God (cf. Rev. 1.3; 22.6-9). Thus we have a case of 'seeing ourselves as others see us': what we have is John's perception of her, expressed in polemical language. 'The teaching of Balaam' is more ambiguous: the biblical record has positive as well as negative traditions about the prophet Balaam, and it is possible that the name was adopted by the 'opponents' themselves, though in a positive sense,[42] and that Revelation has seized upon the negative connotations.

Whatever the case, Balaam is the name of a pagan prophet with a rather double-edged reputation, evidenced by the fact that Philo (*Vit. Mos.* 1.276) can describe him as a μάγος. Though remembered in the J and E traditions[43] somewhat positively as a pagan prophet, to whom God spoke, and who was inspired to utter a blessing rather than a

---

41. A similar stance is found in *Did.* 6.3: περὶ δὲ τῆς βρώσεως, ὃ δύνασαι βάστασον· ἀπὸ δὲ τοῦ εἰδωλοθύτου λίαν πρόσεχε· λατρεία γάρ ἐστι θεῶν νεκρῶν.

42. See J. Roloff, *The Revelation of John: A Continental Commentary* (ET; Minneapolis: Fortress Press, 1993), p. 52.

43. M. Noth, *Numbers* (ET; OTL; London: SCM Press, 1968), pp. 171-94.

curse on Israel (Num. 22–24), the P portrait is somewhat more sinis-
ter, making him into a seducer of Israel by attributing to him the
apostasy of the Israelites at Shittim/Peor (Num. 31.16; cf. 25.1-9). In
other words, Balaam the pagan seer has become the vehicle for idolatry. It is this negative tradition that became dominant in post-biblical
Jewish literature,[44] and that found its way into the New Testament, not
only in Revelation, which explicitly mentions the Baal-Peor incident
('…who taught Balak to put a stumbling block before the people of
Israel', Rev. 2.14b), but also 2 Pet. 2.16 and Jude 11. On the other
hand, Josephus for one (*Ant.* 4.100-158) has preserved something of
the more positive portrayal of Balaam, as a pagan who nevertheless
spoke the true word of God, and this portrayal is shared by at least
some New Testament traditions deriving from Jewish–Christian circles.[45] It was, after all, to Balaam that one important messianic
prophecy was attributed (Num. 24.17; cf. Mt. 2.2; 4QTest 9-13), thus
establishing him as a true prophet. It is possible that this more positive
portrait was seized upon by Gentile Christian prophets within the
church at Pergamum, finding in it a fitting biblical role model for
their own prophetic ministry, particularly if their prophetic ministry
was under attack from their Jewish Christian contemporaries. If this is
the case, then the author of Revelation has transformed a positive
image into a negative one, by reminding his hearers of the Baal-Peor
tradition.

That Balaam was adopted as a role model for Christian prophets of
non-Jewish origin remains a plausible hypothesis. But even if, as in
the case of 'Jezebel', the phrase 'some there who hold to the teaching
of Balaam' has been coined by the author of Revelation himself,
rather than reflecting their own self-understanding, this can still tell us
something of the relation between John and his rivals on the spectrum
of early Christianity. From his perspective, they are false prophets, no
better than pagan prophets, whether or not they come from Gentile
backgrounds themselves. Like Balaam, they are perceived as essentially 'outsiders', non-Jews, though they may well appear to fellow

44. For rabbinic references, cf. *TDNT*, I, pp. 524-25.
45. This more positive Balaam tradition almost certainly underlies the story of the
magi in Mt. 2.1-12 (cf. Num. 24), and therefore seems to have been preserved by
Jewish Christian communities with a positive attitude towards the Gentile mission.
See R.E. Brown, *The Birth of the Messiah* (London: Geoffrey Chapman, new edn,
1993), pp. 190-96.

Christians as typical 'insiders'. They are certainly advocating a position which blurs the distinction between the surrounding culture of Roman Asia and the people of God, akin, according to Revelation, to that attributed to Balaam at Baal-Peor (Num. 31.16), which undermined the clear boundaries separating Israel from the Moabites/Midianites.

This is a position which is readily attributable to Paulines and other 'radicals' with an accommodating stance vis-à-vis Gentiles. Moreover, this may suggest something about the stance of John himself. His negative appeal to the story of Balaam, as one who 'put a stumbling block before the people of Israel',[46] echoes not only much of the Jewish tradition about this figure, but also the picture found in Jude, a work rooted in non-Pauline 'primitive Jewish Christian apocalypticism'.[47] Though there are differences between the two works, the same kind of hostile use of pagan biblical figures can be found in the Johannine Apocalypse, and would suggest a similar, if not identical, Jewish Christian position.[48]

What, then, of Jezebel? Jezebel, the daughter of the Sidonian king and wife of King Ahab of Israel (1 Kgs 16.31), is one of the most notorious figures of the Jewish tradition. According to the Deuteronomistic Historian, it was as a result of his marriage to Jezebel that Ahab 'went and served Baal', erecting an altar and temple to the Canaanite god in Samaria, and making an Asherah (1 Kgs 16.32-33). Jezebel herself is portrayed as a violent opponent of Yahwism, castigated for her 'many whoredoms (LXX πορνεῖαι) and sorceries (φάρμακα)' (2 Kgs 9.22; cf. Rev. 17.1-6; 18.23), and as an enemy of Elijah, particularly after the latter's slaughter of the prophets of Baal on Mount Carmel, as the result of which she was determined to seek Elijah's life (1 Kgs 19.2). She is also remembered as a figure of injustice, given her role in the episode of Naboth's vineyard (1 Kgs 21), and of

46. On υἱοὶ Ἰσραὴλ as a description of Christians, see Rev. 7.4; 21.12.
47. J. Knight, *2 Peter and Jude* (NTG; Sheffield: Sheffield Academic Press, 1995), p. 26. The reference to Balaam in 2 Pet. 2.16 is almost certainly due to literary dependence upon Jude 11.
48. Indeed, it has often been proposed that the reference to 'Balaam' in Jude 11 is a veiled attack on Christians in the Pauline tradition, whether Paul himself, those influenced by the theology of Colossians, or Pauline radicals interpreting his gospel in a 'libertinistic way'; see R. Bauckham, *Jude and the Relatives of Jesus in the Early Church* (Edinburgh: T. & T. Clark, 1990), pp. 165-66.

bloodshed, being held responsible not only for the death of Naboth but for 'the blood of my servants the prophets, and the blood of all the servants of the Lord' (2 Kgs 9.7; cf. Rev. 18.24).

Allowing for the stock language with which individuals and groups 'demonize' their opponents, John has chosen the name 'Jezebel' because of its appropriateness for this particular situation. We have seen how the story of the pagan queen of Israel fits John's concern about the 'compromise' of the Thyatiran prophetess over idol meat, which in his eyes is tantamount to 'playing the harlot', just as it also fits his portrayal of the Great Harlot, Babylon the Great (Rev. 17–18). But can we go further? I want tentatively to suggest that there may be further parallels to be drawn.

First of all, Jezebel was a Gentile, an outsider to Israel, whose marriage to Ahab was seen as detrimental to the people of God. Though 'Jezebel' of Thyatira is clearly a member of the Christian community,[49] could it be that she is a Gentile member, regarded by John as too closely tied to her former life, and encouraging others, including Jewish Christians, to live 'like a Gentile and not like a Jew' (cf. Gal. 2.14)? Even if we cannot be sure about her own pagan origins, at the very least this is how John chooses to perceive her: her radical Christian stance is no better than that of a pagan, infiltrating and deceiving the people of Israel.

Further, the uneasy relationship between the author and this Christian prophetess may reflect a further feature of the biblical story of Jezebel. Throughout Revelation, there is a battle being played out between true and false prophecy, between the true prophet (of which John is put forward as a shining example, Rev. 1.2-3) and the false prophet, too closely wedded to an idolatrous and oppressive culture (typified by the 'beast from the earth', 13.13-15; 19.20). But in subtle ways, John makes clear that this battle is also being played out within the church itself. The prophesying of 'Jezebel' is connected not with the things of God but with τὰ βαθέα τοῦ Σατανᾶ (2.24); thus she is like the second beast, the false prophet, the mouthpiece of Satan. She 'beguiles' (NRSV) or 'leads astray' the servants of God (πλανᾷ, 2.20)

---

49. Some have claimed that 'Jezebel' is not a Christian but a pagan prophetess (see Charles, *Revelation*, I, p. 70); however, the fact that she is 'tolerated' by the angel of the church (2.20) and that she has been given time to 'repent' (v. 21) provides compelling evidence that she is an 'insider'. This is further clarified in certain MSS by the reading γυναῖκά σου.

just as the false prophet leads many astray (πλανᾷ, 13.14). Note also Christ's promise to the victors in Thyatira (2.26-27): the division in that church would appear to be a concretization of the conflict between the Rider on the White Horse and the 'nations/Gentiles', whom he smites with a sharp sword and rules with a rod of iron (19.15). In both situations, it is the battle for the true word of God (19.13), true prophecy (19.10), which is at issue. Likewise, just as the Divine Warrior smites the nations with the sharp sword from his mouth (19.15), so will the 'one like a son of man' wage war with the Balaamites and Nicolaitans of Pergamum with 'the sword of my mouth' (2.16).

It would appear, then, that the biblical story of Jezebel plays a larger role in the book than has often been recognized. Indeed, it has frequently been proposed that one of the archetypal 'two witnesses' in the vision of Revelation 11, able to 'shut the sky, so that no rain may fall during the days of their prophesying' (Rev. 11.6a; cf. 2 Kgs 17), is in some sense an Elijah figure. Does John see himself, in uttering 'the words of this prophecy', as playing 'Elijah' to Thyatira's 'Jezebel', the fierce defender of Yahwistic purity in the face of a Christian accommodation to pagan society which some of his fellow Christians, not least those in the Pauline stream, could advocate? If this is so, then John of Patmos finds his place not on the Pauline fringe, with its radical tendencies, perhaps not even with the 'bridge-builder' Peter (cf. Gal. 2.11-14), but further along the spectrum in the company of James, Jude and their conservative Jewish Christian contemporaries.

Locating the Opponents

The thesis, then, is as follows: John, the seer of Patmos, is a Jewish Christian prophet who is at least partly engaged in a prophetic critique of Christians in the Pauline tradition, whom he believes to have accommodated themselves too closely to their pagan environment, seduced, perhaps unwittingly, by the *Pax Romana* and its local benefits in the province of Asia. We have seen how Pauline Christians could well have appealed to Pauline principles (1 Cor. 8–10) in support of a practice which the author of the Apocalypse roundly condemns, and how John could respond with a vehemence to rival anything that Paul could muster. Indeed, it is possible that further polemic is to be found within the pages of Revelation, specifically directed against the claims of the Pauline tradition. Let us take, for example, the vision of the New Jerusalem in ch. 21. Against an appeal, on the part of certain Asian Christians, to the authority of the great apostle to the Gentiles (cf. Gal. 1.1; 2.7), has not John undermined any such authority by his insistence on only *twelve* apostles of the Lamb (Rev. 21.14), thus echoing those challenges to Paul's apostolic claim found elsewhere in the early period (e.g. 1 Cor. 9.1)?

A further divergence between Revelation and Paul is to be found in their respective attitudes to the Roman state per se. The Apocalypse represents an uncompromising attitude, 'unmasking' the satanic nature of the Empire in all its aspects, and warning fellow Christians of the dangers of its seductive charms (e.g. Rev. 19.4). Not only does Rome appear thinly veiled as Babylon, the infamous enemy of Israel and destroyer of Jerusalem (Rev. 17; cf. 1 Pet. 5.13; *4 Ezra* 3.1); she is also associated with the beast, the terrestrial ambassador of the diabolical Dragon. Whether written in the reign of Domitian or Galba, the Apocalypse demonizes the Roman Emperor as one of the seven heads of the beast (Rev. 17.10), contrasted negatively with 'our Lord and God' (4.11), the one who sits upon the throne, and with the Lamb, who is 'Lord of lords and King of kings' (17.14).

Such an uncompromising attitude is difficult to square with the Pauline injunction to 'be subject to the governing authorities' (Rom. 13.1),[50] an injunction which surely must have been understood by some of its first Roman hearers to include the current emperor, Nero. Admittedly, Paul is writing at an earlier period than John of Patmos,[51] and it is not impossible that later Roman antagonism towards Christians, including persecution, may have changed the minds of his disciples. However, in the first place, the evidence for first-century Roman persecution of Christians has been much overstated, and it is far from clear that Revelation arises out of such a situation.[52] Secondly, an

---

50. It has been proposed that this section of Romans is an interpolation, but such a proposal is not compelling: see J.A. Fitzmyer, *Romans* (AB, 33; Garden City, NY: Doubleday, 1993), pp. 662-65.

51. Depending upon which dating is preferred for Revelation, anything from between 10 and 40 years.

52. See L.L. Thompson, *The Book of Revelation: Apocalypse and Empire* (Oxford: Oxford University Press, 1990), for a radical reassessment of the Domitianic persecution theory.

equally favourable attitude towards the ruling authorities has survived in Pauline writings contemporary with, or even later than, John's Apocalypse (writings, moreover, which may well derive from the same geographical area),[53] namely, the Pastoral Epistles.

The first letter to Timothy, for example, apparently addressed to Ephesus, urges that, in public worship, 'supplications, prayers, inter-cessions, and thanksgivings be made for everyone, for kings and all who are in high positions, so that we may lead a quiet and peaceable life in all godliness and dignity' (1 Tim. 2.1-2). This is a far cry from Revelation's denunciation of the Roman Empire as Babylon the Great, seated on the beast! But it is an appropriate summary of a Pauline Christian stance marked by a positive use of Graeco-Roman household codes, and prepared to borrow insights from contemporary non-Christian philosophy and morality, advocating what some have called a Christianity of 'good citizenship'.[54]

I do not wish to claim that Revelation is explicitly attacking the ideology of 1 Timothy: the author of this epistle would have been even more reluctant to accept the prophetic ministry of 'Jezebel' than John (1 Tim. 2.12)! But the Pastorals do show the extent to which the Pauline tradition, spurred on by elements within Paul's own teaching, could foster a gospel of 'openness to the world' which other Christians might regard as unacceptable compromise, and this is partly echoed in the use of household codes in Colossians and Ephesians. Moreover, these same epistles testify that this attitude was present in certain Pauline circles in late first-century Asia. Such an attitude, present no less among the Asian followers of 'Balaam' and 'Jezebel', and possibly also the Nicolaitans, is one which the seer of Revelation roundly condemns.

Conclusion

Space has not allowed for a fuller exploration of the issues of common concern to Revelation and the Pauline tradition. Nor have I attempted

53. E.g. J.L. Houlden, *The Pastoral Epistles* (TPI New Testament Commentaries; London: SCM Press; Philadelphia: Trinity Press International, 1989), p. 44.

54. M. Dibelius and H. Conzelmann, *The Pastoral Epistles* (ed. H. Koester; Hermeneia; Philadelphia: Fortress Press, 1972). It has also been noted that the Pastorals, unlike the authentic Paulines, omit the mention of idolatry from their vice lists (compare, e.g., Rom. 1.29-31; 1 Cor. 5.10-11; 6.9-10; Gal. 5.16-24), and utilize vocabulary more at home in Hellenistic philosophical writings.

to pursue the equally important question of the relationship between the Apocalypse and the Johannine writings. Nevertheless, I have sought to show, however inadequately, some of the problems associated with the 'Pauline' identification of John of Patmos. The Asian picture, even allowing for developments throughout the New Testament period, is a complex one, suggesting a crossing of, and dynamic interplay between, traditions, rather than general opposition between them. Likewise, the situation in the churches addressed by Revelation is far from simple: admitting the simplest solution, John appears as a Jewish Christian prophet, whose disciples are undergoing hostility from fellow Jews on the one hand, and on the other, attempting to uphold principles enshrined in the Apostolic Decree (or something very like it), in the face of Christian accommodation to a society which he sees as increasingly 'Satanic'. But the situation was probably more complex than that, with different rival groups in the different churches (including rival 'apostles' in Ephesus), even if some of them shared common traits. In the midst of this, we find the prophet John, and likeminded Christians. They know themselves not to be 'of the world' (cf. Jn 17.16), even though they find themselves within the world. Though still considering themselves to be Jews, they can already speak of other synagogues as 'a synagogue of Satan'; how far removed is this from a Christian stance which can say, 'You are of your father the devil' (Jn 8.44)? If we must attach Tübingen labels, it would appear that John's main Christian opponents ('Balaam', 'Jezebel', perhaps the 'Nicolaitans') are the ones most appropriately described as 'Pauline', while he is the uncompromising 'Petrine' or 'Jacobite'. But do such labels really do justice to the rich tapestry of early Jewish and Christian practice and experience in the Province of Asia? Or do they serve to obscure the singular witness of John the seer on his Greek island, and, indeed, the uniqueness of the Johannine sheepfold?

THE TROUBLE WITH THE RESURRECTION

Trevor Williams

In an age of increasing specialization it might seem wise for a teacher of systematic theology to keep to his own territory and not venture into the heavily mined (in every sense of the word) fields of New Testament scholarship. This would certainly seem to be the most sensible course if he could claim as friend and colleague a New Testament scholar of such distinction as John Ashton, on whose learning he could call as often as it was needed. That has been my happy position, as a member not only of the same faculty, but of Trinity College, which has been privileged to claim John Ashton ever since his arrival in Oxford as College Lecturer in the New Testament.

However, specialist or not, no Christian theologian could ever rightly say that the New Testament was not his or her field. Those engaged in the task of trying to understand and to interpret Christian doctrine today must always engage not only with the text but with scholarly exegesis and interpretation of the New Testament, however troublesome that can be for those who would prefer to have sure and certain foundations on which to raise their doctrinal structures. This is especially true in relation to that central and yet utterly mysterious event described as the resurrection of Jesus, on which so much depends, but yet is so hard to fathom.

So in a collection to mark and celebrate John Ashton's sixty-fifth birthday, I hope he will be tolerant of my attempt to identify and grapple with the problems posed by the New Testament witness to the resurrection of Jesus.

These problems were brought into focus many years ago when there was a TV series on 'Jesus of Nazareth'. In a moving scene after the crucifixion, Jesus' almost naked body was laid in a tomb. But a few moments later he was shown seated in a room with his disciples. A little girl of seven or eight at the time at once asked, 'Where did he get his clothes from?!' I have not seen that particular point raised in print till recently by Paul Badham.[1] It's true that Westcott alludes to the question when he writes, 'A little reflection will show that the special outward forms in which the Lord was pleased to make himself known were no more necessarily connected with His glorified person than the robes which he wore',[2] but that simply evades the issue.

One might instinctively reply 'You're missing the point!' Maybe, but it's a perfectly fair question to put to those who uphold the empty tomb tradition and who, like Michael Ramsey, C.F.D. Moule and many others ascribe a spiritual body in some way continuous with his physical body to the risen Jesus. The idea of a spiritual body poses various familiar problems, such as how could it pass through locked doors yet eat fish, as Luke reports? What happened to the fish Jesus ate? More pointedly, what happened finally to the physical body Jesus died in and/or the spiritual body he rose in?[3] Christopher Rowland in the same volume seems to me to dodge the issue. He defends the empty tomb tradition and goes on to say, 'While not deterring the quest for answers to that kind of question, it seems to me that the New Testament indicates that our concerns ought to be primarily elsewhere.'[4] Of course! But those who do defend the empty tomb owe that little girl an answer. Without one, that tradition may be rather more open to question than Rowland appears to admit. Anyone advocating a strong version of physical resurrection certainly owes an answer. Stephen Davis argues one of the strongest. He goes so far as to say that not only was the tomb empty, but that the risen Jesus had a body that was not only touchable but would have shown up on a photograph![5] To his credit, he addresses a great many of the problems and objections to his views, but rather surprisingly not the question of clothes.

I do not think it will really do for John Muddiman to make attack the best defence, when he writes

> Jesus' tomb belonged to Joseph of Arimathea and was discovered empty by Mary of Magdala. It is almost impossible to deny the truth of these two

1. 'The Meaning of the Resurrection of Jesus', in P. Avis (ed.), *The Resurrection of Jesus Christ* (London: Darton, Longman and Todd, 1993), p. 28.
2. Quoted by A.M. Ramsey in *The Resurrection of Christ* (Glasgow: Fontana, 1961), p. 47.
3. Cf. Badham in Avis (ed.), *The Resurrection*, pp. 28-29.
4. P. Avis (ed.), 'Interpreting the Resurrection', in *The Resurrection*, p. 78.
5. S.T. Davis, *Risen Indeed: Making Sense of the Resurrection* (London: SPCK, 1993), p. 24.

points. For if so, we would have to suppose not just the wish fulfilment born of devotion, but deliberate falsification backed up by the invention of two quite fictitious characters.[6]

Davis even more strongly thinks that if there was no physical resurrection, then 'the first disciples were charlatans and dupes'.[7]

We need not think those are the only alternatives any more than we need think that the New Testament writers who used false names or invented stories were charlatans. To project our ideas of falsification to New Testament times would seem to be dangerously anachronistic. But if Muddiman's two points are to stand, where *did* Jesus get his clothes and what happened to them?

There are many other problems, which can be listed briefly, because they are familiar, and some of them at least may be open to solution. They come under two headings, biblical and doctrinal.

1. *Biblical*

Problem 1: On what day did the resurrection take place? Mk 8.31 reads 'The Son of Man must be killed, and after three days rise again'. That would suggest Monday. 'After three days' recurs on Jesus' lips again in Mk 9.31 and 10.33-34. Elsewhere as early as Paul in 1 Cor. 15.4 we have 'on the third day', which is not quite the same thing; perhaps it reflects an attempt at harmonization, or more likely the influence of Hos. 6.2, 'After two days he will revive us; on the third day he will raise us up, that we may live before him'. (Interestingly the Septuagint reads not 'he will raise us' but 'we shall arise'.) But 'on the third day' only works if Friday counts as the first day. Both Luke and Matthew changed Mark's 'after three days' into 'on the third day' (Mt. 16.21; 17.23; 20.19; Lk. 9.22; 18.33; 24.7) Yet Matthew reverts to 'after three days' in 27.63. In fact the time between the crucifixion on Friday afternoon till dawn on Sunday was barely 36 hours, a day and a half.

Problem 2: Where did the resurrection appearances take place? Mark hints at Galilee. Matthew puts the emphasis there. John 20 places them in Jerusalem, but John 21 in Galilee. Luke firmly locates them in Jerusalem. Paul tantalizingly does not say.

6. 'I Believe in the Resurrection of the Body', in S. Barton and G. Stanton (eds.), *Resurrection: Essays in Honour of Leslie Houlden* (London, 1994), p. 131.

7. Davis, *Risen Indeed*, p. 14.

Problem 3: In relation to the Jerusalem empty tomb stories, how many angels featured? Paul of course has no tomb or angels. The Gospels differ over their number or time of appearance. Mark has one young man dressed in white. Matthew has an earthquake and an angel descending from heaven, his arrival apparently witnessed by the women. Luke has two men in dazzling apparel; so does John, though they only appear and speak to Mary after Peter and the other disciple have been and gone—the latter interestingly believed before any heavenly vision.

Problem 4: How many women? Their names and numbers vary, though Mary Magdalen always features. Did they see the risen Lord in the garden? No, according to Mark, and also Luke, surprisingly, given his Jerusalem focus. Perhaps he wants to restore the disciples to pride of place despite their flight. In Matthew, equally surprisingly, given his Galilean focus, the women do meet and are addressed by Jesus near the tomb, though in a strangely superfluous way—just repeating the angel's message. In John, Jesus meets Mary Magdalen alone on her second visit.

Problem 5: The well-known fact that Paul does not mention any women at all in relation to appearances of Jesus, and adds others not mentioned in the Gospels, and of course himself in the same sequence.

Problem 6: I have already touched on the question of Jesus' spiritual body, which could apparently pass through locked doors. In which case why did the stone have to be moved from the entrance to the tomb, as reported in Mark, Luke, and John? Matthew offers a simple solution. The angel rolled away the stone in the women's presence to show that Jesus was not there, not to let him out. But just what is meant by 'spiritual body' and what sort of objectivity should be ascribed to it?

One might ask, if Caiaphas or Herod had been in the house opposite, could they have seen Jesus through the window in the upper room? We may well think not, if the appearance of the risen Lord and faith go together. Davis is at his weakest here. His suggestion that the risen Christ was photographable would seem to make his whole case suspect. Even Pannenberg accepts that the resurrection appearances were not visible to one and all,[8] but then what were they? What sort

8.   W. Pannenberg, *Jesus God and Man* (London: SCM, 1968), p. 99: 'Because the life of the resurrected Lord involves the reality of a new creation, the resurrected Lord is in fact not perceptible as one object among others in the world.'

of reality did Jesus' spiritual body have?

We are familiar of course with Paul's metaphor of the seed, 1 Cor. 15.36: 'what is sown is a physical body, what is raised is a spiritual body'. I cannot resist referring to a critique of this idea from an unusual source, an African chief called Commoro whom Sir Samuel Baker conversed with on his travels to find the source of the Nile, in about 1870.[9]

> Baker: 'Do you think that a good man and a bad must share the same fate, and alike die, and end?'
>
> Commoro: 'Yes; what else can they do? How can they help dying? Good and bad all die.'
>
> Baker: 'Their bodies perish, but their spirits remain; the good in happiness, the bad in misery. If you have no belief in a future state, *why should a man be good*? Why should he not be bad, if he can prosper by wickedness?'
>
> Commoro: 'Most people are bad; if they are strong they take from the weak; they are good because they are not strong enough to be bad.'

One doubts if Commoro had read Nietzsche—who was in any case barely 26 at the time! Baker continues:

> I tried the beautiful metaphor of St. Paul as an example of a future state. Making a small hole with my finger in the ground, I place a grain within it... I continued, 'That grain will decay, but from it will rise the plant that will produce a reappearance of the original form.'
>
> Commoro: 'Exactly so; that I understand. But the original grain does not rise again; it rots, like the dead man and is ended; the fruit produced is not the same grain that we buried, but the production of that grain; so it is with man—I die, and decay, and am ended, but my children will grow up like the fruit of the grain. Some men have no children, and some grains perish without fruit; then all are ended.'

Baker concludes: I was obliged to change the subject of conversation... Giving up the religious argument as a failure, I resolved upon more practical inquiries.

The conclusion to be drawn of course is that metaphor and religious imagery should not be taken too literally.

Problem 7: To return to the New Testament. Matthew poses another problem which we tend to evade. When Jesus was crucified there had been another earthquake, the rocks split and the graves opened, and

9.   Sir S. Baker, *Albert Nyanza, Great Basin of the Nile* (London: MacMillan and Co., 1877), pp. 157-58.

(preferring the RSV to the NEB's watered-down paraphrase), 'Many bodies of the saints who had fallen asleep were raised'. If Matthew can say that, one might think that he would not have had much difficulty with Jesus' risen body. Yet to his credit, although he lets the women grasp Jesus' feet in the garden, his final portrayal of Jesus on the mountain rises above any crude physicality.

Those are some but not all of the problems that arise from the biblical accounts. There are also doctrinal problems.

Problem 1: The resurrection is commonly linked to recognition of Jesus as Lord and God. But why should it be?[10] It is sometimes argued that, Jesus' life having ended in apparent failure, God raised him from the dead to vindicate him in the face of all that had happened. But that would suggest that God saw that Jesus had failed in terms of his earthly human ministry and had one last desperate throw, one last super miracle to salvage the disaster, to prove that Jesus was the Messiah after all!

But this sort of *deus ex machina* is not a Christ-like *deus* at all. This argument postulates not merely an interventionist God, but an interventionist God of the worst kind, who achieves by *tour de force* what could not be achieved by Jesus' keeping faithfully to his vocation. In effect, it betrays his and our humanity.

Problem 2: The second problem with a physical resurrection is that it seems also to involve a miracle that looks like a conjuring trick (to echo the former Bishop of Durham) which can then all too often be appealed to so as to legitimate every kind of irrationalism and superstition: 'If the miracle of resurrection is possible then any kind of miracle is possible'. There is then no need for critical reflection in the light of our present scientific understanding or of a profounder understanding of religious language as metaphor and symbol. Instead, the argument seems to be, if you can believe the resurrection you can believe anything—any miracle. This appears to be at the heart of N.T. Wright's argument.[11] Despite his protestations that the resurrection does not open the door to a miscellaneous appeal to the supernatural and despite his edifying words about the challenge of a new worldview grounded on the resurrection, he uses it to defend belief in a literal virginal conception. 'We can't satisfy post-enlightenment

---

10. B. Hebblethwaite raises this question in 'The Resurrection and Incarnation', in Avis (ed.), *The Resurrection*, p. 157.

11. N.T. Wright, *Who Was Jesus?* (London: SPCK, 1992), p. 82.

scepticism,' he says, 'But in the light of the resurrection we are called to be sceptical about scepticism itself.'[12] Well, yes and no! Stephen Davis admits that two radically different worldviews are in conflict. So does Michael Ramsey,[13] but merely because both can be argued rationally does not mean that the one that accords most closely to a literal reading of the text has the best claim to be accepted.

Maybe if you can believe in the resurrection, you can believe anything; the trouble is that if you can't, you can't. The resurrection may indeed be fundamental to Christian faith and life, but a misrepresentation of it may be a fundamental and unnecessary obstacle to Christian faith and life. To suggest, as Michael Ramsey does, that 'if the evidence is pointing us towards a miracle, we will not be troubled' is to gloss too easily over real difficulties.[14]

Problem 3: A third doctrinal problem is that, taken as it stands, Jesus' resurrection to glory, especially if he is identified with the pre-existent Son and Second Person of the Trinity, can result in his sojourn on earth being regarded as an unpleasant interlude in his heavenly existence, necessary for him to do what he had to do to deal with sin and death, but now happily behind him. So his followers can share in his present glory, and justify the triumphalism that has tarnished the church for so long, as Leslie Houlden has remarked. He criticizes the common tendency (since Luke wrote his Gospel!) 'to see Jesus' resurrection as somehow cancelling his death and ensuring that the story has a happy ending'. He also criticizes 'that kind of attention to "the risen Christ", as an independent object of devotion, which is the breeding ground of all manner of triumphalism, the nourisher of qualities the very reverse of those that mark the life of Jesus'.[15]

But are these problems real problems, or are we somehow missing the point because we have allowed ourselves to be misled by the Gospel accounts and by our historical methodology, as Carnley intimates?[16]

It is widely accepted now that Mk 16.1-8 is the primary source for the story of the empty tomb, and that the discrepancies in Matthew

12. Wright, *Who Was Jesus?*, p. 85.
13. Ramsey, *The Resurrection*, p. 56.
14. Ramsey, *The Resurrection*, p. 57.
15. J.L. Houlden, *Connections* (London: SCM Press, 1986), pp. 150-51.
16. P. Carnley, *The Structure of Resurrection Belief* (Oxford: Oxford University Press, 1987), p. 25.

and Luke are to be explained as kerygmatic and apologetic expansions of the Markan original.[17] Within these expansions one sees an increasing concretization of the risen Lord, in Luke especially. His motive may have been anti-docetic, but the result is to bring Jesus back into mundane history[18]—not completely, as elements of the supernatural do of course remain in Luke's account, but too much. In effect, Luke's resurrection account re-historicizes Jesus with the result that he has to de-historicize him again with the ascension, an episode not needed in the other Gospels where Jesus' resurrection is left a mystery, as in Mark, or is much more closely tied to his exaltation, as in Matthew (and in a different way in John).

But Luke has set the trap into which historical critics fall by presenting the resurrection as if it were, even if only temporarily, an event in mundane history open to the methods of historical investigation; so that such questions as 'Was the tomb empty?' and 'What kind of body did he have?' and 'What happened to his clothes?' can be raised as the object of empirical enquiry, rather than in terms of what religious meaning might be derived from these accounts viewed as symbolic vehicles of truth, as Robert Morgan suggests they should be.[19]

Insistence on the objective historical character of the resurrection traditions in Luke's day and in our own would seem to have at least one thing in common: a concern to emphasize the reality of the resurrection against any kind of docetism. That was almost certainly one of three factors at work in Luke's account, and it may indeed have served that purpose well. It does not follow that this is the only way or the right way by which that purpose can be served now. A second factor may have been a conscious or unconscious resort to the rapture motif which would be familiar to a Roman audience.

This is suggested by Edward Schillebeeckx and taken up by Spong. To quote the latter,[20] 'In this model, when a pious or heroic person

17. Carnley, *The Structure of Resurrection Belief*, p. 46.

18. Carnley, *The Structure of Resurrection Belief*, p. 76.

19. 'Flesh is Precious: The Significance of Luke 24:36-43', in Barton and Stanton (eds.), *Resurrection*, p. 18.

20. J.S. Spong, *Resurrection, Myth or Reality?* (San Francisco, 1994), pp. 76-77. Cf. E. Schillebeeckx, *Jesus: An Experiment in Christology* (London: Collins, 1979), pp. 340-44. 'The "rapture" motif eases the Greek conception of Christian resurrection'.

died, all of his or her earthly remains would disappear totally, because that person was believed to have been snatched up to heaven… (whence) this now divine life would regularly materialize', as 'recognizably human', 'especially to those carrying out the earthly work of the departed one'. In one Roman story the glorified Romulus revealed that Caesar was 'Lord of the world'. Thus Luke's counter-claim would be 'not Caesar but Jesus'. Spong concludes: 'In the service of this image Luke had to recast the resurrection tradition. It would never be the same after Luke had finished his work.'

A third factor can be illustrated with the analogy of the title 'messiah' in the Caesarea Philippi episode.[21] Peter calls Jesus 'messiah', and is blessed, according to Mt. 16.17. Peter then remonstrates over Jesus' talk of suffering and death and earns the incredibly violent rebuke 'Away with you, Satan. You think as men think and not as God thinks!' In other words, Jesus seems to be saying 'You are right to call me messiah if that means you respond to me as the agent of God's kingdom. But if so, you'll have to redefine messiahship in terms of what I am and do. Don't try to force me into traditional messianic preconceptions about military victory and worldly triumphs.'

This serves or should serve as a warning to those over-inclined to think that the resurrection has to be understood strictly in terms of Jewish or Pharisaic preconceptions. Something obviously happened, and one of the best words to express it was 'resurrection', but it was not the only option. As often noted, 'resurrection' does not appear in Hebrews. In Tillich's terms, the cross is event before it is symbol, the resurrection is symbol before it is event.[22] In other words, 'resurrection', like 'messiah', is a symbol of Jewish hope. Like 'messiah', when it is applied to the event of Jesus, it is both blessed and condemned. It can express the reality of hope fulfilled and life transformed better perhaps than any other word. It can also, like 'messiah', intrude into that event undeconstructed concepts of hope and ideas about Jesus, and indeed preconceptions about God, which need radical reconstruction if we are not to go on thinking 'as men think'. Indeed one of the worst troubles with the resurrection may be that it drags God back into undeconstructed human preconceptions at the very moment when, in and through Jesus, he was about to die to his old self and rise in Christ. I speak figuratively of course. What

21. Carnley, *The Structure of Resurrection Belief*, p. 53.
22. P. Tillich, *Systematic Theology* (London: SCM Press, 1978), II, p. 153.

were to die were human misconceptions about messiahship and therefore about God. Perhaps the former, messiahship, did die and rise
transformed to some extent. In the latter case, traditional ideas about
God were not allowed to 'die'—to be surrendered, and so did not have
the chance to rise anew, transformed.

And Luke, I am suggesting, may have helped to contribute to this
failure by not letting the concept of resurrection 'die' with Christ. He
pushes the risen Lord back into Roman or Jewish preconceptions that
have saddled the church not just with the mystery that is proper but
with semi-superstitious or mythological ideas that are a barrier to the
mission of the Christ and too big a concession to 'Satan'. Hence when
Tom Wright[23] affirms the church's belief that 'Jesus was the true and
final revelation of the one true God of Jewish monotheism', I can only
say a very big 'yes' and an almost equally big 'no'. Marcion had a
point though he put it badly.[24]

So I can only half agree with Christopher Rowland when he says 'I
believe it is impossible to understand the resurrection in the New
Testament without resorting to the future hope of Second Temple
Judaism'. He continues, 'Early Christianity shared with the Pharisees a
belief in the resurrection of the dead (Acts 23.6), but regarded this as
fulfilled in the case of the Messiah, but awaiting completion for the
rest of humanity.'[25] But if that fulfilment did not make all the difference, it should have done. If the early Christians could not escape far
enough from their existing worldview, we can sympathize, but need
not therefore tie ourselves to it.

Now Rowland may be right to say that the early Christians could
have talked about exaltation without mentioning resurrection, but his
examples of Enoch and Elijah are scarcely relevant. Unlike them,
Jesus had just been killed publicly. Certainly he could hardly be
exalted if he was still considered dead in every sense of the word.
Hebrews fully recognizes Christ's death, and so his rising to life in
some sense is indeed implicit in his Lordship, but not resurrection as

23. Wright, *Who Was Jesus?*, p. 75.
24. The influential second-century heretic who overstated the discontinuity
between the God of the Old Testament and the God revealed in Christ and was condemned by the church. See G. Filoramo, *A History of Gnosticism* (Oxford:
Blackwell, 1990), pp. 164-66.
25. 'Interpreting the Resurrection', in Avis (ed.), *The Resurrection*, p. 70.

portrayed in Luke: not a return to mundane history, let alone with an empty tomb.

It may be that resurrection talk arose as a seemingly natural consequence of exaltation talk, just as talk of an empty tomb was probably consequential on resurrection talk. Barnabas Lindars[26] and Anthony Harvey[27] make much the same point. Trouble comes when consequential talk takes on a life of its own, so to speak. Then we get what Lindars[28] and Tillich[29] call rationalizations and Leslie Houlden calls dispersal of belief.[30] We see a shift from 'God raised Jesus from the dead' to 'Jesus doing his own rising' and taking centre stage in a quasi-historical drama instead of being given centre place in the divine drama. As Spong writes, 'The importance of the tomb was no longer a sign that Jesus was reigning in heaven by the action of God, but a sign that the deceased person had come out of the tomb and was a walking, talking and eating person who was back in life as one who had been resuscitated.'[31] To add Spong's later comment, '[i]f resurrection cannot be believed except by assenting to fantastic descriptions in the Gospels, then Christianity is doomed!'[32] Possibly.

In contrast, Pannenberg asserts, '[i]f this [argument for the resurrection of Jesus] collapses, so does everything else which the Christian Faith acknowledges'![33] And for good measure to quote Westcott as quoted approvingly by Michael Ramsey, '[i]t is evident that if the claim to be a miraculous religion is essentially incredible, Apostolic Christianity is simply false'.[34] But perhaps Christianity can survive our ideas about it better than we imagine!

Turning to the insistence in our own day on the objective historical character of the resurrection traditions, this may well stem from anti-docetic concerns again, the fear that the only alternative is to surrender to the subjective vision or hallucination theories of Strauss and his

26. 'The Resurrection and the Empty Tomb', in Avis (ed.), *The Resurrection*, p. 129.
27. 'They Discussed Among Themselves what this "Rising from the Dead" Could Mean (Mark 9:10)', in Barton and Stanton (eds.), *Resurrection*, p. 75.
28. Avis (ed.), *The Resurrection*, p. 119.
29. Tillich, *Systematic Theology*, II, p. 127.
30. Avis (ed.), *The Resurrection*, pp. 61-62.
31. Spong, *Resurrection*, p. 82.
32. Spong, *Resurrection*, p. 238.
33. Pannenberg, *The Apostles' Creed* (London: SCM Press, 1972), p. 97.
34. Ramsey, *The Resurrection*, p. 37.

followers. But to see this as the only alternative is perhaps to betray
the fact that one is still in the Lukan trap, and offering the only alternative which would be acceptable to the historical critic on his or her
own terms.

This I think is what Francis Watson is getting at when he says that

> a revisionist interpretation of the event of the resurrection in terms of the
> disciples' experience of renewal has in effect rejected Marcan reserve by
> locating this event within the general category of 'religious experience',
> thereby asserting its essential clarity and intelligibility to critical reason.
> But then it becomes a fundamentally different event to the one that is just
> beyond the bounds of the Marcan narrative.[35]

It might not be as alarming as some people seem to imagine if we
suppose that human psychology was and is involved in relation to the
resurrection. Nevertheless, what resurrection signifies may involve
much more than mere subjectivism without having to be miraculously
materialistic. A recurrent fault of so-called 'objectivists' is their
assumption that God is on their side and that any supposedly subjective
account is necessarily reductionist. But I do not see why a God who is
thought to be able to act objectively in the most miraculous way is
deemed to be unable to act subjectively, i.e. in human subjects, in a
way that is miraculous but in a different mode.

Be that as it may, it is interesting that biblical critics have recently
been suggesting not merely the priority of Mark's resurrection
account and its expansion in the other Gospels, but also that the
primary theme of the resurrection in the New Testament was the exaltation of Jesus to heaven, by the divine act of God, hence his vindication. Inevitably this was expressed, and one might say experienced, in
terms of Jewish apocalyptic hope. Returning to the foundational theme
of heavenly vindication may allow us to cast off or at least loosen the
mooring lines that have tied the resurrection too closely to mundane
history and so allowed too much legendary or mythical material to be
attached to it and then to be taken too literally.

Schillebeeckx in fact argues that the most primitive strand in the
New Testament (the speeches in Acts in particular) simply proclaim
Jesus' vindication in the face of victimization by the religious lead-
ers.[36] The second primitive note presents Jesus as the passive subject

35. '"He is not here": Towards a Theology of the Empty Tomb', in Barton and
Stanton (eds.), *Resurrection*, p. 101.
36. Schillebeeckx, *Jesus*, pp. 274, 278-80.

of God's resurrecting action, which in Spong's words 'meant that resurrection was seen not as a resurrection back into life but as an exaltation of Jesus into God and God's heaven by God's divine action'.[37]

Barnabas Lindars argues that Mark 'preserves the sense that the
resurrection is a theological statement about Jesus rather than an item
in his life story'.[38] Francis Watson in his talk of Markan reserve goes
on to say that

> [t]he manner of narration suggests an ultimacy which in Mark is left
> undefined, while in Matthew's narrative it eventually takes shape in the
> commission to make disciples of all nations, baptizing them in the name of
> Father, Son and Holy Spirit, and in the promise of the risen Jesus' eternal
> presence.[39]

Anthony Harvey is the strongest advocate of the view that heavenly
vindication is the heart of the matter: 'The more profoundly one
believed in Jesus, the more firmly one would believe that this vindication had taken place. No resurrection (*outside heaven*) [my emphasis]
would be necessary.'[40] He reminds us that there is no mention of resurrection in Philippians 2 or Hebrews, and that it plays no part in the
argument of Peter's sermon in Acts 3. 'No belief in the resurrection
[into earthly life, one might add] is called for; only that the Christ,
after his suffering, is now in heaven ready to return.'

Harvey suggests that 'resurrection' came to prominence because of
the happy ambiguity of the Greek word *anastasis*. It could convey the
immediate personal experience of the witnesses that Jesus had returned
to life, and 'the faith of all his followers that...he had been vindicated
by God and given a place in heaven'.[41]

This leaves us with three important questions to be considered.
First, in the light of what has been said, are there any solutions to the
problems posed earlier? Where did he get his clothes? And can we say
any more about how and why the Gospels were written as they have
been written?

Secondly, what started it all off? What happened that had such a
tremendous impact on Jesus' followers? Can we get anywhere near the
source? Despite Morgan's counsel of caution that '[i]t seems better to

37. Spong, *Resurrection*, p. 119.
38. Avis (ed.), *The Resurrection*, p. 131.
39. Barton and Stanton (eds.), *Resurrection*, p. 104.
40. Barton and Stanton (eds.), *Resurrection*, p. 73.
41. Barton and Stanton (eds.), *Resurrection*, p. 77.

insist that how the disciples became convinced of God's vindication of
Jesus is a secondary question which cannot be answered for sure',[42]
can we answer it all?

Thirdly, where and how do *we* stand in relation to that event?

To return to the biblical problems: both 'after three days' and 'on
the third day' may be interpreted in conventional Jewish terms in
accordance with the Scriptures (1 Cor 15.4) as a short period of time,
which posed no problem until the empty tomb tradition established
itself. Until then the location of the resurrection experience in Galilee
could be accepted without any trouble, and its date left open. But that
Peter and also Mary Magdalen were involved in an originating experience would seem hard to deny.

It may be hard to decide between different explanations of the
empty tomb, if it is not historical, but the crucial point would be to
see it as consequential to resurrection faith, and not its source or necessarily part and parcel of it, as James Dunn has rather unconvinc-
ingly argued.[43]

By consequential I mean that it might seem to have followed necessarily from the gospel message 'Jesus lives', taken too simply in this-
worldly terms: 'If he has been raised to life then he can't still be in a
tomb'. Ps. 16.10 in the Septuagint could reinforce the idea that Jesus'
body did not suffer corruption ('Neither wilt thou suffer thy holy one
to see corruption', in contrast to the Hebrew '...let thy godly one see
the pit'). This psalm is quoted in Acts 13.35 and seemingly misquoted
in Acts 2.31.

This logic might have facilitated the transfer of the resurrection
scenario from Galilee to Jerusalem. Jesus died in Jerusalem and was
buried there. So presumably his tomb, if he had a tomb, is there, and
if he is alive, it must be empty. But where is it? By now nobody
knows, but to contribute my own piece of speculation, perhaps Joseph
of Aramathea offers his own *unused* tomb as a meeting place for a
symbolic celebration, at Easter, or possibly more regularly on the
first day of the week, very early, and with no worries that Sunday is
only two days after Friday. Only later might one try to harmonize by
changing the formula to 'on the third day'.

Carnley hesitates over the idea of a liturgy at the tomb, because this

42. Barton and Stanton (eds.), *Resurrection*, p. 12.
43. J.D.G. Dunn, *The Evidence for Jesus* (London: SCM Press, 1985),
pp. 65-69.

explanation has to overcome a natural Jewish revulsion from tombs as unclean places,[44] but this problem would not arise if, as I suggest, an unused tomb was provided by the man who does feature in all the Gospel accounts. In any case Lindars refers to Jewish evidence for tomb gatherings held outside the tomb of a loved one to show respect.[45]

The involvement of the women is another contentious issue. It is often argued that this must be historical because women's testimony was not valid in Jewish Law, so why invent such an embarrassing anomaly? As Hebblethwaite writes, this was 'a detail no one would invent in a culture which despised the testimony of women'.[46] But that argument would only have force if one accepted the historicity of the resurrection appearances in Jerusalem two or three days after Jesus' crucifixion, when of course Jewish cultural conventions would still have prevailed. But we know from Paul's letters how quickly women came to play a leading role in the Christian community. Are we to think of it remaining so rigidly tied to the Jewish Law and custom at the later date when these stories may have emerged? On this interpretation one might understand why, although Paul makes no mention of women, they could play such a prominent part in the resurrection stories at the later date when the Gospels were written.

There is much to suggest that women, Mary Magdalen in particular, were close to the original resurrection experience, which may explain why they were accorded a significant role in the early Christian community. This role, as Leslie Houlden suggests,[47] was reflected in the stories written later in the Gospels, despite women's absence from Paul's list. The women's testimony is only an anomaly and therefore 'uninventable' if it is tied to an empty tomb event immediately after the crucifixion, not if the story of the women emerged in the later Christian community where women were held in high respect.

Their involvement in those later stories may also have been felt necessary to fill the gap left by the fleeing disciples. Mark left them in flight, Matthew finds them in Galilee, Luke covers their shame and keeps them in Jerusalem, but by now the women are safely in the story and need not be excluded.

The very notion of burial is not as straightforward as it sounds. The

44. Carnley, *The Structure of Resurrection Belief*, p. 50.
45. Avis (ed.), *The Resurrection*, p. 129.
46. Avis (ed.), *The Resurrection*, p. 158.
47. Houlden, *Connections*, p. 147.

allusion in 1 Corinthians 15 certainly does not imply that Paul knew of an empty tomb. 'Burial' might well be taken as simply confirming death. There is no instance in the Old or New Testaments where a dead person who has been buried is raised to life, apart from Lazarus, an exception that does indeed prove the rule. And as Spong notes,[48] there is the surprising passage in Acts 13.29 where Paul ascribes Jesus' burial to the rulers of Jerusalem who had him killed: 'They took him down from the gibbet and laid him in a tomb'. This does not quite fit the account in Luke as well as in the other Gospels of Joseph of Aramathea taking the initiative for burial, having opposed Jesus' crucifixion.

If we do locate the original Easter experience in Galilee, then there is a price to pay. The empty tomb, the angels, the women's visits, Thomas, the physical appearances and the clothes all follow the wise men, the shepherds and the angels out of actual history. Was their inclusion in the first place a result of misguided speculation at best, or a gross act of falsification at worst? Spong finds a much more positive answer by attributing it all to midrash. N.T. Wright dismisses the idea out of hand, 'Spong has followed a blind alley to a dead end. The Gospels are not Midrash.'[49] Michael Ramsey at least allows the possibility of its use in Matthew. But even if the Gospels are not midrash, it does not follow that Spong was wrong about the creative input of the Gospel writers. If it is not midrash, what is it when Matthew attaches the journey to Egypt to Hos. 11.1, or when, as John Fenton argues, they engage in their different ways in answering the question, 'Where is Jesus now?'[50]

And finally, what did really happen? I will offer a tentative answer, not with the conviction that it is right, but as a possible solution to some of my troubles. First, I assume that whatever resurrection is, it is revelation of the Lordship of Christ. Revelation is, as Tillich rightly said, two-sided, fact and reception. For that reason alone Caiaphas would not have seen anything through the window, nor I suspect would we, because we have not been shaped in the same Jewish apocalyptic mould. And because we are all different anyway, no single account could do justice to the reality which can never be identical for

48. Spong, *Resurrection*, p. 224.

49. Wright, *Who Was Jesus?*, p. 73.

50. 'The Four Gospels: Four Perspectives on the Resurrection', in Avis (ed.), *The Resurrection*, p. 49.

any two people. As Peter Selby rightly argues, single accounts are ruled out.[51] Yet despite our diversity, we do also share a common milieu, and there may be ways of articulating the resurrection that can speak to us in community and not in isolation, especially as what we are as human beings is persons in relationship.

This then is my final suggestion. Jesus mysteriously broke the mould of existence, the inherited mould in which not only human beings, society, and religion, but even God, or at least ideas of God, had been shaped. Jesus lived and spoke for his vision of God and by doing so shattered the humanly constructed conceptual obstacles which barred humanity from God and hid God from humanity and concealed true human being from itself. In so doing he opened the floodgates for the divine Spirit to pour into the human spirit—into those at least who let themselves be broken open and allowed themselves to be filled with the divine. This was an experience which was only possible for those who acknowledged Jesus the Christ as exalted Lord. In other words, it could only make sense if Jesus' name, his very being was at one with. the ultimate source of being. If that is true, then Jesus is involved in every resurrection experience. Resurrection is not just something in the life of his disciples. Jesus sharing the life of God is not left behind, dead and buried, even if his body is still in an unmarked grave.

This I suggest is far from subjectivism in the usual reductionist sense, when it is taken to refer to the natural response of some already existing human subject. Resurrection experience is conditional on a Good Friday experience, on the shattering of the subject, its death, before it could begin to experience the new possibilities of life. A shattering fact had to precede the transforming reception. If something like that happened to Peter and Mary Magdalen, and Paul, and many others at the time, perhaps it is not wholly removed from what can happen to human beings today, even in Oxford!

The trouble with the resurrection is that we do not like having our moulds broken, or to put it another way, being stripped bare and being offered new clothes.

51. Quoted by Paul Avis in 'The Resurrection of Jesus: Asking the Right Questions', in Avis (ed.), *The Resurrection*, p. 7.

Ἰωάννης συγκοινωνός...

Christopher Rowland

As friendships develop, there are sometimes issues which tend to be ignored as other matters of common concern are pursued. So points of difference get put on one side, perhaps because the areas of mutual interest are such that there is little need to accentuate what might divide rather than what unites. In two areas I am aware that we have not yet sat down and explored our differences: the importance of the liberationist perspective and the centrality of historical exegesis.

Ever since I gave my inaugural lecture (which was in effect an attempt to marry what I had learnt from liberation theology with the historical method in which I had been formed) I have wanted to have a conversation about some of its hermeneutical implications, particularly in the light of your valedictory lectures in Oxford during Trinity Term 1996.[1] That course of lectures on history and exegesis has given me an opportunity to begin to explore some of the differences between us, discussion of which, I hope, will be part of conversations in the years ahead.

You firmly believe that study of the meaning of an ancient text is not only a legitimate object of enquiry (as I do), but also the essential prerequisite *before* the exegete embarks on contemporary application. In *Studying John* you put the matter as follows:

> ...the old distinction between meaning and meaning for must be upheld. Feminists and liberationists, and any whose programme is based on or prompted by current ethical concerns—whether or not these have a direct biblical input—may be perfectly entitled to seek for further inspiration and encouragement in the Bible itself. They will have their own agenda and will usually, no doubt, focus their attention upon texts they think likely to yield some dividends, by way of inspiration or argument, to the cause they are eager to promote. But in so doing they should not pretend that they are attempting to *understand* the biblical text. Provided that they

1. Also in *Studying John* (Oxford: Oxford University Press, 1994).

declare their interest openly, having already decided what they wish to find in the text (resembling the majority of Christian readers in the pre-critical era), then they may go their own way without fear of being disturbed by any of the findings of traditional exegesis. The two tracks may be parallel but they will never converge.[2]

You suggest that exegesis involves two steps: understanding and interpretation. I agree with you in this but think that the order should be reversed: interpretation, finding meaning in texts (with all that this involves in terms of 'reading in' via illustrative parallels or the insight of experience) is always going to be an experimental affair which will run the risk of misunderstanding in the quest of understanding. Understanding, knowledge of what ourselves, a text or even God may be, is a quest, an eschatological goal.

Liberation theologians (and I along with them) would want to dispute your twin-track approach, which may be neat and tidy but masks the extent to which in 'traditional exegesis' contemporary issues motivate the interpretative agenda,[3] and runs the risk of ignoring the difficulties which attend our attempts to understand the text on its own terms. What is more, it seems to me that understanding a text may be enhanced by the process of application (to put it simply: how you live or act conditions the way in which you interpret). Critical reflection enables us to become aware of at least some of our prejudices and to make allowances for them in our interpretation. That is just one way of learning to read with an attentiveness to possible socio-economic and psychological conditions in contemporary culture and is the basis of the art of criticism. Like you, I think that a shared human predicament enables a degree of resonance between biblical texts and readers. If our interpretation of a text depends on 'getting it right first', we shall, I think, inevitably find ourselves resorting to the experts who can adjudicate on this until such time as we acquire skills which enable us to understand rather than misunderstand a text. At the heart of liberation theology is the conviction that the experts may not always be

2. Ashton, *Studying John*, pp. 206-207. Your contrast between understanding and application is paralleled (though coming from a very different philosophical starting point) in Nick Wolterstorff's distinction between 'authorial discourse interpretation' and 'performance interpretation' in his 1993 Wilde Lectures, *Divine Discourse* (Cambridge: Cambridge University Press, 1995).

3. This is one of the points made by Nicholas Lash in his essay 'What Might Martyrdom Mean?', in his collection *Theology on the Way to Emmaus* (London: SCM Press, 1988).

in the best position to understand. This is the implication of that amusing incident recorded in the Anabaptist chronicle, the *Martyrs' Mirror*, which I quoted at the beginning of my inaugural lecture in 1992.

In Flanders, in the middle of the sixteenth century, a chandler called Jacob was detained for his Anabaptist activities and subsequently questioned by a certain Friar Cornelis in the presence of the recorder and clerk of the local court. During the discussion Jacob quoted the book of Revelation in support of his views which provoked a heated response from his interrogator:

> 'What do you understand about St. John's Apocalypse?' the friar asked the chandler. 'At what university did you study? At the loom, I suppose? For I understand that you were nothing but a poor weaver and chandler before you went around preaching and rebaptizing... I have attended the university of Louvain, and for long studied divinity, and yet I do not understand anything at all about St John's Apocalypse. This is a fact.' To which Jacob answered: 'Therefore Christ thanked his heavenly Father that he had revealed and made it known to babes and hid it from the wise of this world, as it is written in Mt. 11.25.' 'Exactly!' the friar replied, 'God has revealed it to the weavers at the loom, to the cobblers on the bench, and to bellow-menders, lantern tinkers, scissors grinders, brass makers, thatchers and all sorts of riff-raff, and poor, filthy and lousy beggars. And from us ecclesiastics who have studied from our youth, night and day, God has concealed it.'[4]

What is particularly disconcerting is the implication that the academic endeavour might not, in some instances at least, offer an understanding of the text and that one who is engaged in 'meaning for' (like Jacob the chandler and the readers in the basic ecclesial communities of Latin America) might, in certain circumstances, be better equipped to understand the text.

Of course, what can never be excluded, nor should it be ignored, is the role of experts in enabling those like Jacob to hear or read the Bible in the first place. So the comparison of the biblical manuscripts with manuscripts from the ancient world, which has enabled us to make sense of the vocabulary and syntax of the Bible, remains indispensable. The texts we read, in Greek and even more in translation, are themselves the product of intellectual activity in the modern world. However much some of us want to promote grassroots Bible study as

---

4.	The passage from *Martyrs' Mirror* is quoted in my '"Open thy Mouth for the Dumb": A Task for the Exegete of Holy Scripture', *Biblical Interpretation* 1 (1993), pp. 228-45.

an indispensable foundation for Christian pedagogy, it is impossible entirely to write that dimension out of the hermeneutical script.

You suggest that one cannot be an exegete unless one is also a historian and suggest that a major weakness of some current biblical criticism is a neglect of the situation in which a document was written. Since the understanding of texts is a complicated business, we need all the help we can get. So to forego the insights of historical research is to deprive ourselves of an important dimension of study because it happens to be problematic. But I have some qualms about the relationship between history and exegesis. First of all, there is often not a sufficient recognition of the extent of the circularity in which we are involved when we engage in historical exegesis of the New Testament. There is no escape from this and we need to be constantly aware of the various, necessary, *eisegetical* measures which are required to make sense of a text.

I have grown increasingly uneasy about neat distinctions between exegesis and eisegesis. Without some of the latter the former is impossible. Barth is, I think, in this respect absolutely right: 'why should parallels drawn from the ancient world be of more value for our understanding of the epistle than the situation in which we ourselves actually are and to which we can therefore bear witness?'[5] Why, indeed. And yet the skills of the exegete can help the readers to see what they are doing with the text and point to the alternatives; to remind those who may want to use the text in a more allusive or allegorical manner that attention to the letter may yield a rather different sense. Indeed, I suspect that attention to the particulars of the text continues to be an exegete's major function, thereby placing a check on easy systematisation or a use which fails to recognise the awkwardness of the biblical text in all its diversity.

That exercise in pursuing the literal sense of the text is to be separated from the historical method. Indeed, the latter seems to be much more akin to the allegorical method of the ancient church.[6] The extant literature is used in the imaginative reconstruction of the life of particular Christian communities, another story which functions as a

---

5. K. Barth, *The Epistle to the Romans* (ET; Oxford: Oxford University Press, 1933), p. 11.

6. See J. Barr, 'The Literal, the Allegorical, and Modern Biblical Scholarship', *JSOT* 44 (1989), pp. 3-17, but cf. B. Childs, 'Critical Reflections on James Barr's Understanding of the Literal and the Allegorical', *JSOT* 46 (1990), pp. 3-9.

determining commentary on the literal sense of the text. The biblical texts become a window onto the life of the church in which characters in a text can become ciphers for different groups. One might just-ifiably view this approach as a modern form of spiritualising or alle-gorical exegesis, though of course the referent to the hidden story is history rather than the higher truths of divinity. Historical study is at heart an exercise in comparative literature. It is a process which needs careful handling. The parallels which are trotted out so readily by us all in our commentaries on the New Testament do manifest at times a 'parallelomania' which may obscure rather than assist interpretation.

Why should a text, merely because it is contemporary with, say, Revelation, be any more illuminating than a piece of eighteenth- or even twentieth-century prophecy? I think that reading William Blake is more likely to enable me understand Revelation than reading the Mishnah, and that understanding the mind-set of the antinomian radi-cals of English protestantism will better equip me to get into the minds of Paul and his converts than will hours spent poring over contemporary Hellenistic and Jewish texts. This may reflect not only certain assumptions that I make about the affinity in religious and political terms between Blake's writing and parts of the New Testa-ment, but also the challenge I find in his work to engage the imagina-tion in reading, to often shunned by mainstream exegesis.[7]

Blake's work may assist our New Testament exegesis in other ways too. Because we have access to so much more material on the late eighteenth century we are able to catch a glimpse of the complex rela-tionship between history and myth. Take Blake's allusions to con-temporary events in his Continental Prophecies. Eighteenth-century historical events are taken up into the imagination to form part of the prophetic narrative which transcends the particularity of the late first or eighteenth centuries.[8] Precise allusions cease to be of importance for understanding the general drift of the text. In 'America' Washing-ton, Franklin, Paine and Warren, for example, who appear as symbols of a colony's resistance and harbingers of change, have ceased to be historical personages but have become part of that awesome scene of upheaval which Blake conjures up in his imaginary, yet profoundly

7. There are some pertinent comments in N. Frye, *Fearful Symmetry: A Study of William Blake* (Princeton: Princeton University Press, 1947).

8. D. Erdman, *Blake: Prophet against Empire* (Princeton: Princeton University Press, 1977), p. 217.

insightful, description of the unpredictable effects of revolutionary change. There is no neat correlation between text and reality, and for that matter no denying the problematic character of the construal of that relationship.[9]

Gershom Scholem appreciated the greater significance of much later ideas and historical movements for interpreting Christianity when he noted the parallels between the messianism of the Sabbatian movement in the seventeenth century and early Christianity.[10] One of the prime reasons for distinguishing the early Christian literature, particularly the New Testament, from most of the ancient literature known to us is that this material represents the ideology of a group which had ceased merely to express certain beliefs as articles of faith but also now asserted that some of the apparatus of Jewish eschatology was now in the process of fulfilment. While the messianic beliefs of the early Christians did not in the main diverge too widely from those shared by other groups, the fact that the early Christians believed that they were either actually living in the eschatological age, or were very close to it, meant that their focus of attention and their way of handling those common features of the tradition would have been bound to be different. Thus, the fact that hope was in the process of fulfilment gave that group a particular distinctiveness for which the mere citation of parallels can hardly do justice.

While the specific messianic and eschatological beliefs in the New Testament are not particularly unusual (a point reputedly made by Paul in Acts 23), the conviction that these beliefs had been fulfilled led to the Christian movement ending up with rather different conclusions about the meaning of the tradition as compared with others of their contemporaries. The charismatic or messianic movement, which we believe early Christianity to have been, probably made it prone not only to schism but also to idiosyncratic interpretations of the Bible. It is in this area in particular that the investigation of similar millennial movements is so important.[11] It is a pity that study of millenarian movements among those scholars who have wanted to take on board the insights of social anthropology has not concentrated on movements

---

9. F. Jameson, *The Political Unconscious* (London: Methuen, 1981), pp. 98, 299.

10. G. Scholem, *Sabbatai Sevi* (London: Routledge & Kegan Paul, 1973).

11. See W.D. Davies, 'From Schweitzer to Scholem', in *Jewish and Pauline Studies* (London: SPCK, 1984).

whose ideological pedigree is much closer to home than the cargo cults.[12] The seventeenth-century radicals in Judaism and Christianity would provide fertile soil for the kind of comparative study which social theorists suggest. Thus, the work of Christopher Hill on the fate of the seventeenth-century radicals is a suggestive guide to the debate about the similar problems of unfulfilled hopes within early Christianity and Judaism, a reminder of the important place you would want to attach to *Wirkungsgeschichte*.[13] We tend to forget that the millennial tradition has a long history within the church,[14] and the development and problems initiated by such groups not only within their own organisation and practice but also in relation to the parent body is a study which presents many typological similarities to early Christian messianism.[15]

This affirms the continuing centrality of a historical perspective for our biblical interpretation: a focus on how texts were interpreted, and, in particular, what kind of effects they had and why, prevents an exegesis which ends up in a textual fantasy world all too easily cut off from the social formation which determines all reading. But it is the *interpreters'* history which is important, as well as the text's. This is more or less the position adopted by most liberation theologians. Clodovis Boff, for example, offers a hermeneutical model which he describes as 'correspondence of relationships', an interaction between reader(s) and their context and the text and its context. The dialectic between modern and ancient struggle, to which the biblical texts bear witness, involves him in the historical study with which we are familiar. The same is true of those who read the Old Testament following in Norman Gottwald's footsteps.[16]

---

12. J. Gager, *Kingdom and Community* (Englewood Cliffs: Prentice–Hall, 1975); and P. Esler, *The Social World of the First Christians* (London: Routledge, 1994).

13. E.g. C. Hill, *The World Turned Upside Down* (Harmondsworth: Penguin, 1972); *idem*, *The English Bible and the Seventeenth Century Revolution* (London: Allen Lane, 1993); and on Muentzer and Winstanley see Rowland, *Radical Christianity* (Oxford, 1988).

14. See N. Cohn, *The Pursuit of the Millennium* (London: Paladin, 1970), and Rowland, *Radical Christianity* (Oxford: Polity Press, 1988).

15. I have often thought that Stuart Hall's account of the origins of Rastafarianism casts light on the emergence of Christianity; see his essay 'Religious Ideologies and Social Movements in Jamaica', in R. Bocock and K. Thompson (eds.), *Religion and Ideology* (Manchester: Manchester University Press, 1985).

16. E.g. I.J. Mosala, *Biblical Theology and Black Theology in South Africa*

Despite the emphasis on the importance of history in modern biblical exegesis I wonder whether the concern with history is serious enough? Your recognition of the importance of the Gadamerian proposal for a concern for *Wirkungsgeschichte* (exemplified in New Testament studies by the recent work of U. Luz, some of which you have expressed great sympathy for) indicates that you too recognise that there is not just one historical dimension to the interpretation of a text. As interpreters we have a history which has helped to form us and that history is also important in understanding the way in which the text is read.

I am also uneasy about the relegation of theology to a secondary place. Theology (in the widest sense of the word) has been an indispensable part of making sense of the text. Despite the widespread exegetical reaction to Lutheran readings of Paul, Luther and his followers did not entirely misunderstand Paul (nor for that matter did Marcion). The 'enlightened' modern exegete has her or his own insights to offer, but they are part of the constellation of interpretations which contribute to the ongoing struggle for the understanding of texts. In one central respect a theological dimension is crucial to understanding these texts. The biblical texts have formed the basis of communities of faith who have seen in them and have used them to express convictions about the divine dimension to the reality which confronts them. To exclude this as part of any historical criticism worth its salt is to impoverish interpretation. We may think that interpreters in the past may have been wrong to think in the way they did. We may on philosophical grounds decide that they were mistaken to think thus, but that is not an adequate reason for rejecting their approach to the text or declaring that a primarily theological approach should be subordinate to the historical. The possibility remains that the theological approach can offer an approach to the text which can be denied to the historical.

The Pontifical Biblical Commission has recently offered what is, I think, a judicious survey and review of methods of biblical interpretation.[17] Surprisingly, however, it is, in my opinion, rather too sanguine about the historical method (indeed, you would be in general

(Exeter: Paternoster Press, 1989); and C. Rowland, 'In Dialogue with Itumeleng Mosala', *JSNT* 50 (1993), pp. 43-57.

17. Reprinted with commentary in J.L. Houlden (ed.), *The Interpretation of the Bible in the Church* (London: SCM Press, 1995).

sympathetic to the line it takes). It is critical of any kind of exegesis
(particularly of a liberationist or feminist kind) which is in danger of
'proceeding from a preconceived judgment, and running the risk of
interpreting the biblical texts in a tendentious and debatable manner'.
Yet this seems to me to be a not entirely inappropriate description of
the historical-critical method, which the commission regards as
'indispensable', because, in its view, it operates with the help of scientific criteria that seek to be as objective as possible. There is a
naïveté about such a view of the historical-critical method, in particular, the view that scholars who practise it 'have ceased combining this
method with a philosophical system' and are somehow free of the
'preconceived judgments' of other methods. This is a good example of
the exponents of a dominant ideology thinking that what they do is
normal or common sense. In the report the liberationist and feminist
interpretations are both given the label 'contextual approaches' as if
the historical-critical method is not contextual! The processes of
reconstruction and hypothesis as key determinants of a text's meaning
are the bread and butter of the historical-critical method, and their
approaches are circumscribed by the intellectual climate of modernity.

    The dialectic between interpreters and texts demands the highest
level of awareness, and attempts of interpreters to understand themselves and their circumstances, parallel that attentiveness to the historical setting of text, author and original readers, which has been so
characteristic of biblical exegesis over the last two hundred years. A
critical reading involves the ability to acknowledge our prejudice,
which leads us to adopt parts of a text and reject others, and thus
enables the peculiarities and 'otherness' of the text to become more
apparent. Thereby the text can be ' heard', if not precisely on its own
terms then at least with sufficient respect for its own integrity, to
ensure that it does not merely mirror the prejudices of the reader and
so may question them. Where I differ from those of you who argue
for a separation of exegesis from application[18] is in my belief that the
historical method is neither indispensable nor the only tool necessary.
The process of the application of a text may in itself have an important role in the quest for understanding.

    A critical awareness is for me as much a spiritual as an academic
exercise. The reading of the Bible in the Christian community as well
as the academy can offer an alternative critical perspective which I

18. K. Stendahl, 'Biblical Theology', in *IDB* I, pp. 418-31.

think we are wrong to ignore. In this respect I have learnt so much from the Spiritual Exercises of Ignatius of Loyola.[19] It can also be a reminder to pause before we allow ourselves to be carried along by a particular way of reading a text, the product of conditioning and complacency. Modern exegesis has enabled us to develop resistance to a text (with all that says about us and our prejudices) and in this the hermeneutics of suspicion have proved invaluable. We have resisted both co-opting the text, in order to allow space for it and its own world, and being co-opted by it, in order to allow space for ourselves and our experience of the world. We have refused to be 'taken in' by the text; we have resisted its demands, or, in the case of contextual theologies, have demanded that experience (of oppression, doubt, suspicion of androcentrism) set the interpretative agenda. Yet it seems to me that biblical scholars (or at least most 'northern' exponents) in the last two hundred years have invested an enormous amount of time and energy in the pursuit of *one* pole of the hermeneutical process: the elucidation of the text and its historical context. The text's 'pathology' (and I use the word advisedly) and contradictions have meant that it has been the major object of our critical concern. It is the text that is 'the problem' and the interpreter who is 'enlightened' and able to view with detachment its shortcomings. I have become uneasy about treating Scripture as presenting the problems, which the 'enlightened' interpreter can solve. Part of the process of reading is that critical self-awareness and attentiveness may mean that interpreters may themselves be interpreted by the text.

The debt to 'southern' interpreters has slowly begun to alter our perspective in the 'north'. The demand that we take seriously the diachronic perspective when it comes to the 'interpreter' pole is long overdue. So we need to set the interpretations of the giants of biblical scholarship of the last hundred years in their historical and philosophical context,[20] to understand the interaction between text and reader which has taken place at different periods of history. While believing that we have much to learn from Third World liberationist exegesis, I do not want to assert that everything about it is to be slavishly followed. Yet at the end of the day I think that liberation exegesis has in common with mainstream biblical study a concern to be critical. We

19. C. Rowland, 'The Revaluation of all Values', *Supplements to The Way* 79 (1994), pp. 85-92.
20. E.g. J.C. O'Neill, *The Bible's Authority* (Edinburgh: T. & T. Clark, 1992).

need to be reminded of the ideological character of our study, in particular imagining that we in the 'northern' academies are just reading the text on its own terms.

So, John, despite the superficial differences between us I think that we both accept that hermeneutical reflection is an essential part of the exegetical enterprise. You write in your magisterial book on the Fourth Gospel that you have avoided 'high hermeneutics', though it seems to me that these are evident in myriad ways throughout the book. Indeed, in the very same footnote in which you disavow any high hermeneutical concerns you quote evocative words of Hugh Kenner, which themselves suggest that you recognise that you too stand in a long tradition of interpretation which is shot through with the complexities of high hermeneutics:

> With John's gospel we are also deep in what Hugh Kenner calls 'the whispering forest of all traditional poetries, where the very words to which millions of minds respond have helped to form the minds that respond to them'.[21]

It is in that κοινωνία in the traditional poetries that women and men seek to illuminate and alleviate the human predicament that we share. But there cannot be any escape from 'high hermeneutics' when we are immersed in such a 'whispering forest' which has formed us. We long to find our own way out, not merely following the behests, however benign, offered by some authority. There are many, perhaps too many, signs pointing a way, confusing and none compelling. But in our common quest I have come to the conviction that an indispensable part in criticism is the practice of Christian discipleship with the grace of humility it requires and offers, and the insight into Scripture which has come from those who seek to apply it as a way of understanding it. As we have to walk by faith and not by sight, what we seek to do as critics is to learn to attune our ears to the whispers, struggle to decipher those faint sounds and then choose between them, without being so preoccupied with these attempts that we fail to notice the still small voice of our brothers' and sisters' blood crying out to heaven. It is by attending to them that our understanding of Scripture may be immeasurably enhanced.

21. *Understanding the Fourth Gospel* (Oxford: Oxford University Press, 1991), p. 3.

NIKEPHOROS BLEMMYDES ON JOHN:
A BYZANTINE SCHOLAR'S REACTIONS TO JOHN'S PROLOGUE

Joseph A. Munitiz

The sermon in which Nikephoros Blemmydes comments on the Prologue of John's Gospel aroused considerable interest when it was delivered (c. 1250), so much so that it was denounced to the Patriarch of
Constantinople as heretical, but it had to wait until 1989 before
appearing in a critical edition for the service of scholars.[1] Its author
was famous in his day as a 'philosopher', and had won fame as imperial tutor and as founder of a monastery dedicated to Christ, 'The One
Who Is'. His introduction to minor logic (very much in the later
Aristotelian tradition) had great success as a school book, but he was
also known as an apologist for the Orthodox faith, acting as spokesman
in two discussions with the Latins, and in one with the Armenians.[2]

In his 'Encomium on John', delivered above the tomb of the Evangelist in the great basilica at Ephesus, Blemmydes breaks with tradition in that he abandons the traditional lay-out of such speeches,
referring only briefly to the hero's life and deeds and adding quite an
extended commentary on the Prologue. Thus in the modern edition,
divided into 72 paragraphs, the central section (§§24-54) consists of
the commentary, preceded and followed by introductory and explanatory biographical comments. Blemmydes is clearly aware that this is
an unconventional approach:

> ... it is appropriate that the present sermon, which appears after so many
> others, should exalt the theologian from his own words rather than from
> his deeds (§33).

1. J.A. Munitiz, 'Blemmydes' Encomium on St John the Evangelist (BHG
931)', *Analecta Bollandiana* 107 (1989), pp. 285-346.
2. There is a handy introduction to Blemmydes in the English translation of his
autobiography: J.A. Munitiz, *Nikephoros Blemmydes: A Partial Account* (Etudes et
Documents, 48; Leuven: Spicilegium Sacrum Lovaniense, 1988).

So much, then, for what we have to say in honour of such a great saint. Let others recount how much this mighty one strove for the proclamation of the saving word (§55).

His comments concentrate on certain aspects of the Prologue, and it is their choice which is of interest, if only as a foil to the commentaries of our own day. In order to obtain an overall picture of Blemmydes' commentary, the simplest approach will be to reproduce the Prologue, and to pick out the parts that attracted Blemmydes' attention.

The text of John has been set out in stichometric pattern,[3] with the phrases underlined that are commented upon by Blemmydes. Italic type is used to highlight those parts of the Prologue that are thought to have been part of 'the early Christian hymn, probably stemming from Johannine circles, which has been adapted to serve as an overture to the Gospel narrative',[4] with ordinary type used for John's additions.

ἐν ἀρχῇ ἦν ὁ λόγος,
καὶ ὁ λόγος ἦν πρὸς τὸν θεόν,
καὶ θεὸς ἦν ὁ λόγος.
²Οὗτος ἦν ἐν ἀρχῇ πρὸς τὸν θεόν
³Πάντα δι᾽ αὐτοῦ ἐγένετο,
καὶ χωρὶς αὐτοῦ ἐγένετο οὐδὲ ἓν
ὃ γέγονεν.⁵
⁴Ἐν αὐτῷ ζωὴ ἦν,
καὶ ἡ ζωὴ ἦν τὸ φῶς τῶν ἀνθρώπων·
⁵καὶ τὸ φῶς ἐν τῇ σκοτίᾳ φαίνει,
καὶ ἡ σκοτία αὐτὸ οὐ κατέλαβεν.
⁶Ἐγένετο ἄνθρωπος
ἀπεσταλμένος παρὰ θεοῦ,
ὄνομα αὐτῷ Ἰωάννης·
⁷οὗτος ἦλθεν εἰς μαρτυρίαν,
ἵνα μαρτυρήσῃ περὶ τοῦ φωτός,
ἵνα πάντες πιστεύσωσιν δι᾽ αὐτοῦ.
⁸οὐκ ἦν ἐκεῖνος τὸ φῶς,
ἀλλ᾽ ἵνα μαρτυρήσῃ περὶ τοῦ φωτός.

---

3.   The importance of stichometry for the study of early texts, and in particular for John's Prologue, has been underlined by J. Irigoin, 'La composition rhythmique du Prologue de Jean (I.1-18)', *RB* 78 (1971), pp. 501-14.

4.   R.E. Brown, *The Gospel according to John: I–XII* (AB; Garden City, NY: Doubleday, 1966), p. 1.

5.   From his comments it is clear that Blemmydes read a punctuation sign here (colon or full stop), despite its absence in the earliest witnesses.

⁹ Ἦν τὸ φῶς τὸ ἀληθινόν,
  ὃ φωτίζει πάντα ἄνθρωπον,
  ἐρχόμενον εἰς τὸν κόσμον.
  ¹⁰*ἐν τῷ κόσμῳ ἦν,*
καὶ ὁ κόσμος δι' αὐτοῦ ἐγένετο,
καὶ ὁ κόσμος αὐτὸν οὐκ ἔγνω.
  ¹¹*εἰς τὰ ἴδια ἦλθεν,*
καὶ οἱ ἴδιοι αὐτὸν οὐ παρέλαβον.
  ¹²*ὅσοι δὲ ἔλαβον αὐτόν,*
ἔδωκεν αὐτοῖς ἐξουσίαν τέκνα θεοῦ γενέσθαι,
τοῖς πιστεύουσιν εἰς τὸ ὄνομα αὐτοῦ,
¹³οἳ οὐκ ἐξ αἱμάτων
οὐδὲ ἐκ θελήματος σαρκὸς
οὐδὲ ἐκ θελήματος ἀνδρὸς
ἀλλ' ἐκ θεοῦ ἐγεννήθησαν.
  ¹⁴*Καὶ ὁ λόγος σὰρξ ἐγένετο*
    καὶ ἐσκήνωσεν ἐν ἡμῖν,
  καὶ ἐθεασάμεθα τὴν δόξαν αὐτοῦ,
  δόξαν ὡς μονογενοῦς παρὰ πατρός,
  πλήρης χάριτος καὶ ἀληθείας.
¹⁵ Ἰωάννης μαρτυρεῖ περὶ αὐτοῦ
    καὶ κέκραγεν λέγων,
    Οὗτος ἦν ὃν εἶπον,
ὁ ὀπίσω μου ἐρχόμενος
    ἔμπροσθέν μου γέγονεν,
    ὅτι πρῶτός μου ἦν.
  ¹⁶*Ὅτι ἐκ τοῦ πληρώματος αὐτοῦ*
    ἡμεῖς πάντες ἐλάβομεν,
    καὶ χάριν ἀντὶ χάριτος·
  ¹⁷ὅτι ὁ νόμος διὰ Μωϋσέως ἐδόθη,
ἡ χάρις καὶ ἡ ἀλήθεια διὰ Ἰησοῦ Χριστοῦ ἐγένετο.
¹⁸θεὸν οὐδεὶς ἑώρακεν πώποτε·
    μονογενὴς θεὸς ὁ ὢν εἰς τὸν κόλπον τοῦ πατρὸς
    ἐκεῖνος ἐξηγήσατο.

Blemmydes begins by stressing the 'philosophical' importance of John's opening words: 'the first principle of his teaching, the most original philosophy of all' is that 'logos' (here clearly *reason*) precedes all things, so that 'all the activities and achievements of irrational living things, even of the smallest and most despicable, cannot be found bereft of *logos*. There is a *logos* that somehow illuminates them' (§24). As with all human activity, reason (mind?) in some sense must come first, and must always have been there. Blemmydes uses the logical argument of the need to avoid a *regressio ad infinitum* to show that reason must always have existed, or there would be no 'reason' for it ever to have begun (§26). The 'reason for' things gives them a share in the mind that produces them. Thus human beings have something of the divine, just as a tree is related to its roots (§27).

But there is a further step: this 'reason' is God himself, eternally present to, and eternally to be identified as, God (§28). Blemmydes makes an interesting distinction between what is 'confessed' as a matter of faith, viz. that there is a God, and what is 'theologized', namely that the Logos was God (ὡμολόγηται as opposed to τεθεολόγηται §30).

John is unlike the other Evangelists, who can be grouped together, in that for him the emphasis is always on the 'significant', in so far as it is the 'teaching' aspect that he is stressing. He provides a direct channel to the source of all divine wisdom and true theology (§§31-32).

There is an echo of the controversies with the Latins when Blemmydes claims that the phrase καὶ ὁ λόγος ἦν πρὸς τὸν θεόν 'is true of the personal individual... and shows that the Father is first as causer' (ὡς αἴτιος §34), thus going, however justifiably, beyond John's words.

His next comment concerns the words πάντα δι᾽ αὐτοῦ ἐγένετο, to which he adds 'thanks to the Father, because it is from there that the Son possesses both his being and his creativity' (§35). As Blemmydes pointed out in his *Partial Account*,[6] this addition is perfectly orthodox, but some critics claimed that the preacher was subordinating the Son to the Father. In fact he goes on to stress that because 'In Him was life' the Logos was absolute life, who preserves 'quintessential substantiality' (πολλῷ ἂν μᾶλλον διατηροίη τὸ οὐσιωθέν); this term, from the verb οὐσιόω 'to invest with substance', appears to have a Plotinian origin.

The Logos is both life *and light*, this last epithet referring to the constant teaching function: 'Just as the water in the source is ever welling up, so in the Logos there is as an inexhaustible teaching full of life and light' (§36).

From v. 4 Blemmydes jumps to v. 10, omitting all commentary on the text that some have identified as Johannine commentary on the original hymn, and then links it at once with v. 14: 'The Logos was "in the world", although not seen... But later he has appeared to us also with flesh, "becoming flesh". Here was complete union... τοῦτο τῆς ἄκρας ἑνώσεως᾽ (§38).

6.   *Partial Account*, II, pp. 67-74.

However, he does not stay for long even on v. 14. Instead he develops a long rhetorical coda (§§40-45) on the enigmatic words καὶ χάριν ἀντὶ χάριτος. The exact meaning of the preposition here is far from clear,[7] but Blemmydes seems to favour 'in place of', rather than 'upon' (in the sense of accumulation) or 'for' (in the sense of matching or correspondence). The contrast is between the Old and the New Testaments, the latter 'taking the place of' (ἀντὶ) the former, as is suggested by v. 17. Commenting on the latter Blemmydes expatiates on how Christ goes beyond Moses, drawing a detailed parallel between the two, intended to show the superiority of Christ (§46-51).

The conclusion to all this takes us back to the initial *point de départ*: John was 'the first real philosopher (πρῶτος ὄντως φιλόσοφος), handing down the first principles of the noblest theology' (§53), even if there is no human capacity fully capable of grasping them (μερικὴν ποιούμεθα τὴν ἀνάπτυξιν, οὐ τὴν ὁλικὴν κατεξέτασιν) (§54).

John Ashton himself in his comments on the Prologue has emphasized that even if this hymn is partly about 'creation, culminating in incarnation', still

> it would be closer to the mark to say that it is a hymn about *revelation* that culminates in incarnation...The most marvellous insight of this extraordinary passage is that divine revelation, hitherto manifested intermittently in the lives of God's messengers, the prophets, and in a Law that has not been kept, has now actually taken flesh and dwelt among men—indeed in a community of which the writer is himself a member.[8]

There is no sign that Blemmydes was aware of the existence of any special 'community', as distinct from that of all Christians, and another insight of John Ashton that finds no echo in Blemmydes is the realization that the Prologue of John is closely linked with the hymn to Wisdom by the writer known as Ben Sira (Ecclesiasticus).[9] However, there is much in Ashton's remarks with which Blemmydes would be in sympathy: he resonates with the same admiration for John's mental depth and vision; he is convinced that the Logos is so-called because his prime function is to speak:

7. Brown, *John*, pp. 15-16.
8. J. Ashton, *Understanding the Fourth Gospel* (Oxford: Oxford University Press, 1991), p. 528.
9. *Understanding*, p. 527.

> The *Logos* is for ever a tutor (παιδαγωγός), one who explains for those in need. That is why he is named the *logos*, since his locutory role is uninterrupted in the uttering of what will draw away from all opposed to the *logos*, through the Gospels, through the prophets, through the written law and through the law of nature, through all manner of revelation. At one and the same time <he is *logos*>, both as announcer of the Father's affairs and as proceeding from him impassively (§36).

Where Blemmydes differs radically from Ashton is in the attempt to make of John a new 'Plato/Aristotle/Plotinus', names that are never pronounced in the encomium but figures that stand firmly in the background. It is to Hellenic philosophy that Blemmydes is looking when he claims that John is the real 'philosopher', the man with true wisdom. He begins from the grandiose vision that Reason permeates and enlightens the whole of creation, which comes into being guided and created by Reason. That eternal Reason is the Godhead, generated from but abiding in the Eternal Mind: νοῦς γὰρ ἄλογος, οὐκ ἠκούσθη ποτέ ('A mind without reason has never been heard of!', §26). But it is this Divine Reason that has 'taken flesh', and has surpassed the wonders worked by Moses—law, circumcision, sabbath, manna, walking through the sea: 'He will accomplish all the outstanding deeds of Moses, but do so in more perfect and sublime fashion' (καὶ ταῦτα, τελεώτερόν τε καὶ ὑψλότερον, §46). It is the cosmic breadth of John's vision that impresses Blemmydes: 'Lifting himself on high, and observing all around from that vantage point, he could encompass the whole cosmos in his gaze' (κόσμον ἅπαντα τῷ ὄμματι συμπερι-λαβών, §52). At the same time, it is John the Teacher that appeals to him: light and vision enable John to formulate the principles that empower others to engage in the work: 'we have the expressions, axioms and definitions, thanks to which we can reason out religious knowledge. We can advance slightly further led and guided by those same phrases, provided we hold fast to them' (§54).

Given the broad lines of Blemmydes' own life, it is not surprising that these aspects of the Prologue should have appealed to him, and that the more humdrum approach of the Synoptic Gospels should not. His delight in his monastic solitude lay in the study of earlier philosophical writings, which he had collected at some cost to himself, travelling in Northern Greece and going as far as Ochrid.[10] His fame, as mentioned earlier, was as a philosopher and teacher. However,

---

10. *Partial Account*, I, pp. 63-64.

there may also have been other motives. The message of his encomium is that among the apostles John held the commanding position (τὸν δὲ θεολόγον, τῶν ἀποστόλων ἐξάρχοντα, §71), because it was to him that the Lord entrusted his breast and his heart ('which is the first principle—that is from where all life and movement come', §71). When Blemmydes delivered his encomium he was coming fresh from the conversations with the Latins and the Armenians. The problem of true authority in the church was uppermost in his mind. Although unspoken, the message is clear enough: the Prologue of John is the proof that the knowledge of God does not come from any administrative head, any Pope or Patriarch, but through the revelation given by the Logos. So, perhaps not so far from the thinking of our honorand.

INDEXES

INDEX OF REFERENCES

OLD TESTAMENT

NEW TESTAMENT

INDEX OF AUTHORS

Davis, S.T. 220, 221, 225
Derrett, J.D.M. 49
Dibelius, M. 217
Dietrich, A. 181
Dodd, C.H. 9, 94, 98, 140-42
Downing, F.G. 37
Dunn, J.D.G. 61, 113, 144, 151, 162,
    232

Edwards, J.R. 20, 177
Ellis, E.E. 125
Emerton, J.A. 183
Erdman, D. 240
Esler, P. 242
Evans, C.A. 93
Evans, C.F. 38

Faierstein, M. 15
Farrer, A. 20, 202
Fee, G. 131
Feuillet, A. 38
Fiddes, P. 149
Filoramo, G. 228
Fitzmyer, J.A. 26, 38, 40, 41, 142, 151,
    216
Fjärstedt, B. 111
Fleddermann, H.T. 37
Fletcher-Louis, C.H.T. 49
Ford, J.M. 198
Foucault, M. 179
Fox, R.L. 155
Foxe, R. 189
France, R.T. 122
Freud, S. 146
Friedlander, G. 57
Frye, N. 240
Fuks, A. 60, 61
Fung, R.Y.K. 116

Gadamer, 9
Gager, J. 242
Garlington, D.B. 62
Gaster, T.H. 54
Girard, R. 145, 146, 148, 150-54
Gnilka, J. 162
Goedt, M. de 74, 75
Goldin, J. 65
Gooch, P. 125

Goodman, M. 61, 155
Gottwald, N. 242
Goulder, M. 32, 33, 46, 198, 199
Grocyn, W. 189
Gundry, R.H. 19, 21, 22, 24, 25

Hahnemann, G. 177, 178
Hall, S. 242
Halleux, A. de 184
Hamerton-Kelly, R.G. 149
Hammer, R. 18, 26
Hanson, A.T. 141, 142
Harnisch, G. 49
Harvey, A. 231
Hawthorne, G.F. 120, 163
Hebblethwaite, B. 224, 233
Heinemann, J. 67
Hellholm, D. 199
Hemer, C.J. 203
Hendricksen, W. 94
Héring, J. 170
Hill, C. 242
Hofius, O. 116
Hooker, M. 20, 25, 151
Houlden, J.L. 162, 217, 225, 229, 233,
    243
Hughes, P.E. 166
Hurd, J.C. 120, 209
Hurtado, L. 120

Irigoin, J. 248

Jameson, F. 241
Jeremias, J. 25, 26, 48
Johnson, L.T. 207
Joosten, J. 187

Kagan, N. 100
Kaiser, W.C. 18
Käsemann, E. 109, 110, 143, 144
Kenner, H. 246
Kloppenborg, J.S. 42-44, 105
Knight, J. 213
Knowles, M. 17, 18
Koester, H. 111, 125, 204
Kuhn, H.-W. 86

Lane, W.L. 165

JOURNAL FOR THE STUDY OF THE NEW TESTAMENT
SUPPLEMENT SERIES